RUN
FOR YOUR
LIFE

To Ed & Sally
Best of Luck

Charlie Space

RUN
FOR YOUR
LIFE

engineers don't idle well

CHARLES SPACE

Tate Publishing & Enterprises

Published by Tate Publishing & Enterprises, LLC

127 E. Trade Center Terrace | Mustang, Oklahoma 73064 USA
1.888.361.9473 | www.tatepublishing.com

Tate Publishing is committed to excellence in the publishing industry. The company reflects the philosophy established by the founders, based on Psalm 68:11,
"The Lord gave the word and great was the company of those who published it."

Book design copyright © 2007 by Tate Publishing, LLC. All rights reserved.
Cover design by Jacob Crissup
Interior design by Stephanie Woloszyn

Published in the United States of America
ISBN: 978–1–60247–896–1
1. Autobiography
2. Engineers, Christian
07.10.18

DEDICATION

This book is dedicated to the following:

Our children Suzanne and Steve who experienced many of the adventures first hand, and our grandchildren Riley and Courtney who have patiently listened to the tales, wishing they had been there.

Those who have guided me, inspired me and made my life the blessing that it has been.

My Lord, who, in spite of my wandering into and out of His will, has always watched over me to assure that all would turn out for the best. His patience in drawing me back to Him has sustained me for many years. Even my most painful experiences turned out to be but stepping stones in the path to the faith, joy and happiness we now enjoy.

Linda, my faithful wife who joined me early in my journey and stayed by my side during the good and bad times. Linda has been always ready to support me when I was low, to quietly celebrate our victories and to patiently encourage me to stay the course. Without her strength, faith and love, our life together would not have been the blessing our family received.

As we approach our twilight years together, the many joyous years of our marriage should be an example to all couples that faith, honesty and perseverance do have great rewards. No prize comes without a struggle, so chart your course, be ready to accept detours and hold fast to your principles. Without them any victory will be hollow and temporary.

Finally, Ma Perkins, my English teacher at Landon High School. She motivated me to make something of my life and to step out of the gloom that had almost swallowed me up. As I look back at the many blessings in my life, I know this great lady had the most significant influence in those early years. She helped restore the faith and self-confidence I lost early in life and convinced me that honesty and perseverance pays off in the long run.

TABLE OF CONTENTS

INTRODUCTION

Unlike many people, my life has seldom been dull. The mid 1930s to today have been amazing years, filled with unparalleled advances. I have been greatly blessed with a family and career that has taken me through many of these uncharted waters of progress, requiring doing something new continuously, many times things that had never been done before. I wish I could say all were successful, but they weren't. Both the good and the bad were adventures, and I hope to share the best of them with you.

But life is not all work and career. The adventures continued during family times of rest and relaxation. My ancestors were adventurers, too—from Jean de Brienne, the thirteenth century Crusader King of Jerusalem to the early settlers of America, the roots had been planted for my reach into the unknown.

In 1996, we purchased property on Lake Chatuge in the foothills of the Smoky Mountains and began the latest adventure—retirement and rebuilding an old cabin. As completion neared, my wife, Linda suggested I build the model railroad that had been my dream ever since my childhood Lionel Flyer set was given away by my mother when I was eleven. Linda's suggested theme was to build a model railroad trip through my career, with hand-built scale models of projects from those days past, partly for me but also for my children and grandchildren to enjoy. I am now over half way through that task and enjoying every minute. Several illustrations in this book are photographs of models I constructed for that model railroad.

It was not until my seventieth year that I finally got around to writing this book, after years of procrastination. Many of these stories have been told to friends and family over the years, but in spite of hearing, "You should write it down for your family to enjoy, especially your grandchildren," I delayed. For me, it was always easier to tell the stories and watch the facial expressions as the story unfolded.

I think my seventieth birthday was a wake up call. It was looking like I wasn't going to live forever, and details of the stories were starting to dim. From my earliest years, I have never been able to feel comfortable unless I was finding how things work, doing some project or thinking about doing another, always looking for a better way. I use the old saying "engineers don't idle well" as the subtitle for this book. It is a perfect description of my life. Even today, sitting still is difficult.

For you, the reader, I hope you can join in on the smiles of my family and friends.

RUN FOR YOUR LIFE

There was only one hope—to reach the underground storm pipes before they caught me.

Run for your life!

I knew the pipe location from last year when we played hide and seek and I stumbled upon the eight foot high pipe under Empire Blvd. with its miles of neat tunnels—a perfect hiding place. But I was only seven then—much smaller—and never went back after getting lost far back in the system. The thought made shivers run up my spine, for in that earlier episode it was dark and as I went deeper onto the maze of pipes it got darker and I got lost. The pipes had gotten much smaller, and the only light came through the street drain openings far above. It had begun to rain and I cried for help, but only the echoes of my voice responded. As the water rose, I could hear the rats as they ran screeching and running into my legs trying to escape the rising water. Finally, in a panic, I ran too, following the flow of water until it reached the entrance. I was out! On the way home, the rain soaked me thoroughly and most of the mud was gone so I wouldn't have to explain my narrow escape. You could hardly smell the foul odor of stagnant water. Mother and Dad would never know or I'd probably be grounded for life.

Now though, the squad of Nazi soldiers was closing in fast, and I was exhausted. Some had machine guns, others Lugers. There it was—just as I remembered, and just in time! I ducked into the pipes and ran, pausing every few minutes to listen. They were behind, but with it getting darker with every step further into the maze, I was sure they would never find me. Oh no! They had a spotlight—and a siren. They were riding on a red truck and coming my way—fast. I ran deeper and deeper until the pipes were too small for them to ride further, and they were now on foot. By the time I reached pipes too small to stand in, I had lost them. I huddled in the dark, hoping they would give up before I did. With my arms over my face I gasped for air.

Something is brushing my cheek! Should I look to see if it was one of the feared rats? No! There it was again, and again! I slowly opened my eyes. There was light—and a window curtain? That's what was brushing my cheek. I was home in bed! Today was one of the first cool October Saturdays in Florida when the windows could be opened. The breeze was moving the curtain across my face. This was one of the rare days off, as my job required extensive travel and workweeks regularly included sixty or more hours. Saturday usually was just another workday.

It was still there after almost thirty years—the nightmare that had haunted me since I was nine years old. But now I was almost forty, had a wife and children, and had a successful career. The old nightmares should be gone by now.

As I lay there, memories of those days during World War II flooded back. Our family of four lived just outside Rochester, NY, within shouting distance of Lake Ontario—Canada on the other side. When the day of infamy arrived in December 1941, I heard the hushed conversation of my parents, and later the radio blared out "war." President Roosevelt announced that Pearl Harbor had been bombed and we all would now join the war. Life changed from then on, even for a six-year-old.

Thanks to my mother's tutoring, I had learned to read and write by the time I went to public school in 1940 just before turning five, so when the paper announced Pearl Harbor on Monday, I could tell and, even better, spread the exciting news to the other first graders. My parents didn't like our listening to the war news on the radio, but it came on just after *The Green Hornet*, *The Lone Ranger*, and *The Shadow*, so I listened to what I could before being sent to my room while the folks listened. Until that day, news of the war in Europe was exciting—brave Allied soldiers fighting the war to end all wars. Now, the news was scary! America had been attacked!

Poland, France, Belgium and Denmark had already surrendered, and even neutral Norway and the Netherlands were invaded and occupied by Germany. Germany and Italy and the Axis Powers expanded into Asia, Europe and Africa. Most of the rest of central Europe joined them, under threat of invasion or through political maneuvering. Britain and the United States joined in an oil embargo of Japan. Japan retaliated by invading and occupying the oil and rubber rich Dutch East Indies. Talk was that England would be next to surrender. We never thought the war could ever come to America. War news was the start of our class day, so we would get beyond whispering about it and get to our studies.

Now, with England on the verge of being overrun, we were told of the threat to us if Canada surrendered too. Invasion across Lake Ontario would be probable, now that we were no longer neutral. In early 1942, we began air raid drills in class, starting by hiding under our desks, then into the halls, crouched with arms over our heads when someone realized flying glass would more of a threat than the roof caving in.

In Asia, the Japanese seemed to be unstoppable. Early in the twentieth century, the Japanese had declared that it was their destiny—to free the western Pacific basin from European and American domination. The fascist government emerged during the Great Depression, and Japan was dominated by its military. Manchuria had fallen years earlier, Burma, Indo-China, Thailand, the Philippines, and parts of China had also surrendered by 1942.

German industries had influence in Mexico, and their plan was to convince the Mexican government to join them and open the southern flank for an Axis attack on America. Japanese plans for the invasion of Mexico were discovered—to be implemented if Germany failed to recruit Mexico—but neither plan worked.

An oil refinery in California had been shelled by a Japanese submarine, and rumors were flying. One of the Aleutian Islands in Alaska was invaded, and German submarines were torpedoing and shelling tankers off Florida and the rest of the east coast. Most of our parents tried to keep bad war news from the younger children, but bad war news was all there was. As soon as we got to school, the older kids delighted in scaring us with the news, often enhanced enough to get us to cry.

Up until the war, the neighborhood boys were divided into gangs, not like those of today, but groups that played together, mostly playing war games like Commando and Guard the Fort. In our subdivision, Orchard Park, there were two—The Big Kids and The Little Kids. Because we had none old enough for high school, the only other group was the Babies. My sister was a Baby, and I was a Little Kid. It was the social order for the Little Kids to tag along behind the Big Kids, but far enough behind to be out of stone throwing range. Occasional bullying was normal, but only pushing and teasing were allowed. Babies were not allowed near either gang, especially girl babies.

By that time, I had fully bought into the war effort, collecting and turning in everything I collected to the collection point at the Socony Vacuum Gas Station on Empire Boulevard. "Bring your war materials to the Flying Red Horse" was the motto for our neighborhood. Gas stations were few and far between in those days, and because of gasoline rationing, the stations were set up as collection points. The government was paying ten cents per pound for rubber, the most critical material.

The Dutch East Indies, which was a major supplier of natural rubber, had been captured after neutral Netherlands was invaded by Germany in 1940. Shortly after the invasion, all the Dutch holdings in southeast Asia were occupied by the Japanese. America was neutral at that time and was still receiving rubber, but our leaders knew the supply was in jeopardy. Synthetic rubber was in the developmental stages, and not yet available in large quantities. Recycling was difficult, far more costly than using virgin rubber and yielded a lower quality, sometimes called Camelback. It was used for recapping worn tires. The government had begun an ambitious program of building refineries for the production of aviation gas and butadiene, a main ingredient in synthetic rubber. One of these refineries was Eastern States Petroleum in Houston, mentioned here only because after high school, it was my first employer. America had geared up for the war by shipping food, all kinds of military equipment, ammunition, and supplies to England and Russia. As relations with the Axis Powers deteriorated, the supply of rubber was threatened.

At least our family could enter the war with ease. We had a set of new tires coming on our new Oldsmobile that had just been delivered to the dealer. But we had a surprise coming. Dad was informed that our car was being shipped off to war, but we would be first in line for the first new car after the war was over. We would have to make do with the 1935 Ford for the duration, and the tires on that car were bare. Tires were rationed four days after Pearl Harbor, but by calling in a favor, Dad had purchased a complete set for the Ford just in time. After the government called in all tires except those on the car and one spare, our new tires were covered and hidden in the woods behind the house until Dad could install them and turn in the worn tires. Too bad he didn't tell me that. I proudly put the brand new tires on my wagon one at a time, took them up to the Flying Red Horse collection point, and collected the money. Up to that time, I had earned many spankings, but none compared with this one. Dad went to reclaim the tires, but somehow, there was no record of them ever being turned in. I was given strict orders to stay away from Mother's Wear Ever aluminum pots.

Spankings, first with the hand, sometimes a belt, and later with a board were frequent. Anything not strictly done as Mother ordered earned a "Go to your room, close the door, sit on your bed and just wait until your father comes home." When he did, we always got a spanking, whether guilty or not.

It was rare for only one of us to get a spanking. One was always peeking around a corner while it was administered to the other. It was forbidden to laugh at your sibling "getting it," but Nancy couldn't resist, and neither could I. After the crying was over, it was common to get Mother's makeup mirror and inspect to see if the redness was accompanied by blisters. Neither the redness nor the blisters were the worst part though, being forced to look straight into Dad's eyes during the lecture that went with the whipping was far more terrifying. Looking away meant he would start over after placing his hand on your head, turning it back and holding it long enough for it to stay in position. Look away twice, and you got another swat. A blink was allowed.

As I watched his eyes, he would pause for the required "yes, sir." I would keep it on the tip of my tongue to repeat at the proper time and in a respectful tone. Occasionally, "yes, sir" would slip off early and interrupt. That was "murder," our term for the worst offense. He would start over from the beginning, and as he repeated the lecture, his eyes would gradually get larger, and they seemed to get closer too. Dad always started with, "This is going to hurt me more than you," then the spanking, then the lecture. One time I responded to his "…hurt me more than you" using Dad's favorite term, "The hell you say!" (after all, I was trying to grow up like him). This time it was a spanking, a lecture on language that was okay for grownups and not for kids, followed by another rear end reminder. Nancy had apparently run off when she heard "the word" because she escaped the session.

Outside, the other war was going on. By 1942, tires, rubber products, butter, coffee, meat, sugar, and gasoline all were strictly rationed. The "A" gas sticker we got only allowed 4 gallons a week, so the Sunday drive in the country and church took a big hit. Almost all travel was now by bus, streetcar, bicycle or on foot. We didn't know it at the time, but gasoline rationing and the mandatory nationwide speed limit of thirty-five miles per hour was actually more to conserve rubber than gasoline.

A grocery wagon came to the neighborhood every week bringing much of the food that we couldn't raise in our victory garden, but meat was a rarity on the dinner table. Fish, chicken and eggs were not rationed, but the demand was high and you were lucky to find any. Occasionally we had Spam—always fried and then topped with brown sugar after any grease was saved for another meal. Sugar was strictly rationed, but just before it went on the list, Dad bought a hundred pound sack and stored it in the basement. That left the ration coupons for trading or for brown sugar. One of my jobs during the war was to chop off hunks of the sugar, which had long before turned to a solid block in the damp basement. It had to be broken up with a hammer, but I got to lick the hammer afterward, before I washed it. We had lived for a short time on a farm nearby, and Mother was able to get an occasional string of sausage which she fried and used the grease to drip on waffles to replace the butter that was no longer available. All the left over grease was saved for her secret weapon "Utzaputz," but that didn't count as food.

Every week we had at least two meals of the stew we called Utzaputz. Mother had her own special version of this traditional Dutch dish we all learned to despise. Hutsepot was its real name. It was originally a boiled vegetable stew, sometimes with meat added. With meat rationing, Mother improvised. The leftover sausage grease was added to the mushy vegetables, along with whatever used cooking grease was available. The only seasonings in the Dutch version were salt, pepper and onions or garlic, the latter two forbidden in our house. Extra pepper was substituted. After eating grease-saturated "Utzaputz," you never needed a laxative, and Utzaputz seemed to last for days because we ate sparingly. Whatever wasn't eaten at dinner went back into the pot for the next meal.

Years later, on Mother's eighty-fifth birthday, my brother David brought a five gallon pail marked "Industrial Strength Utzaputz" to the party as a joke. Everyone roared in approval. Mother just smiled—a little.

We did save enough gas to pick up Dad from the bank on Fridays and stop by Flick's Fish House restaurant to pick up a meal of fried fish and French fries. Neither fish nor potatoes were rationed, but the cooking oil was. We couldn't get oil, and they could.

A game we used to play during pleasure drives in the country before the war was "Horse, Horse" where the first person to spot a horse called it out, and the kid with the most "horses" at the end of the drive won. With the trips limited to the weekly trip to pick up Dad and dinner in town, seeing horses was rare, except for the occasional ice wagon. Nancy and I invented "Blue Star" instead, counting all the blue star flags displayed in the windows of those families having members off fighting the enemy. After a few months, gold stars started to replace the blue. Mother knew we had little concept of death, so when I asked about the stars, she whispered, "Remember your Dad's heart attack, and that all men in our family die early? Those are for soldiers that died." It was the same warning I would hear from her for the next forty years, "You are going to die young, just like they do."

I had been to a cemetery before. Mother and I placed flowers on the grave of her brother, Jack, who was poisoned during a fraternity initiation prank. Mother explained that Jack just went to sleep and didn't wake up. That didn't seem too bad to me. I remember vividly asking why his marker was a blue Noxzema jar with his name on a slip of paper instead of the stone markers on the other graves. She answered that it was temporary, until the real one came. Other trips to the grave revealed the jar with the fading name and a rusting lid. I never did see another marker.

It was during one of the newsreels before a movie that I saw wounded and dying soldiers. Death wasn't just going to sleep as I had been told! From then on, the gold represented the death of a serviceman. It was then I realized death didn't mean just going to heaven. These guys were not just dying, they were being killed! After that, the Blue Star game was no fun. If the attack came, some of my friends and maybe even my family might be killed, or worse, we might die like the men who were being tortured. The Big Kids even told us to expect our fingernails to be pulled out or being put in a room full of bees.

Between the collections, garden work, and school, there was little time to get into trouble, but I was able to manage regularly. Selling my mother's rubber shower cap and all the family winter boots was an example of that ability. This time, it was not just the whipping, I had to return the money, climb the pile of scrap rubber and dig them out. It took all day Saturday.

Next was the flying lesson. It was a constant battle to keep Nancy from wanting to be with the guys. If we couldn't keep her away, who knows if Shirley Connelly or some of the other babies would try to tag along? Our Gang would never be the same. She whined to be let into our tree hut we built to watch for German bombers if the attack came. I knew if she went to Mother, I would "get it." I decided to let her halfway up and teach her to fly. Gullible Nancy climbed the tree, hung upside down, her skinny legs bent over a limb. As we all watched, she spread her arms out like wings, straightened her legs and flew—straight into the ground. She cried as all the guys rolled on the ground in laughter. "You did it wrong," I shouted. "You forgot your Batman cape." The next try with a bath towel tied around her neck proved no better, but the fluttering towel did add a different touch. That evening was one of those rare times there was a single spanking, but by the time it was over, I had gotten the equivalent of two. At least she went back to her dolls for a while.

In those more innocent days, there was no fear of children being harmed when away from their parents, so after reaching eight years old, I was allowed to take the bus to the movies on Saturday with the Gang (four of us). A Tom Mix or war movie, a cartoon, candy bar, and bus fare—all for a quarter, with enough for a Coke later in the week. Allowance of a quarter a week was supplemented by collecting bottles for the two-cent deposit and sale of scrap (although I knew tires, boots, and shower caps were off limits). We got our exposure to more war news through the Movietone News shown at the theaters.

By 1943, the war outlook was dismal. Even headlights on cars were partially blacked out to keep enemy bombers from spotting them from the air. Air raid drills were common, and occasionally a plane was flown over during the blackouts to add reality. Once a neighbor's house was not blacked out, and a bag of flour was dropped on the roof, resulting in a fine and grumbling of "unpatriotic" from the neighbors. Shortages were widespread, even if you had ration stamps. A thriving black market was operating, and until 1943, Dad was able to get his "spuds" as he called cigarettes from under the counter. He smoked four packs a day, Mother smoked two, and filling that need was a constant struggle. I remember Dad smoked Old Gold and Lucky Strikes. Soon even Lucky Strikes showed the effects of the war when the green dye used on the pack was discontinued "to make the green available for uniforms." After his supply dried up, he taught me to roll cigarettes for them.

War bond drives were held to raise money for the war. Morale was sagging, and we kids knew it. Constant watch for spies was encouraged. "Loose Lips Sink Ships" posters and similar sinister warnings were everywhere. Dad even took us to see a captured Japanese submarine that was paraded through downtown Rochester in 1943 for a war bond drive.

The Gang was always waiting for the invasion that never came. One afternoon during a bow and arrow hunt to shoot at muskrats, one of the Gang lost an arrow in a shallow cave along Irondequoit Bay, an arm of Lake Ontario, and when he reached for it, his hand hit a locked steel box! He took it home and broke the lock so we could see if it was buried treasure. It wasn't. It was photographs of Kodak Works where all their film and chemicals were destined for war, the Bausch and Lomb plant where binoculars and bomb sights were manufactured, and the plant that made delayed action fuses for bombs. I recognized that factory because one of my prized possessions was an actual delayed action bomb—no explosives, but it was complete with the delay action fuse. Dad had gotten it for me when we toured the factory, courtesy of one of his customers at the bank. There is no way to count the times I took it apart to show buddies and explain how it worked. The box also contained many photos of the rail yards, with war materials ready for shipment. Even we knew what we had found.

German spies and saboteurs from Canada! They were here! One of the fathers called the authorities, and we were each interviewed by a "government man" in a black suit, black tie, black hat and sunglasses. "There are spies everywhere, and if they find out you were involved, they will come across the lake and *get you*. Stay away from the Bay." Everyone was told to tell no one, *not even parents, and don't talk about it to other kids*. (Two out of three was all we could manage. The kids all knew.) The photo drop site was staked out and the spies were captured, but it was never in the news. We were all scared enough to keep our mouths shut, and the bay was off limits from then on—by choice.

So, that's where the dream started. It had haunted me for years, but now that I realized where it came from, it finally faded away.

THE WAR
YEARS

After the saboteur experience, both the gangs now shared a common secret and became closer. With the age difference, just a little closer though. We talked anyway. All decided we would have to do more if invasion came. As was common in the hierarchy of kids, the Big Kids did the planning and the Little Kids did the work. The plan was to build a circular defense fort in the woods, and when the attack came, we would all head for the fort and use the pile of rocks for throwing, and the Big Kids would bring their BB guns for defense. With imagined spies everywhere, we covered the fort at night with an old piece of canvas. Some of our parents came to see our fort, which was designed after the snow forts we built for snowball fights in the winter. We got a little praise for our bravery and quite a few smiles. When someone asked if BB guns would stop an attack from bombs and hand grenades, we had to reconsider our mission.

A bomb shelter! We had seen the movie news of the British going into the subways during attacks, and they were still holding out. We could do the same. With a homemade rope ladder to get in and out, we could go deeper. The excavation continued half of the summer, finally down about twenty feet, but by then, it was only a couple feet in diameter. The kids developed good muscles lifting all that dirt out of the hole, but now it was too small for us all to hide. We built a side cave at the bottom, one that eventually had a ceiling about four feet high and was large enough for about eight kids. Fortunately, the soil was rock and clay and didn't collapse on us and bury us all. A major problem during construction was disposing of the dirt. If the shelter was to be secret, we couldn't leave a big pile of dirt to give us away. Bucket by bucket it was all scattered in the woods. With the canvas roof, we were invisible.

One of the neighbors had been following our progress and reported to one of the parents. "Fill it in before somebody gets hurt!" we were ordered. "But there's no dirt," we replied. Mr. Benzing (David's dad) threw tree limbs and brush into our shelter, blocking the entrance. We took them out the next week. After a second filling and removal, the parents won. They trapped a skunk and dropped it in. We gave up.

The next winter filled the mouth of the shelter with snow, and with the spring thaw, the roof caved in and it was over.

As the war news got worse, the bullying slowed down. We were now working together collecting tinfoil, tin cans, newspapers, rubber, scrap metal, aluminum pots and pans—even string for the war effort. One class a day was devoted to knitting squares for hospital blankets. We learned to fold paper cups, roll up bandages, write letters to the soldiers, and even collect any grease left over from meals. Saving grease proved to be one tough job. Butter and meat were strictly rationed, and all the mothers saved grease to use over and over for cooking. We only got it if it was spoiled. With silk stockings one of the first thing to disappear from stores, straining the grease through a silk stocking to extend its useful life slowly gave way to using old diapers (washed of course).

Oleomargarine was available, but it was against the law to sell anything but white oleo. Legislators were concerned that grocers would sell it as butter, so each package included a packet of food coloring for mixing with the oleo. It was my job to mix the color in, and then lick the bowl. Later on, the coloring was in a capsule packed in with the oleo. That way, one could break it and mix in the color by kneading the sealed package and eliminate the waste from mixing in a bowl. The name oleo was a reminder of the war, so after the victory, we called it margarine.

Butter rationing really hit Mother's uncle ("Unkie" to us) hard. He had been financially ruined in the Great Depression and refused to work again for the past thirteen years. Auntie Ann was just barely able to support them in her typing job, but she was expected to cope with rationing without compromising his taste. Oleo was forbidden at his table, it made him deathly ill! It would be butter and *no excuses*. She traded ration coupons, begged, or paid black market prices—whatever was necessary. Finally, in desperation, she started mixing oleo with the butter—one cup to the pound at first, then two, then three, finally all oleo. She carefully hid the wrappers in cereal boxes before putting them in the garbage. Unkie never got deathly ill, not even a sign of trouble. He even bragged to his friends how resourceful Auntie Ann was. It was several months later that an oleo wrapper fell out while he was emptying the trash can. That evening right after eating a "buttered" biscuit, he jumped up from the table, ran to the bathroom, vomited and exclaimed, "It must have been something I ate."

Auntie Ann's great grandfather emigrated from Holland in 1848 with few possessions, but as a Dutchman, he brought his temper, and Auntie Ann inherited a full dose. Her temper won out over her timidity. She told him in no uncertain terms that he was a fake! He had been eating it for months, and if he didn't like it, he could cook for himself! She stomped out of the room and slammed the door behind her. He couldn't believe his ears, but he finally gave in when the next meal time came around, but now he used much less "butter" on his biscuits. "I'm using less to help the war effort," he exclaimed. We knew better, though.

Their lives were bleak. Unkie smoked his pipe and tended the roses—his favorite flower from his days as a wealthy nurseryman. Auntie Ann went to work every day. We visited them every week. Mother and Dad played pinochle with them, and they both accompanied us on vacations each summer. It seemed enough for them. Unkie even broke down and got a job at a defense plant during the war "to beat the Krauts" but quit as soon as it was over. He wanted his butter back and was willing to work to end this "foolish rationing." He also missed his hard cheese. It was scarce and finally disappeared from stores. "Sent it all to the Brits," he complained. "They're going to surrender, so why not keep it here?" We could get plenty of Velveeta, but Unkie swore it wasn't cheese, just a bunch of chemicals. Unkie swore a lot!

It was time to take matters into his own hands. One weekend he decided to drive across the border and get some real Canadian cheese. Off he went and got his case of cheese. It was wrapped in a blanket and hidden in the trunk behind the spare tire to avoid customs. He had gotten his cheese, even though he had been caught at the border. He paid a fine ($75.00 according to Mother), and they let him keep his prize. It was worth it for a case of cheddar.

The unwrapping of his prize on the kitchen table was a ceremony to show how he had beaten the system. Off came the blanket, then the paper. There it stood—*Velveeta*; he had been swindled! This time Unkie swore more than usual, got a beer and went sulking to his chair to listen to the radio. I wasn't there to hear what words he used this time, but I bet there were some new ones I'd never heard.

I got my first chance to try an "invention" the next year. Dad taught me to mow the lawn with our push mower. I asked him if it could be fixed to run by itself. He laughed and replied, "Just how do you think we could do that?" I had worked in the basement shop with him on several projects and knew a motor turned the table saw.

"What if we added a motor to run it?" I responded.

Well, for the first time, he said, "Let's see if we can." Up till then, he always planned the work and let me watch as he built it. Occasionally, I got to drive a nail or apply some glue. I did get to paint the finished product, but I always wanted to do more. This time we would plan and build it together.

We took the motor off the saw, and he let me see how it worked, which way it turned, and how the pulley and belt turned the saw. A light went on in my head. "We can put the motor and pulley on the mower," I proudly exclaimed.

"Right," said Dad, "but to put it on the mower, the blades are in the way. We'll have to saw off an inch of the end of each one for the pulley to fit."

"What saw can cut steel?" I asked. Instead of answering, he introduced me to a hacksaw and let me "cut" on the first blade. He finished the blade removal after I gave up half way through the first one. He then cut two strips of steel to bolt to the mower for mounting the motor. After marking them for bending to shape, he invited me to try to bend them to fit. He put one in his vise and gave me a hammer. No matter how hard I hit the steel bar, it wouldn't bend.

"If you aren't strong enough to bend it, let's see if we can make the steel weaker," he suggested. "I'll show you how." Up to the kitchen we went, and he heated the steel to a cherry-red color on Mother's gas stove. Quickly we returned to the basement, and I easily hammered the bar to shape. Dad finished with his favorite expression: "That's using your head for something other than a hat-rack. If you are stumped by a problem, figure out a way around the problem. Don't just give up." I never forgot that advice.

The mower was finished and worked fine. Dad even let me help assemble it so I would remember how the parts worked. All the kids marveled at the new machine. I even learned to mow the lawn without cutting the 100 foot extension cord I used. The next few summers I earned spare money by mowing lawns. Most went into buying war bonds.

Our tolerance by the Big Kids died out especially after Mother ordered, "Let your little sister tag along with your friends." Oh no, a Baby tagging along—that's as close as we would let her come. It was great sport to outrun her or make her cry and go home, but new methods were in order to discourage Nancy. Even Dad, who understood the difficulty of a girl tagging along, couldn't get Mother to back down.

One place we could always get away to was Bowman's Farm and Orchard, a block from the house. Our subdivision Orchard Park had been a part of the farm before being subdivided into lots about 1935. Our house was the last built before Pearl Harbor. Vacant lots were everywhere because building of new houses stopped during the war. Many still had peach, cherry, apple, and pear trees growing and producing fruit, but it was much more fun to sneak into Bowman's. The pasture and remaining apple orchard were fenced off with a new fangled fence. It was electric, and with each hum, a short jolt of electricity rushed through. The pulse was intermittent and we could hear it, so we could sneak through the fence between pulses if we counted properly. Nancy couldn't, so for a while we were okay. The apples in his orchard were much better than those on the vacant lots because he sprayed and fertilized them, and we got used to the manure smell. Farmer Bowman had one rule—only eat apples off the ground—never off the tree. For awhile that was fine, until a new kid moved in to a vacant house in the neighborhood. We told him of the initiation ceremony every kid had to go through. It involved seeing if a newcomer could taste the difference between red and green apples. First was the taste test on the fence.

His initiation to the gang was short. We went to the fence, and each kid grabbed the fence between pulses and licked the wire. "It tastes like chocolate ice cream today."

"No, it's strawberries. What do you think?" we asked the newcomer. *Zap.* Laughter, a little crying, and he was in.

As we picked up apples, he saw the worms in some.

"We just eat around them."

"If we throw an apple into the tree and one falls, why can't we eat that one too?" he asked. That seemed logical, so from then on few worms bothered us. A few weeks later, we had rationalized that climbing into the tree was just as good, and no worms or manure.

Shortly after that, it was common to wait for the lull between electric charges, cross the fence and climb the apple trees. But that stopped abruptly when the story of the shooting circulated through the neighborhood.

Two Big Kids were up in the apple tree, enjoying their favorite flavor— *bam!* They were out of the tree on the ground. From several yards away Farmer Bowman with shotgun in hand yelled, "I told you boys—now *git!*" They *got*—rock salt in the rear, torn pants and all. Pre-teens are not known for their brilliance. Everyone had left apple cores on the ground, never thinking that he would notice.

We may not have all known to hide apple cores, but everyone knew confessing to parents always brought worse punishment. A spanking on a wounded pride would be too much. Both boys went to a garage and with tweezers pulled out the salt from each other's rears. Little damage, but according to the wounded, it sure burned. After ditching underwear into the garbage and waiting for the bleeding to stop, they both went home. Neither thought mothers counted underwear when doing laundry, but they did. Mothers were used to snagged pants, but not lost underwear. Clothes were too hard to replace with rationing. One of the mothers noticed. At school, the son bragged about his ducking the belt. Remembering that he frequently lost socks and underwear under the bed, he took out a clean pair, wiped his dirty hands on the seat, threw it under the bed, retrieved it, and told his mother he got it from under the bed. True, but just barely.

Years before, in 1940, my dad left for Florida for several weeks. Before that trip, we seemed to be inseparable, I was always tagging along and trying to help. (It was okay for me to tag along with him, but not Nancy tagging along with the guys.) Mother told us he was at his mother's house recovering from a heart attack but would be back soon if he got better. She also told me of the family problem that followed all males on both sides of the family.

"For six generations, all the men on both sides of the family died before sixty-five. Not one had beaten the curse." She continued, "You will face the same fate—dying young." For a four-year-old, that was a heavy load. All I knew about death was it was going to heaven, and I had little concept of what that meant. Two playmates had run their wagon under a truck and had been killed, but to me, they just went away.

When Dad returned, I had been overjoyed. Mother had been unusually sad during his absence and spent a lot of time in her room. Mother, Nancy, and I took the family car to meet his train and brought him home.

Dad was back! Before he left, he was always supportive, but that support seemed to drift away. He spent more time alone now. Mom said it was his fear of dying, but forty years later, I found out otherwise. He had left her, only to return "for the kids" but under protest.

I was relieved when he got back, but for most of my life, that family curse followed me, affecting many decisions. Every time I had indigestion or a chest pain, like Fred Sanford on TV, I wondered, "Is this the big one?" Dad never mentioned the curse, and after Mother's warning while he was away, I never did either. Our closeness returned eventually, and I was determined to be just like him, even to becoming a banker. He participated in scouts, school activities, church, hobbies, and was the model father.

The constant presence of the war faded away once each year as we continued the pre-war practice of two weeks vacation on the banks of the St. Lawrence River, along the Thousand Islands area. Each year Dad saved, traded, or bought enough gas coupons on the black market to allow us a vacation at Cedar Point State Park. The family along with Auntie Ann, Unkie, and Gram set off for camping, the highlight of every year.

Our WWII Thousand Islands Camping Rig

We all slept on canvas cots in a tent, cooked out and enjoyed fishing, hiking, and cave exploring in the small shale caverns eroded by weather and passing ships. I always had a little devil in me and was looking forward to pranks. With company along, Mother was always cheerful.

I learned to swim at six during the 1942 vacation at Cedar Point. Dad rented a rowboat and towed me around the cove near our tent, and I would let go and paddle a little, then grab hold of the boat. After a few confidence-building swims, Dad told me to swim to shore, and he rowed out of reach. Off I went paddling toward shore as he rowed away. Near shore, I tested the water depth, and it was just about eyeball level. I tried to walk to shore, but it was just a little too deep. I didn't know how to start swimming again from a standing position. I remember seeing Nancy running up the hill, and each time my eyes rose out of the water, so did my ears. "*Swim!*," Dad yelled. Nancy was screaming! What was all the fuss? I was trying to walk to shore, but was just bobbing like a fishing line cork. Suddenly, as I started to "go to sleep," Dad grabbed me and pulled me to shore. He had jumped in, new watch, wallet and all, and swum about 100 yards to rescue me. Then he had to swim back to get the boat, which was drifting away. I was sure I was done for when he got back to the tent, but all he said was, "Tomorrow we learn to start swimming from a standing position."

I learned how a watch worked on that trip, too. I got to take the watch apart, dry and oil the insides. I also got to dry and iron paper money. Nancy watched the whole scene unfold and from then on was terrified of the water. In spite of encouragement, threats, offers of money (that always worked before, but not this time) she was not going to swim—ever!

The next summer, Dad had had enough of her stubbornness and insisted she swim. When she refused again, he took her to the end of the stone pier and calmly threw her in. I watched her bob, just like I had, then I jumped in and pulled her out. Dad cursed and walked off. She might never have learned to swim if we hadn't moved to Florida five years later, where the salt water made it easy to float.

This particular summer, 1943, we had taught Nancy to fish. There were no rods and reels then, so we used a drop line, simply a line with a sinker and hook, baited with a worm. As we held the line over the side of the rowboat, we waited for a nibble, and with a flick of the wrist, he was hooked. I was shocked when Nancy's reflexes beat mine and she caught more fish than I did. I was jealous of the attention she was getting and tried to think of a prank to take her down a notch or two.

My opportunity came when a camper caught a large pike, and just like a girl Nancy "eeeyewed" and ran back to the tent as she saw the guts of the fish on the ground after cleaning. The camper suggested that I tie one of the large eyes on a string and surprise Nancy by swinging it around my head until it got her in the face. That seemed like fun to me, unfortunately it was not amusing to the folks. This time the expanded family got to see the spanking (with my pants down), mortifying me, but not reforming me.

Something was wrong with Dad, though. Ever since we drove to the train station to pick him up from his "heart attack," his temper outbursts became more frequent as did the beatings, many times for nothing I did. If I whined or sniffled, it was "If you're going to cry, I'll give you something to cry about." During the frequent squabbles with my sister, I had impeccable timing, and Nancy knew how to use it. If she teased me, or we got into a shoving match, I got even—just as one of the parents saw me. Now, she didn't start them all. Nancy can testify that as big brother, I had a large number to my account.

One time while I was getting a whipping for ruining the shower curtain that Nancy had cut with the scissors, she watched and started laughing that she had "gotten me in Dutch," as we called trouble. She laughed so hard that she had an accident. When Dad asked what happened, she said, "Charles wet my pants." He almost believed her. She sat there looking into his big eyes, thinking, *He believes me!* I couldn't even tell the truth with as straight a face, but she could fib! I looked guilty, even if I was not. At least after that I wasn't automatically guilty anymore. I thought to myself, *I should have sold that rubber shower curtain for the war, then she wouldn't have been able to cut it.*

My hero worship was fading fast. One afternoon the gang decided to have a contest to see how fast we could pedal, then jump off our bikes and the bike that coasted the farthest would signal the winner. I won and rushed home to show Dad. As I entered the driveway and jumped off, running to the garage, my bike coasted even farther! Dad grabbed me by the arm and said, "You're running from Bill Teefle again!" (He was one of the big kids that liked to push little kids around.) "I told you to stand and fight." He was always warning me not to be a sissy. As I denied running away, the beating started, and finally, as he dragged me across the yard still beating me, I lied, and he quit. That was the first time I lied to stop a beating, and I decided that day I would no longer be like him.

VE (Victory in Europe) day came in 1945, and the newsreels showed the liberation of the Jewish concentration camps—one of the most horrifying shocks of my youth. Dad was anti-Semitic and anti-black, but I had never seen a Jewish person or a black, so I had no concept of prejudice. I just let him ramble on. Even his favorite Mussolini–Hitler joke, "If I knew you were coming I'd have baked a Kike," went over my head. He had still been my hero in those early days.

The "sub-human animals" my dad always joked about were actually *people*. The image of their bodies stacked in huge piles burned into my mind, and I became terrified of what my dad might do to me. His temper had become more heated and punishment more severe. After that, I was sure I would be killed during a temper outburst and distanced myself from him.

It was not until a family reunion in 1992 that I learned the source of one of his deep prejudices. We were in Beemerville, NJ, along with about 400 Spaces. I had received the invitation after meeting Fred Space, the patriarch of the New Jersey Spaces during a search for family ancestry in 1979. Fred, then in his eighties, owned Space Farms and Zoo, and he spent several hours telling of his adventures growing up in the mountains of the Delaware Water Gap. After the picnic featuring barbecued buffalo from his herd, I heard a voice calling, "Does anyone have information on a George Austin Ashley Space of Georgia?"

He was my great-great grandfather, and I had seen his grave outside Darien, Georgia. As I looked for the source of the voice, I was shocked. *Aunt Helen? Here?* It wasn't her, but a lady who could have passed for her twin. After a short conversation and exchanging family tree information, she asked if we had an account of the lynching of my great-great grandfather. He had moved from New York to Darien in 1867 after the War to work building shrimp boats and was lynched by a gang of runaway slaves. Grandma Space had always forbidden talk of the Civil War and had relived the agony and bitterness of her husband over his loss. Dad had learned his hatred from the family.

The camping trip that summer of 1945 saw the return of my devilish side. I was nine, and Nancy had just turned eight. Baby Jill was born three months earlier, and she came along with the family. She even accompanied us on fishing trips in the rowboat. Jill would lie in a wicker basket on the boat bottom, cooing as we fished. Some of the other campers complained that we shouldn't take her, but Mother just told them to mind their own business.

About midway through the camping trip, Nancy and I were walking to get the thermos jugs filled with water. There on the ground was a wasp nest. She asked me what that strange thing was. I told her it was a fairy toadstool, and if she danced on it barefoot, they would come out to sing for her. Running for cover, I watched her begin her dance. It was "neat" to see her dance, then jump and run screaming back to the campsite. Some time later when I got back to the campsite, I saw a doctor giving her shots for the stings. I tried to back out, but Dad was quicker. This was serious. It was the end of spankings and the start of beatings. I was sure he would kill me that time. I was reformed (a little) on that trip, and Nancy and I got along better.

All was forgotten a few days later, as VJ day was announced at the campground, and a large celebration ensued with fireworks, a huge bonfire, and the singing of patriotic songs. Germany had surrendered in the spring and Japan now followed. The two atomic bombs dropped on their homeland broke their resolve.

Both the war and sibling rivalry died away. I was nine, Nancy was eight, and she had developed her own friends, no longer interested in the boys.

Rationing went away and so did the OPA—the government agency that froze prices and wages. Shortages remained and prices rose. But at least we could have bananas on our cereal again, and no more dried, salted codfish, a two day per week meal for the past four years.

School went on, and by then I was making top marks, started to get interested in girls, and because of my photographic memory was the star of all the school plays. I was not particularly talented in acting, but at least I could memorize the lines. Dad's moodiness and temper outbursts continued, and I just stayed as far away as I could. I now detested being called "Chuck Space's son."

Over the past few years I had acquired the habit of saving everything for the war, and in parallel with that, I collected everything. My allowance was minimal, but I was able to earn extra by mowing lawns with the power mower Dad and I built. Baby sitting, feeding our next door neighbor's dog, and redeeming the two-cent deposit on drink bottles added to my savings. We lived a short walk from a fishing spot on the Bay, and fishermen always left their beer bottles, probably so the wives couldn't count them when they got home. By 1947, I had model trains from before the war, hundreds of comics, an Erector set, chemistry set, model airplanes, several scrapbooks of war headline stories I collected each day along with those comic strips related to the war. I also had a coin and stamp collection, a collection of several hundred antique shoe buttons used before shoelaces were common, and a collection of Indian head pennies, Buffalo nickels, Lincoln pennies—including the galvanized steel issue when copper was all used for ammunition. My prized coins were those coins from the 1700s and 1800s given to me by Unkie and "Daddy Scott," father of Aunt Lucy of bathing suit knitting fame. My artillery shell with the delay action fuse was hidden in my closet. Much of my earnings from selling collected things for the war effort went into buying War Bonds. After our country's source of kapok was cut off, milkweed pods were purchased by the collection centers. They were plentiful and the fluffy blooms were being used to fill life jackets for sailors and aviators. Every week, we all bought as many ten cent war stamps as we could and pasted them into a booklet, then exchanged the stamps for a $25.00 bond. When the war was over, I had many of the bonds in my name.

Friendships were close, and with gas rationing over, Sunday school and church resumed. I was a happy kid. I was especially interested in the Bible. At school, my beliefs were attacked by kids who claimed that the only people who go to heaven were from their church, and we were all going to hell. When I questioned this at Sunday school, my teacher told me to study God's word in the Bible and "see for yourself." After a few weeks of study, the taunts no longer mattered.

It was about that time I realized that all churches didn't teach the same things, and I began to question my parents why. They didn't know—"That's just the way it is!" I was told.

"Don't they use the same Bible as we do?" I asked.

"Go ask your father."

"Each church has its own rules to go along with the Bible."

"Are their rules as important as the Bible?"

"Yes, you can't question church rules."

It was clear that I was getting nowhere, so I gave up asking. But I didn't agree.

HISTORY

Dad was born Charles Collier Space in 1908 in Ridgeville, an outskirt of Darien, Georgia. His parents were Julian Austin Space and Penelope Collier Space. He was named after his two grandfathers. Charles Austin Space moved to Georgia from New York in 1867, and Thomas James Collier was a Civil War veteran who served in Butts Volunteers under Robert E. Lee and was wounded at the victory Malvern Hill southeast of Richmond on July 1, 1862. Grandma Space was especially proud of her father's role in the war and still harbored some of the pain from the ordeal. Both families had come from pioneer stock starting their ventures into America in the 1600s. Most had been farmers.

Dad was the middle child of seven. His father worked in the local bank in Darien. Dad spoke little of his growing up beyond the normal squabbling of siblings and part time work sweeping out the bank. The family moved to Lakeland, Florida, some time around 1920, and he graduated from high school in 1924. He had been a bright student and had skipped two grades, but Grandma Space made him stay in high school an extra year because he was so young. He spent hours during these years taking apart and reassembling anything he could—to see how things worked. He was even skilled enough to get them back together. His dream had been to go to Georgia Tech, to be a mechanical engineer, but as the third son, there was no money for that opportunity. Neither of his older brothers was able to attend college, and one, Uncle Julian, was working full time to help support the family. Grandma Space worked as a schoolteacher. Grandpa Space and his father both lived until 1936. Years later Dad admitted they had been heavy drinkers who did little to support the family.

Because it was not considered appropriate to be poor or to discuss family secrets in those days, the "Georgia Tech Story" was created. According to this version, it was not because of lack of money or family problems that he was unable to attend. A few months before school was to start, he "came down with pneumonia, and during the recovery period, all the college money was used for medical expenses."

After this "recovery" he left for Detroit to seek his fortune. The Roaring Twenties were in full swing, and the economy was booming. He was sixteen and ready to join the thousands who were getting rich. He got off the train, checked into the YMCA, and looked forward with excitement to the career that was ahead as soon as he got a job.

The Good Humor Ice Cream Bar had been patented the year before, and he started his career selling the new fangled treat. The inventor, Harry Burt, sold his Good Humor bars from a fleet of white trucks equipped with bells and uniformed drivers. At sixteen, Dad wasn't allowed to drive, so he started with a three-wheeled bicycle–driven white cart outfitted with the standard uniform and bell. His first job was not the glamorous one he sought. That summer was unusually cool, and as Dad described it, "If I hadn't been able to eat the ice cream bars, I would have starved to death."

Dad left Detroit and began anew in Rochester, NY, as a bookkeeper for Burroughs Company, where he met my mother in about 1930. She was a stenographer at Burroughs. They married in May 1931, during the depths of the Depression. Dad had changed jobs and was then working as cashier of Security Trust Company. Many lost jobs during that trying time, but Dad was fortunate that Security Trust survived the bank closures, partly because George Eastman, founder of Eastman Kodak, kept his funds there. Dad's only sacrifice for the Depression was a pay cut of $5.00 per month, but the remainder was enough to enjoy a better living than most in those trying times.

◆ ◆ ◆ ◆ ◆

Mother was born in 1911 to Frank Palmer Hilliard and Christina Pietronella Van der Koorde, both second generation Americans. The Hilliards immigrated to America from Ireland, and the Van der Koorde family immigrated from Middleburg in southern Holland in 1848, a few years after the defeat of Napoleon. They were Protestant refugees from the still prevalent persecution in Southern Netherlands.

The Reformation Movement that swept northern Europe after Martin Luther's break with the Roman Catholic Church in 1521 had caught on in the Netherlands, but not without embroiling the country in wars with Spain (lasting almost 100 years) and France, which dominated Holland until 1815. By 1848, the southern part of Holland was still under some French domination, and the original Van der Koorde family passport that I located a few years ago is in French. At the time Hubertus Van der Koorde was a preacher who had lost two of his four children in Holland. Because of the religious persecution in southern Holland, the family left for the new world.

Hubertus, his wife Joanna, and the two surviving children moved to Rochester, NY, and began their new life in America. Unfortunately, after arriving they lost two more children who were born in New York. Surviving son Hubertus and three sisters were the only remaining members of the original family. Grandmother and her sister Johanna were born in Rochester to Hubertus Jr. and Tannetjie Adrianse, also from Holland. There were no sons, so the family name through that line died out.

Mother was one of nine children. Her father, Frank earned his living weaving cane chairs, and feeding a family of eleven soon became more that he could manage. Her aunt, Johanna, had married a prominent Rochester businessman Leonard Hall, but they were not able to have children, so "Auntie Ann" and "Unkie" took Mother in to raise as their own. At that young age, being given away was more than she could understand.

The new life had many advantages—she was now a rich kid, respected in school and wherever they went. Unkie owned a large landscaping business with many wealthy customers, and years later he often bragged to Nancy and me of doing work for the Rockefeller, Vanderbilt, Eastman families, as well as many other people he knew but we didn't. They bought a new car every year. Mother was active in school and was enrolled in the Eastman School of Music where she studied ballet. She often told of one occasion when she danced on the same program and met Enrico Caruso, the famous opera star of the early 1900s. Every year included a grand vacation, and Mother used to show us her awards. Her favorite was a photo of Mother as she stood between President Hoover and his wife, Lou all three posing in front of the Washington Monument. It was taken in 1929 during a 4-H Club trip to Washington. She was careful to point out to everyone who saw the photo out that the purse Mother was holding was Mrs. Hoover's.

The fact that her siblings lived nearby and visited often continually reminded her of being given away. They also delighted in reminding her. Mother also saw dark days while growing up in the big house. Auntie Ann and Unkie had no experience raising children and had little tolerance for anything that bothered them. She was often punished by being locked in a closet, sometimes for hours at a time. Even as an adult, she was uncomfortable in a dark room.

The stock market crash of 1929 wiped out Unkie's fortune, and hard times for Mother returned. He lost everything, with only enough for a small house remaining. He was so broken in spirit that he refused to work at all, and except for three years work during the war, never worked again until his death in the 1950s. Auntie Ann took a job typing to support the family. Mother was eighteen when she went to work as a stenographer at Burroughs, a step down that wiped out the only comfort she had for being given away to her aunt and uncle.

After their marriage in May 1931, Mother lost her first son late in the pregnancy. He was to have been named after my father, Charles Sr. This new loss devastated Mother, and it was some time before they were able to start the new family. The Van der Koorde family history of losing infants had followed her.

Mother and Dad had only one adventure that we knew of before I came along in 1935. It was when Mother and Dad took Gram on a vacation to Virginia Beach, Virginia. A drive of over 500 miles in those days was a major trip, especially during the Depression. Tires were reinforced with cotton cords at that time and roads were poor, so one could expect several "flats" on that length trip.

Grandfather Hilliard died in 1933, and this vacation was a good time for Gram to get away to recuperate. In August 1933, they loaded up their luggage and the camping tent and drove in their car, a Ford Model A sedan, from Rochester to Virginia.

While tent camping on the beach, the sky darkened and the wind increased. As the hurricane approached, the sand blowing on the beach began to sting and rain poured down. It got worse, and Dad decided pack up the tent and move to the mainland. By the time the car was loaded, the waves trapped them and the car got stuck in the sand. The weather was worsening, and the only way off the beach was by crawling across a railroad trestle connecting the beach with the mainland. All three, along with another couple, headed across on their hands and knees as waves crashed against the wooden beams. Mother, Dad, and Gram just made it across when the trestle collapsed. They never saw the other family and assumed they were among the eighteen who died that day. When the storm left, they returned to the beach, still in their bathing suits, and found the car with less than a foot of the top showing above the sand. Everything was lost, but they had survived the Great Chesapeake Hurricane of 1933.

Dad didn't tell us how he got clothes, or how they got home, but I know that he bought another Ford after returning to Rochester.

I was born two years later, in 1935, and, as was the custom in those days, was also named Charles. To make up for the loss of their first son, I was the focus of all their attention.

Mother's next near tragedy was in 1936, when she found me in the crib near death. I was just barely breathing and had turned blue, with a fever of 106. They rushed me to the hospital just up the street from their apartment, and I was packed in ice to lower the fever. Immediately afterwards, I was bombarded with x-rays, the standard treatment to shrink my enlarged thymus gland, which was the cause of the episode. "There is no way to tell if restricted breathing and high temperature had caused any brain damage until he is older," Mother was told.

Years later, it was discovered that a high percentage of those x-rayed developed tumors, and even seventy years later, the University of Rochester continues to monitor my condition. During the '30s and early '40s, x-rays were used pretty casually. The equipment was relatively inexpensive, so many machines were available for new uses. From the time I learned to walk until the end of World War II, x-rays were used regularly for a number of common duties, even to fit shoes. The danger of excessive exposure was not understood, and no radiation protection was provided for the operator or the lower body of the customer.

Mother never mentioned the x-ray treatment to me, but other family members recall her fear of losing another child, or even worse, having a brain damaged son. From the time I could walk and talk, she was overprotective and determined to tutor me so I would have a head start by school age. She spent hours reading to me, teaching me to read simple words at the age of three. By Kindergarten age, which in NY public school was four years old (if you reached five by Christmas), I could read, count, spell, print simple words, and add. I still have some of the "Buddy Books" she taught me to read. By 1941, I was reading on my own, and the school recommended I be allowed to skip three grades. Dad refused, remembering that when he skipped two grades, he never was accepted in school activities, and he didn't want me to face that problem. At the time I was disappointed, but later on, I found this decision was one of the best he had made for me.

Nancy came along in 1937 and took part of my center stage, but I was too young to notice. Mother had time for two and stayed busy. By the time Nancy was two, Mother announced it was too much for her and she just had to have help. She was staying in her room a lot and seldom was happy, except when we had visitors or when we went out to the pinochle parties. Dad hired a Dutch immigrant Mena (short for Wilhelmina), and our lives drastically improved, especially the food. Beds were made every day, clothes were always clean, she picked up our toys without complaining, and Mena even sang while she worked. She was a fantastic cook and delighted in playing with us after her chores were done.

One evening at the dinner table, Dad spit his food on the floor, exclaiming, "Onions! Don't you know I don't eat onions?"

Mena was crying, "I didn't know..."

"You're fired. Get out, right now!" I thought fired meant he was going to set her on fire and jumped to her defense.

"Look Dad, I put Hellmann's mayonnaise (Dad's favorite) on the meat loaf, and it's real good!"

He ignored me and shouted, "Pack your things!" I started to cry, and he balled up his fist. "Do you want something to cry about?" he shouted. I went to my room with no more supper. Mena left in the morning. To this day, I only eat meat loaf with mayonnaise, and always Hellmann's if it's available. Each time I do, I remember kind, gentle Mena. Mother never forgave me for missing Mena.

The following year, I made two trips to the hospital, one to remove my tonsils and another after a bicycle accident. I had gotten a bicycle for my sixth birthday with a stern warning not to leave it behind the car. I had lost three tricycles that way. Dad taught me how to ride, and I caught on to everything quickly except the art of graceful stopping. My legs were a little too short. I could pedal with the tips of my toes, but braking was another matter. I would stop by running my bike into the curb and jumping off. One Saturday, I hit the curb a little fast and went over the handlebars—right into a forsythia bush. I remember Mother coming to see what all the crying was about and trying to brush a brown spot off my upper lip. It hurt and wouldn't come off. It was a two inch long twig the diameter of a soda straw, and it passed up through my cheek into my eye socket, just missing the eye.

I remember that hospital trip vividly. Without using any pain killer, the doctor slowly pulled out the twig as Dad held me down by lying on top of me on the operating table. He was so heavy that the pain in my chest blocked out the pain of the extraction. After Dad got off and I could breathe again, I saw the doctor dipping a Q-tip into a bottle of yellow fluid. "We've got to clean it out so it doesn't get infected." He told Dad, "So hold him again, and I'll start." This time Dad's weight was not enough. As the procedure started, I realized the yellow stuff was soap. As he twisted the Q-tip further in, it burned like fire, especially when it reached my eye. I thrashed and almost got away, but it was soon over. The damage to my eye was not serious, but I began wearing glasses after that incident. I also learned to stop the bicycle the right way. I didn't know that the seat could be lowered so I could reach the pedals. I thought Dad would take it back if I complained. When I finally told him of the problem, he cuffed me on the back of my head and used the nickname "Stupie" for the first time. I watched as he adjusted the seat height so I could reach the pedals and decided to learn how things worked so I could fix everything myself.

THE NOMAD YEARS

Life was good before the war. By the time I came along, it was the middle of the Great Depression. Dad continued working at Security Trust, and his career was blossoming. Unlike many in those days, there was enough money, we had moved into the new house, and school was going well. Up to that time, we had lived in several rental houses and apartments, never for long, though. Apartments and rental houses were plentiful during the Depression. When loud parties, drinking and card games resulted in complaints from the landlord, Dad just replied, "The hell with you" and moved the next day. The family had always owned a car, so it was loaded up the next day with help from card party friends, and off we went.

It's unusual for anyone to remember his life before seven or eight, but I can recall isolated facts from the time my sister Nancy was born in 1937. I remember that time primarily because I was no longer the only one making noise in the house. Perhaps the other memories stayed with me because so much changed when Pearl Harbor came into all our lives. Here was a six-year-old remembering and longing for the "Good Old Days"!

Other reminders came from the hundreds of photos that were taken. My dad's best friend from before he was married, Harry Bell, was an employee of Kodak. I don't know if it was from Dad or Harry Bell that I learned to plan pranks. Both were experts at pranks and jokes but not diplomacy. They delighted in sharing their "latest" whenever they got together. I tried to eavesdrop to hear, but those I understood made me laugh and get caught. Two particularly stand out in memory—the tea and the marble cake.

Mother had not learned to cook before her marriage to Dad. Being brought up in a wealthy house with no siblings and with kitchen help didn't require learning cooking or housekeeping. One of her first cooking attempts was to fix dad a cup of Lipton tea. Dutifully, she measured out two cups of water and boiled it, adding a full cup of tea leaves. Well for goodness sakes, when she tried to pour, no tea came out. Unfazed, she took out the orange juice squeezer and mashed the wet leaves until she had a cup full. Dad took one sip, and did he say, "Honey, this is a little strong"? No, he spit it out and poured the rest in his shoe, saying, "This is good only to tan leather." Mother cried.

On another occasion, he and Harry came in a little tipsy from one of their regular celebrations. Mother had spent the afternoon baking a special surprise cake for Dad. It was a marble cake, white cake with marble-like swirls of chocolate throughout. It was her first attempt at cake baking, and it was perfect. Dad and Harry took this occasion to make a joke of the cake.

"Harry, this is a marble cake."

"Really, Chuck, is it real marble?"

"I guess so, let's check." Mother was fuming. "Marble is heavy, so you get on one side and lift. I'll try to lift the other." The rest is history. Like a football halfback, Mother grabbed the cake and passed it right into the chute to the basement incinerator. That night Dad and Harry both sobered up—fast.

Harry and his wife Marion, along with Ann and Bobby, were regular visitors, and on many trips he brought his camera, floodlights (before flash cameras) and what seemed to be a mile of wires. I would have to dress up, pose with the latest toys, and wait in the hot lights while they laughed and fiddled with the camera to be sure the picture was just right. After all, he was using the expensive new color film.

Another vivid reminder came from the card parties that continued each weekend. The games rotated among several friends' houses, winter or summer, interrupted only by illness. Pinochle, drinking, and heavy smoking were no particular bother early on, because I slept in another room on the host's bed alongside the coats, hats, scarves and gloves. Yes, in those days you dressed up to go out—even to the store.

After Nancy was born, the card parties became the dread of my life. With the baby now getting the bed, I had to sleep on the sofa in the living room, which was rearranged to make room for the card table. I was put behind the sofa cushions to shield me from the lights and expected to go to sleep. *Slap!* went the cards onto the table when someone lost, followed by a loud, "Dammit!" I choked and coughed as the cigarette smoke filled the room, burning my eyes and giving me a constant sore throat. The threat, "Stop whining, or I'll give you something to whine about!" followed. I tried to pretend sleeping, but the sniffles gave me away. Hey, give me a break. I was only two when it started! But it lasted until we moved into our house three years later.

Soon, I began getting "sleeping medicine," a tablespoon of awful tasting Scotch, and if that didn't work soon enough, a second dose. It usually worked, but if not, I really got good at pretending to sleep because I always ended up feeling sick after the Scotch. Occasionally, the Scotch came early, and I walked funny afterwards. To the whoops and laughter of the adults, I showed off, the center of attention again. I even begged for a cigarette, but Dad told me they were "coffin nails" and bad for your health. That they were banned made them even more attractive.

Cigarettes were off limits until I was five, when during a ride in the country with my cousins, my aunt got tired of the cigarette begging. "If you want to, then fine!" I was excited! "Aunt Teen" took a big drag on her cigarette, inserted a soda straw into my mouth, held my cheeks so the smoke couldn't escape and blew. I'll never forget seeing the smoke roll out of my nose, burning like fire! I couldn't breathe! Then as I thought I was dying, I saw two small columns of smoke rising in front of my eyes. They were coming out of my tear ducts! She finally quit and let me go. Mother stopped the car, and as I jumped out, I began to vomit violently. Exhausted, I returned to the car and never again smoked a cigarette. I was frequently asked, "Want a smoke?" Laughter came as I refused by "making an ugly face." No way! I was cured for good.

I can remember living in many places in the years 1938–41, even on the Day family's farm, where I delighted in feeding chickens, picking apples, chasing the pigs, and watching apple cider being made. "Uncle Bill" as I called him, let me taste it. It tasted fine, but the fermented Apple Jack burned my throat and made me dizzy, just like Dad's Scotch "sleeping and cough medicine." The farm had no water other than a hand pump lifting it to the kitchen sink from a cistern in the basement. That water came from the roof drains. Mother never pumped the water because sometimes a frog came up, too. We had an outhouse beside a trickling brook, but it was downstream from the place we dipped water when the basement went dry. It didn't take Mother long to cut this adventure short. She preferred reading Earle Stanley Gardner Mysteries to the Sears catalog in the outhouse. We had learned to "sit and git" when the temperature dropped into the teens. At least in the cold weather the flies were gone. I can recall some of the other less pleasant duties, too. Moving the outhouse by dragging it downstream with a team of horses was the worst. Chopping off chicken's heads and plucking off the steaming soggy feathers came in a distant second.

One place we lived stood out in my memory—a multi-story brick apartment on Garson Avenue. Here, Nancy was getting old enough to be part of the fun, but neither of us was old enough to learn the custom that boys were not to play with siblings unless they were brothers. In that apartment, we had no choice. We couldn't go out to play until Mother woke up and approved. Nancy and I would be on our own each morning, as Mother would get up to fix breakfast and go back to bed with a "I don't want to hear a peep out of you two." Sometimes I would say, "peep, peep" so low she couldn't hear.

Apartments in those days didn't have many of the appliances we enjoy, and ours was no different. The laundry was in the basement, and each apartment had a door to the laundry chute, allowing each renter to drop the clothes down on wash day. All clothes were sent down in a bag with your apartment number on the side to prevent mix ups. I discovered the chute had small ladder rungs on one side to allow climbing up or down to reach laundry bags if they got stuck. Mothers tended to pack the bags overly full so that once your turn came, you could get as much laundry as possible into the wringer washer. I suspect the ladder was one reason they got stuck, but for me it was a chance to explore while Mother slept. The door was big enough for a four-year-old, and one of the kids on another floor told me he had climbed down to the basement once and there was a large furnace and coal pile in one corner. You could get dirty without even going outside! If you used the laundry chute, you also had to have a little brother or sister to unlock the apartment door and let you in or your mother would catch you, and it would end the fun for all the kids.

He also told how he had fun by letting go of the ladder and falling on the pile of clothes, but "Be sure they were there before letting go." He had jumped without looking the first time and got a whipping for tearing his pants and skinning his knee. In those days, boys had to wear short pants with suspenders until they went to school. Even in winter, I wore shorts under my snow suit and boots. I couldn't even talk the folks into buying knickers, a compromise some lucky kids wore.

One winter morning, after a pinochle party, Mother wouldn't get up for breakfast, and we were hungry. After two or three tries and loud "go aways," I decided to do something new. With Nancy as my lookout, I entered the chute, climbed upward, checking each chute door as I climbed. The top one was unlatched! I opened it a crack, and no one was there. Quickly, I hopped out, opened the icebox, and there were some apples. Pushing two into my pockets, down I went. We were sitting on top of the enameled table eating our prizes when Mother came out. "You both are making so much noise, I couldn't sleep," she snorted. "And just where did you get those apples?"

"From the icebox," I replied. It was true, at least mostly true.

Another prank using the laundry chute was also related to iceboxes. Refrigerators were relatively new, and most homes and apartments in those days had an icebox, which was an insulated wooden box much smaller than today's refrigerators. As the ice melted, it dripped into a tray under the ice, a tray that had to be emptied every day to prevent flooding.

Ice sawn from Lake Ontario in the winter was stored in ice houses covered with huge piles of sawdust to keep it from melting. Of course, some motor-driven ice machines were working, but lake ice was cheaper. Three times a week, the ice wagon came through neighborhoods to deliver fresh ice. Those needing ice would place an ice card in their window, a circle of four pie shaped slices each having a different color representing ten, twenty-five, or fifty pound blocks of ice. The fourth side was black, signaling "no ice today." By putting the card in the window with the color for the desired amount on top, the iceman could cut the ice to size, deliver it, and collect with one trip up the stairs.

The "fun" came by sneaking into apartments early in the morning and turning the card to "no ice today" or fifty pounds for a small icebox. The iceman didn't think it was fun at all, especially carrying fifty pound blocks up to the top floor and back down. We had no TV showing programs on how criminals avoided getting caught, so it didn't take long to be found out.

The kids' use of the laundry chute had been discovered, and it was now off limits. Mother had asked if I'd ever used it, and I replied "Where?" I was shown, being pulled to the door by my ear. I replied, "Wow that looks scary; do kids use that?"

"Yes, and if I ever catch you in there you'll *get it*." I ran to my room pretending to be scared. I was—scared she would ask any more questions.

Another fun thing to do on freezing winter days was to go to the Commercial Laundry a few doors from the apartment and sit outside the vent from the steam pressing machine. We took turns warming our hands in the steam as it puffed out. Then, I had a bright idea. We could warm our afternoon snacks! Peanut butter sandwiches tasted better warm. All bright ideas eventually get you in trouble as they go into the "what if we…" territory. The large potato we pounded into the pipe did it. I never saw a mad Chinaman before, but this guy was scary. We couldn't understand his shouts, but they were probably Chinese for some of those grown-up words forbidden to children. Guess what? We moved again, this time to a rental house across the street from the house Dad was having built. I thought Gram might move in the spare bedroom when it was finished, but she never did.

Gram lived in a one room apartment with a water heater you had to light each time hot water was needed. Dad gave her money each week for groceries, and one of her sons paid the rent. Several of my cousins lived in crowded row apartment buildings several stories high. None had a yard, and there was no park. The apartments had only a narrow alley behind. Each had a clothesline hanging across the alley to the next building. I remember looking at the lines way up in the air and wondering how mothers reached the clothes.

One day I decided to find out. I waited till Aunt Tizzy did laundry, and then I sneaked out into the alley to see how it was done. I had to hide to keep from being seen because we *never* stayed around when laundry was being done. Diapers smelled bad, and we might get caught and have to help. There were pulleys on each building allowing the laundry to be pinned to the line, put out, and retrieved when dry. I had solved another of life's great mysteries.

Several of my cousins lived in poor surroundings, and they had little money for anything but food. Buying things was Mother's measure of success. All were impressed by how well the "give away" sister had done. The agony of losing her first son, Charles, in 1931, and the panic when she almost lost me in 1936 had faded, was replaced with my survival and their lavishing many toys and gifts, often gifts for older children. Until Nancy was born, I was the center of attention and loved it.

Now that we lived in an actual house, Mother was able to use our car on weekends to pick up her mother, sisters, and most of the nephews and nieces that were our age for a visit at our new home. Visits from Mother's family included lots of play time, and regularly we all piled into the car for a day at the beach. Durand-Eastman Park was just a short drive away on the shores of Lake Ontario. The park was named for two wealthy citizens, Dr. Henry S. Durand and his friend George Eastman, of Eastman Kodak fame. They saw a need for a public park in the area and bought a number of farms on Lake Ontario. They donated their land to the city of Rochester, "to be used as a public park forever, a tract of land of about 484 acres in the Town of Irondequoit on Lake Ontario," land which included nearly a mile of public beach. Dad seemed to disappear on those Saturdays when Mother's family visited us or when we went to the beach.

Dad was playing "golf," whatever that was. I remember finding some golf balls one day and trying them out from the top floor of the Garson Avenue apartment. They would bounce all the way back up to the window if thrown down hard enough. One bounced onto the hood of a truck, and the driver jumped out to catch me. Nancy and I hid behind the curtains and escaped capture, but that was the end of my "golfing." The driver took the ball, and Dad's "big eye" questioning got me to confess.

A few weeks later, he took me to the course to see how the game was really played. I learned two things on that first and last trip to the links. One, the grownup words they used at golf were the same ones I heard during the pinochle card games. Two, don't throw a golf ball on the course. I was playing catch with one as I walked behind Dad's foursome on the way from the tee to the green. Playfully, I lobbed the ball over the four, hitting the ground in front of Dad. He thought the next group had hit it before we were out of range and blew up! "You *** fool!" he shouted. "You almost hit me! I'm coming back to whip your ***!" I panicked and did what any decent son would do. Confess? No way! I stared at the ground in silence. "Charles, did you see that fool?" he said. I had, and I knew that fool well. He and I had gotten in trouble before. Dad's friends convinced him to go on and ignore the "fool." I was glad he did. Dad was too mad to notice he was short another golf ball.

By war's end, Dad received the reward for the government's confiscation of his new 1942 Oldsmobile for the war effort. It had been only a week before Dad was to pick it up, and at the time, he complained bitterly at its loss. Now, he proudly drove our brand new Olds home to everyone's delight and the envy of all his friends.

We never got to visit any of Dad's family because they all still lived in the south, and Grandmother Space only visited once or twice while I was growing up. I never expected to be able to travel that far, but I was in for a surprise!

EXODUS

My passion for knowledge, for collecting, and for building things continued. In the fall of 1946, Dad came down with a constant cough and finally went to the doctor for tests. He believed doctors should be consulted only as a last resort. It was "sissy" for a man to ask for help. He was coughing up blood and that was enough for Mother. He had to go for a check-up. "You have three kids and do it for them if not for me," she begged. Dad gave in and went. When he got home, he was very quiet. They spent most evenings talking in a low voice that neither Nancy nor I could hear, even with ears pressed against the door. Mother cried a lot, and we knew something bad was happening.

We found out in January 1947. Dad came home from work one evening to announce that we were moving! He sat Nancy and me down to tell us that his doctor had told him we had to move. Damage from the years of heavy smoking combined with air pollution in Rochester gave him only six months to live if he didn't stop smoking and move to a climate having clean, fresh air. When he explained the unfamiliar term "air pollution," I recalled the terrible smells in Rochester when we picked him up on Fridays. I had often gotten sick in the car while in town. Almost all industries were fueled by coal, and all but the newest houses had a coal burning furnace. In most neighborhoods snow was black a few days after it fell. Added to the coal were the fumes from industries.

He had chosen Jacksonville, Florida, for his new job and Jacksonville Beach for our residence. It was far away from the power plant and paper mill in town, and he didn't want to chance breathing any polluted air. We would leave in February and drive to Florida. I was heartbroken. I was fine here—friends, family, school, church. I had just learned to dance and had already picked out a girl in my class to dance with. She didn't know it yet, but I was building up courage to ask. Life was over! I began to realize that all of Dad's changes over the past months were not from their marriage. Some came from his health problems. I understood we would have to go, or he would die if we didn't.

He quit smoking "cold turkey," and he became even more irritable for a few weeks, but the advice from the doctor served him well. Instead of dying in six months, Dad lived fifty-five years longer to the ripe old age of ninety-four.

The effect of moving was worse on Mother, though. She was losing her house, her friends, all the family relationships that had been restored, and she had to stop smoking too—something she refused to do until Dad finally stood up to her. Migraine headaches and depression set in. Her treatment of Nancy and me became harsh. Jill, then two, escaped the wrath. Knuckle sandwiches, broom beatings, boxing of our ears kept us terrified and bruised. Octagon soap originally used on our tongues for fibbing began to be administered indiscriminately "just because I feel like it!" When she announced that everything I had saved except my coins and stamps was to be thrown away, my world seemed to end. They were all gone before I had a chance to ask Dad for help. "I'm having to leave here, and you both are going to suffer, too," she exclaimed. We did.

Dad had all the many war bonds I had accumulated so they survived the destruction. At least I hadn't lost those prizes.

February 1947, we left for Florida—Mother, Dad, Nancy and baby Jill. A huge snowstorm earlier that week had stopped most traffic, and crossing the mountainous areas of central Pennsylvania was now impossible. Even those roads that were plowed had snow banks higher that the roof of the car. Dad was scheduled to be at his new bank job on Monday, so with only three days to get there, we couldn't wait any longer. We all piled into the new Oldsmobile along with everything we could pack in and headed east toward New York City. Dad planned to drive along the east coast, away from much of the bad weather. Two days before, I had come down with a fever, which proceeded to get much worse. By Albany, I didn't know where I was, and when we pulled up to the Commodore Hotel in Manhattan, I couldn't walk. The hotel doctor came to the room, checked my temperature at 103, gave me some nasty tasting medicine, and I went to bed.

I don't remember anything more except waking up two days later on Sunday at the Manson Motor Lodge in Jacksonville Beach. The Mansons were old acquaintances of Dad's family, and they welcomed us appropriately. By that night the fever was gone. I had slept it off and was feeling better. During the delirious hours in the car, I had a nightmare about being accepted at school. I even saw that they were studying in the same textbook and on a page that we completed several months earlier in New York. Before I left, I had been kidded by my cousins about the "backward South," and how I would be far ahead of the class, maybe enough to skip school for a couple months while they caught up. I was even told that schools there didn't have indoor plumbing—only outhouses, and all the homes were shacks.

In our new hometown, land had been cheap before the war, and people who had money took advantage of the low real estate prices. Much of the land was swampy and considered worthless. B. B. McCormick saw otherwise, and over the years traded his construction services for hundreds of acres, which he filled and converted to valuable land. This filling, along with the dredging of mosquito control ditches, reduced the insect problem to a reasonable level. The ocean breezes kept what mosquitoes were left to the west of the beachfront, and those summer breezes brought many visitors from Jacksonville and the surrounding areas. The availability of bus and auto transportation to Jacksonville opened the area to a population increase of over 800% between 1930 and 1940.

The Beaches saw many war-related changes. Tankers had been sunk along the east coast—torpedoed and shelled by the German submarines, leaving large areas of the sand saturated with tar-like oil. A group of saboteurs had landed from a sub just a few miles south of Jacksonville Beach and were captured weeks later. Most of the strangers seen during those years were servicemen. The roller coaster and the boardwalk amusement area had been blacked out and a barrier constructed to prevent the submarines from spotting ships silhouetted at night in the city lights. The war was more real to these people than it had been for us in New York. They had actually heard the explosions and watched as the tanker, *Gulf Breeze*, went down just off the beach.

The Casa Marina Hotel was leased to the government to house war workers and converted into apartments. The first hospital at the Beaches was started in an old motel on 1st Avenue South. During my first spring, I got to test the skill of the hospital staff. I jumped off the seawall onto the sand where someone had buried half of a Coke bottle, broken edge up. An artery in my foot was severed, and I ran as fast as I could to the hospital a block away. The blood stains remained until the storm in the fall of 1947 demolished that seawall.

Until after the war, virtually no one moved to Jacksonville Beach, except for those associated with military installations a few miles north in Atlantic Beach at the new Army Combat Team Camp and at Mayport Naval Station. The new Mayport Sea Frontier Base was used for maintenance and refueling of submarines and as a homeport for minesweepers. Construction had continued in spite of war shortages near these bases, but most of the workers had no cars or children. By the time we arrived, most had left.

The day after we arrived, Dad left for work on the bus, and Mother drove Nancy and me to Pablo School. Jacksonville Beach was originally named Pablo Beach, and the school kept the original name. Driving us to school was a mistake. Nobody got driven to school in those days! Who were these people? The license plate said New York! The car was a brand new Oldsmobile! It may be hard to imagine nowadays, but at that time, no student had ever met anyone born outside the state of Florida! Except for kinfolks, most had never met anyone from more than 100 miles away. During the war, no one had a new car.

We walked to the principal's office to receive our class assignment between two lines of strange kids staring at us all the way. Not a confidence builder for someone who had never moved from one school to another. In fact, with almost no travel possible during the war, I had grown up with the same friends and had only met one new family.

As I nervously entered class, there was a lot of giggling, and the teacher introduced me, showed on the map where I had come from, and read my report card to the class. Spelling E, Reading E, Arithmetic E, Deportment E, on it went. The class nodded with approval. No competition from this newcomer—all E's. He failed everything! Then the teacher explained that grades in New York were not the A, B, C, etc. used here, but Excellent, Satisfactory, and Unsatisfactory. The class made faces but remained silent.

Shortly afterwards I realized a basic difference in educational attitudes. Before, it was good to get top marks in school. All the kids seemed to want to excel. Here, it was the reverse. Good marks meant you were not smart but the teacher's pet, the lowest order in kids' society.

At recess, I went to the swings to get away from the stares, but I was invited to join the dodge ball game. Getting bopped with the ball would show me. I was good at dodge ball. Ducking my parents and bullies had sharpened dodging skills.

The second day of school, we opened our Social Studies books, and I saw it was the same one used in New York. That should make it easy, no catching up to do. As I turned to the proper page, the picture at the bottom leaped up at me. It was the same page and picture I had seen during the delirious nightmare in the car. They *were* two months behind! For the first couple weeks, I settled in and I tried to gain acceptance by holding back on answers and even missing questions on purpose. Everyone laughed at my accent, but to keep their attention, I even added more. It seemed to be working, and at recess, I was even staying ahead of most in dodge ball.

A couple weeks into the new class, something happened. People quit talking to me and wouldn't respond if I spoke. I was getting the cold shoulder. For the first time, when I won at dodge ball, instead of getting cheers, two of the larger kids came into the ring, held me by both arms and the class took turns throwing the ball at me. "Damn Yankee," someone whispered. Now I knew using the word "damn" was a cuss word, spoken only by parents—never kids, under penalty of a severe whipping. But what was the word Yankee? The only Yankees I knew of were the baseball team, and they had just started playing again after the war. When I got home, Mother was suffering from another migraine, so I didn't dare ask her what was happening.

At home Dad explained the expression and that it came from families who lost the Civil War, and along with it many lost fortunes, loved ones, homes, and jobs. That war had only ended eighty-two years before, and many parents had heard of the hardships directly from family members. In the South being a Yankee was worse than a being Black, a German, or a Jap. To a sixth grader, that was not a big confidence builder! Dad told me to tell everyone that he had been born in Georgia, his grandfather had been a well known officer in the Confederate Army, and that Dad had moved north to make a living. He was just coming home to the South.

I tried that, but it didn't work. Kids even crossed to the other side of the street to keep from speaking as I walked to school from the Motor Lodge. Even the cute girl who sat behind me stopped tickling my ear with her pencil. I was officially off limits.

I remember one of our first swims in the ocean after we moved to Florida in 1947. Aunt Lucy had knitted bathing suits for Nancy, Baby Jill and me—all three a sissy pink. There was no refusing to wear it. The only hope was to wear it once and spill something horrible on it or just secretly throw it away. My record at keeping secrets with a tattle tale sister was dismal, so I decided that spilling indelible ink would do the trick, but fate was on my side. I ran to the surf with a towel around my neck, started swimming and the suit disappeared. Once wet, it stretched several sizes, and it was gone. Thank heavens for the towel. It was quickly adjusted, and I then looked to see how the other bathing suits were faring in salt water.

Baby Jill sat in a shallow puddle, and her suit gradually sagged to the sandy beach. She was just two, so modesty was not a problem. She just ran naked across the beach as Mother watched in horror! What if someone we knew saw us?

Nancy was not so lucky. She ran out of the surf with both hands full of bathing suit large enough for an elephant. If she hadn't been so skinny, actual flesh would have been showing. Mother wrapped a towel around her sobbing body and the suits were never mentioned again. When Mother wasn't looking, I snuck in a smile. No more pink bathing suit for me!

By then, we had moved to a rental duplex at the south city limits twenty-five blocks from the school on an unpaved road, surrounded by palmettos. To avoid torment, I stopped riding the school bus. I started riding my bike to school along the sandy beach and occasionally into the shallow water. I always got there as late as possible and skipped recess. The bike ride home was often along the beach, and it was fun dodging shells, seaweed and the large patches of black sand left over from torpedoed tankers. I would time getting home with dinner, and after doing dishes with Nancy, I would listen to the radio until bedtime. There were no other houses near ours, so after school there was little to do.

I had noticed a change in Mother during those months. After moving, she went into a deep depression and her migraines worsened. Her friends and family were gone again. She had been so proud of the house we owned and thoroughly enjoyed her sisters' envy when they visited every week. It was now replaced by a rental duplex located on a dirt road in a rattlesnake infested area that was strewn with garbage. Rats roamed the yard regularly, and they terrified Mother. The move to Florida was hard for the kids, but even harder for Mother. Because Dad's lung problems were so severe, she had to stop smoking, and went through terrible times withdrawing from nicotine. There were no medications available then. Dad had been scared out of smoking, but for Mother, it was another in the long string of losses that affected her whole life. During this time, Mother was pregnant again, this time with our brother David, and as time went on she continued to refuse treatment for her depression. She ultimately had a nervous breakdown, and in addition to the regular chores, I was assigned the task of hanging laundry on the clothesline. Nancy had to do housework and take care of Jill, who was two.

One day after school, Mother decided I was capable of washing the laundry in our old wringer washer, and she showed me how to use the washing machine. As a sheet went through the wringer to squeeze the water out, a small frog jumped onto the sheet and was smashed in front of her eyes. She became hysterical and locked herself in her room for days. We made breakfast and lunch for ourselves, dusted and swept the carpets, did the dishes, and took care of Baby Jill until Dad came home. Then miraculously, Mother dressed, came out of her room, fixed dinner, had cocktails with Dad as if nothing had happened! Every day was a repeat, and we dared not talk about it. Her glare warned us that saying anything would be a mistake. By this time, David arrived and now the laundry chore got much bigger—and smellier. I found out that if I slowed down the work just enough to finish after Dad got home, I could avoid getting yelled at.

I knew that if I could hold on for three months, I would be going to Fletcher High School in the fall, and this would all be behind me. Only one more incident marred my sixth grade experience—shoes. It seemed there was an unwritten rule that as soon as it was warm enough, barefoot was the uniform of the day. Beach sandals were okay, but not good. Mother was unconvinced of this "barbaric" custom, and we had to wear shoes. After two weeks of being the "Dumb Yankee" again (at least it wasn't Damn Yankee), I gave in to temptation, and hid my shoes on the way to school. I couldn't win though, now my feet were too white!

Nancy didn't have anyone to play with either, so in spite of our previous clashes, we actually enjoyed a truce, often setting up a blanket on the outside stair handrail, hiding behind it and using my Red Ryder BB gun to shoot rats that frequented the yard. Living on a remote, unpaved road put us close to garbage dumped by neighbors living blocks away. We saw our first rattlesnake when Dad ran over it with the Olds. It was bigger around than my arm and eight feet long! Uninjured, it slithered into the palmettos. That ended hiding in the palmettos.

I formulated a battle plan to prepare for high school:

1. Practice getting rid of the Yankee accent.

2. "Lose" my shoes—they were tight anyway.

3. Boost my self-confidence by reading all the adventure and motivational novels I had been given by relatives. Horatio Alger was one of my favorites, a writer of young men's novels to motivate youth in the 1870s to 1890s. His theme was that honesty, hard work, and perseverance always overcame poverty and misery. *Strive and Succeed* was a typical title. Other books I inherited featured inventions, war novels, and Zane Grey westerns.

4. *Enter Fletcher HS as a new person.*

♦ ♦ ♦ ♦ ♦

One day that summer I saw a strange sign on our door. I looked up "eviction" in the dictionary, and found out we were moving. Dad explained that he and the landlord had a long standing disagreement, and he refused to pay the rent until it was resolved. He explained that we were not "evicted," though. We were moving before the ninety-day limit on the notice. But he still was not going to pay. Mother was devastated that we were being thrown out, and she went downhill again.

We moved to another rental apartment, a duplex located between Nancy's grammar school and the high school I would enter in the fall. The new duplex was also near my aunt, uncle and three cousins, Dick, Ann and Bruce who lived in the McCormick Apartments, so we began to have someone to play with. I would have to walk to school though—riding my bike in salt water had reduced it to useless rust.

The new location was less than a block from a church! We were excited. Mother and Dad had stopped attending before the move to Florida, so this was a chance for Nancy and me to walk to Sunday school each week and meet other kids. We enjoyed returning to church and attended often. My curiosity about "how different churches follow the Bible" remained from the unanswered questions in New York. Neither Mother nor Dad was ready to discuss them. We were too new to this church to bring them up. Mother and Dad seemed to enjoy the free time they had while we were at church.

Summer came, and I went into high gear on my plan to reform myself. I read every day, completing over twenty Alger novels and dozens of adventure books, practiced "y'all," memorized a pamphlet on Southern slang words, got rid of the Northern words and phrases, outgrew my shoes so that I wouldn't get caught throwing them away (mothers somehow always knew if you did something wrong). I even got brown feet and calluses. I was ready.

Confidently, I walked up to the door and entered Fletcher Junior-Senior High School, to receive a shock. These were the same kids! It hadn't dawned on me that they would be at the same high school. At least there were kids from one other grammar school. Maybe they wouldn't find out. But they did.

Another custom I was to learn the hard way was that after being barefoot in grammar school, the first thing a high school student got was a new pair of shoes. I stood there barefoot, and my careful preparation for the new identity went down the drain. Surrounded by laughter, I slumped into my seat. The next day, I hesitatingly walked to school and lost track of the time. I walked into class late, and amid the familiar laughter was sent to the coach and assistant principal's office for a swat with the famous "Ish Brandt three-hole paddle." It raised blisters if you got two or three swats. Back to home room, more laughter. One of the kids whispered, "Better get here tomorrow by 9:00 because the second swat will be worse." I was there the next day at 8:55. Late again, and this time it was a real *swat*.

They say the third time is a charm. Wrong! At 8:45 I walked in, just after a bell rang. Back for a swat that lifted me off the floor and onto the desk this time. Coach Brandt asked, "Don't you know that school bell rings at 8:40 promptly, and you have to be in your seat by 8:45?" On my return to class, there was a roar of laughter. "Gotcha," they said. That was it for me. I got up, left the room and walked out of Fletcher High School. This was my last day of school, even if I had to run away from home.

For the first week as a seventh grade drop-out, I hung around construction sites and watched as swamps were filled in and new apartments rose. Occasionally I was rewarded by seeing an alligator run from the swamp into the nearby apartment complex when its nest was destroyed. Mothers screamed every time one crossed the lawns.

When any of the workers asked about my being there during school, I moved to another site. I was sure I would eventually be recognized if I hung around school or home, so I rode the city bus to Jacksonville every day. It was about half an hour away.

Using transfers, I explored the city. No one would ever know. The first hooky day in town, I ended up in a shopping center in the Riverside area. There before my eyes was a store with Fleers Double Bubble Gum for sale. Not since the beginning of the war in 1941 had that delicacy been on the shelves, and none was available at the beach. I loaded up pockets for a pen-

RUN FOR YOUR LIFE

ny apiece, and headed home. When I flashed my new found treasure to a neighbor kid, he offered a nickel apiece! I sold all I had left.

The trips to the gum store became more frequent after that. I was able to buy full boxes of 115 pieces for a dollar and make it to meet Dad at the bank by quitting time. Dad had sold our new Oldsmobile for a big profit while they were still scarce, bought a 1935 Ford and a vacant lot in the bankrupt 1920s San Jose development in South Jacksonville. He began driving to work instead of riding the city bus. Without a car to escape the kids, Mother went back into her slump. I arrived early enough to hide my gum boxes under the seat of the car, and we went to our new lot in Jacksonville to work. When we got home, the boxes were removed for business the next day. He never found out.

I began selling the gum outside the school fence. Two for a nickel gave me a good profit. Within two weeks, I had enough to discard my beach sandals and buy myself a real pair of shoes. I began buying four boxes of gum a day, and the money was just rolling in. I was even able to begin adding to the coin collections that I had brought from New York. Dad brought home cancelled stamps on correspondence and packages the bank received from many countries for my stamp collection. My other treasures were gone forever.

Life was good—no school, plenty of cash, time to spend on the beach, and I was starting to get a reputation as a neat guy. No longer did I hear "Yankee!" because when I did, the gum sales stopped.

Some days I skipped my "gum runs" and joined the kids in bike riding, beach activities, and roller skating on the remaining floor of a demolished motel on the oceanfront. Roller skating was a favorite activity of mine. I was still not over the disappointment of rejection during those months of 1947, but things were improving.

One of my "non-customers" began tripping me and pushing me down on the concrete one afternoon, and after several bloody scrapes and breaking my glasses, I snapped. Just like Ralphie in the classic movie *A Christmas Story*, I jumped him and began punching him. Then I started banging his head on the concrete. By the time I was dragged off him, he was unconscious and his hair was soaked in blood. I ran and caught the bus for town. I was scared that he was dead. That night while I was packing to run away, Dad got a call. After a few minutes of hushed conversation, he invited me into the other room. I knew I was too late. It was curtains for me.

I was surprised. He knew I had been bullied. Dad congratulated me for defending myself but warned not to take it so far next time. The story was circulated, and the large blood stain on the concrete remained as a reminder of my temper. I got new glasses, and I was able to skate without problems from then on.

A few weeks into my new "gum runner" business, fortunes changed. Someone else found Fleers Double Bubble gum on sale and was undercutting my price, offering them at three for a nickel. Within a week, profits dropped as we started a price war. About then, I was caught by the coach and invited back to the office for a discussion and some seat of the pants re-education. He took the gum but not the pocket full of nickels. "Where have you been for the past several weeks?" I confessed.

"Do you want swats or me to call your folks? It's up to you." I had experienced swats from the coach and punishment at home. The choice was easy. I chose swats. When I told Coach Brandt the "no shoes" story, and that now that I had some I could return, the swats were administered with a smile (not mine) and I returned to seventh grade.

Dad announced we were going to build our own house on the San Jose lot, and I was going to help. He originally planned to build a sod house like those built in the mid west a century earlier, but I suggested building one of concrete blocks after Mother screamed, "I'll never live in a mud hut!" She then locked herself in their room. He gave in and bought a mold for making our own concrete blocks, and I started to cast them—three every day, then four (the most I could make between school and dinner). We had to have about 1500, so it didn't take long to figure out that it would take almost a year, even if he bought another mold and I went to eight a day. I continued riding the bus to town every day, met him at the bank, rode with him to the new lot, and helped clear it of brush and trees. We drove home at dark and ate in silence.

That fall, I got my first taste of tropical weather when a huge storm hit the beaches with high winds and torrential rain. It stalled and pounded the area for days. At first, it was exciting to watch the breakers pound the seawall and rush up the auto ramps to the beach. As the storm continued, the fun began to disappear. Large sections of the seawall collapsed into the ocean, followed by the houses it had protected. Instead of watching, we were all at home, bailing water that had risen above the floor level. We all rolled up blankets and sheets to place about a foot inside the walls to act as a crude dam. The family bailed, mopped and squeezed the soaked rags into buckets as fast as it leaked in through the walls and doors. Anything on the floor was piled on tables and beds, including our rugs. People in low lying areas evacuated, using rowboats where necessary. As the storm began moving away, the kids went to the beach to see the damage. Several houses were gone, the seawall had disappeared in many places, and the mile wide beach (at low tide) was gone! Only a narrow strip remained, but the sea was still above normal level. So much sand had washed away that we were able to walk upright under the concrete steps that led from the top of the remaining seawall to the beach. The steps were hanging from the seawall. The next day the sea receded, and I immediately noticed that the large oil patches left over from the torpedoed WWII tankers were gone. It was time to get back to school. The excitement was over, and the dull routine resumed.

Freshmen regularly were bullied by upperclassmen, but after the skating incident and supplying gum to all classes, I was never again harassed without a big kid defending me. The rest of seventh grade was filled with friends and fond memories. But now that I was established and had new friends, it was time to move and start all over again. The Fletcher annual I bought to help me remember those friends was stolen from my locker the last day of school. It had been our fourth move in eighteen months and my third school.

If anyone ever tries to convince you that a child gets used to moving every few months, tell him he's wrong. Losing old friends and making new ones does not come easy.

STARTING OVER AGAIN

The summer of 1948 was a busy time for all the family. Mother's depression lifted some when we bought the lot in San Jose Estates. Now she could look forward to her own house again. We spent most days at the new lot, and now our builder had started the house. He poured the foundations and laid the concrete blocks for the walls and put in the cast iron plumbing. My effort at hand-making concrete blocks in the afternoons had been abandoned because I was not able to make them fast enough. I did make enough for us to add a large screened porch after the contractor left. But now, Dad had discovered the bathroom plumbing was installed wrong. The sink drain pipe was 1–1/2" too high. Mother had insisted on a new style pop-up drain instead of the standard rubber stopper, and that required the drain to be lower to install the pop-up. After Mother refused to budge, Dad told the plumber to rip it out at his own expense.

There was a huge demand for construction workers then, so after giving Dad some advice that a twelve-year-old dared not repeat, the plumber quit. Wow, I had never heard anyone tell Dad off and survive! It must have shown. "Get that smirk off your face or I'll knock it off, and get into the ditch and start chipping the lead out of the joint." I had watched the plumber caulk the oakum joints and fill them with lead, so I told Dad I could fix it.

Dad rented the lead-melting heater with a ladle to pour the molten lead into the joints. He also bought a cold chisel to pack in the oakum and lead. Then I got to try my skill at plumbing. The horizontal joints were simple, and after a few blow-outs, the vertical joint technique was mastered. We actually finished all the plumbing with no leaks, but my shoes were shot after being splattered with the hot lead. I had hoped that success would get them to stop calling me "Stupie," but the nickname continued until I left home for college.

Mr. Linker, the builder, was let go when we ran out of money, and Dad bought a do-it-yourself book on how to build a house. We were going to build our own house. I was twelve and old enough for us both to do it on our own. Dad had a wood shop in the basement of our house in New York, and he and I often built small projects for school classes and Boy Scouts, but he never had experience in construction. While I was enjoying the "gum smuggling" episode earlier, I had been fascinated with all the new buildings going up and watched to see how they were built. I was able to show Dad many of the techniques I had observed.

With the contractor now gone, we were left with a foundation, concrete block walls and the cast iron sewer pipe in the ground—no windows, floor, interior walls, ceilings or roof. Every day including weekends and all the summer vacation we took Dad to work, went to the lot and worked on the house. After Mother picked up Dad at the bank, he joined us and we continued until dark. The progress was behind schedule because in the post-war building boom, materials were scarce and costs were rising fast. In the year since we bought the lot, materials prices had risen almost 50%. The money from the sale of the new Oldsmobile was now gone. The money from the sale of the house in Rochester had been invested in a new company that had rivaled Kodak in producing film for the war and surely would grab a huge slice of the market after the war. It was a "can't lose" investment that would provide plenty of profits to build the new house. Unfortunately Kryptar used expired Kodak patents, didn't have a marketing network, and with the Kodak giant bringing out new products, the dream of surpassing Kodak using obsolete technology quickly faded away. The house money was gone when Kryptar folded.

By this time, we had run out of money. The developer refused to install the water and sewer lines that were part of the lot purchase, and fall was approaching. We were running out of time. "Materials just aren't available," he told Dad. We had to be in by start of school in the fall, and apply the rent money towards building materials. Thanks to a loan from Dad's sister, we proceeded on.

I think I learned from Dad's attitude, "Don't tell me it can't be done; I'll find a way," that summer. When confronted with the excuse, "We just can't get materials for the water and sewer pipes," Dad went to work. He was in charge of the commercial loan department at the bank and had many contacts. One day a couple weeks later, he called the developer and announced that two truckloads of water and sewer pipes had just been delivered to the lot, and they were charged to him. Would he please see that they were moved off our lot and into the ground as soon as possible? Dad told us that the developer never spoke to him again after that.

I found out quickly that watching construction was easier than doing construction. We started with the floor framing, using a hand saw. I got the "opportunity" to crawl under the framing and paint creosote on every board to prevent termites. It was a hot, smelly job, and wherever the creosote got on the skin, a burn resulted. After the first few days, it became apparent that the hand saw was no match for the dense Long Leaf Yellow Pine lumber. Dad rented a new fangled tool—a Skilsaw—and it was so much faster than the hand saw, we started to believe the August move in date was possible. By August 15, the water and sewer lines were in, the floor joists and two interior walls were framed, the roof framing and 1x6 planking was on (plywood was not available then), and the tar paper was on the roof. We still had not installed the sub-flooring or any doors.

The next week, we installed sub-flooring in all of the house except the bathrooms because the plumbing was not finished. We had one working toilet, the bathroom sink (with the coveted pop-up drain) and the kitchen sink were also in working order, but the kitchen sink sat on temporary framing— we had no cabinets or counter tops. The water heater was working, as was the stove. The minimum wiring was installed, so we moved in. Well, we had no front door, only tar paper nailed to a wooden frame, with a piece of wood to keep it closed. It was hung on canvas hinges. The side and back doors were also tar paper, but they were nailed shut. I think the early move-in really hit Mother hard. She was expecting better and at least a floor and bathtub in the bathroom. The tub was sitting on the open floor joists without the water lines hooked up. The bathroom door was a shower curtain hung over the opening. Except for the sheetrock on the bathroom walls, no other interior walls were covered. You could see from one end to another through the stud walls! And you couldn't wait too late to go to the bathroom. Everyone had to hop from one floor joist to another slowly for fear of slipping or losing your balance on and falling into the crawl space under the house.

This was not the castle Mother envisioned, but to Nancy and me, it was an adventure. Everyone had to dress under the sheets if they were modest, and we were. The one saving feature for us was that there was only one neighbor on the street, and she was not home to watch when the "gypsies" moved in. His two week vacation was over, and it was back to work for Dad.

The "shower curtain door" was the first of our novel features to disappear after the tub was connected and boards laid in for a temporary floor in the bathroom, but for many months, we used a washcloth to wedge the door shut. The doorknob came the next year.

After we moved in, Mother's depression returned with a vengeance, and she still refused to attend church. She couldn't face anyone outside the family while living in "that dump." Her attitude was a crushing blow to Dad. His best was not good enough. Nancy and I walked several blocks to a local congregation.

The fact that the temporary flooring had shrunk and we had almost half inch wide gaps between the six inch wide floor boards bothered her the most. Cockroaches crawled in along with lizards, the wind blew dust up through these cracks, and a clean house was impossible. But worse than that, the mosquitoes found the cracks, too. One night we had a violent rainstorm, and the house was invaded by hundreds of green frogs. The power went out, and Dad and I spent the evening with flashlights catching them in jars and throwing them out the tar paper door. Mother was frantic, Nancy hid under the sheets of her bed, and Baby Jill just sat there and played with the "cute little biddy froggies."

Once they were all gone, Mother came out and lit candles, but Nancy wouldn't believe they were gone and refused to budge from under the sheet. Even when I tried to pull it off, she wouldn't let go. It was then the prankster side of me emerged. I picked up two clothespins, tiptoed into her room, and threw them one at a time on the sheet, then yelled "Frog!" It worked—too well. She threw the sheet up in the air and evacuated the premises, screaming. Right out the tar paper door into the rain. Even in pitch dark she found the way. Unfortunately Dad found me in the dark, too. If I hadn't been laughing so hard, I'd have been able to run outside and escaped the belt.

The rest of the fall was spent working on the house as materials could be purchased. We started hanging sheetrock on one side of the studs for privacy, and a few months later were able to cover the other side. Dad found some aluminum painted tar paper to cover the cracks in the floor, so I had to find other things than frog throwing to amuse me. As cold weather approached around Christmas, Nancy and I learned to use a Two-Man Cross Cut Saw for sawing firewood for the fireplace. Nancy learned quickly that she could hold onto one end and let her arms move with the saw without pulling or pushing. Central heat came a year later.

In September, Nancy and I went to the new Dupont School two blocks from home. This was my fourth school in twenty months. School was a relief from the constant work and tensions at home. After the previous summer practice at changing my accent and a year in junior high school at the beach, I got to try out my revised character on the new class. This time I had no witnesses from the year before. I was equipped with the necessary shoes, a few "y'alls"s, some Southern slang, tanned feet, and now I could say we moved from Jacksonville Beach—not New York. For the first time in almost two years, I felt comfortable at school. Almost all the students came from schools at least five miles away, so they were "new" too.

Early in my new school, I discovered that good grades were not on the top of the list for acceptance any more than they were at the beach schools, so I tried to fit in by laying back and getting average grades, which put me at odds with the parents. Nancy was getting excellent grades and the accompanying praise. My excuse was "My grade is harder—just wait till she gets to this class." But when she got there, she continued to get "A's." I was always being pushed to be better, but I pushed back, but never let them know why. Until I moved away from home five years later, I was nicknamed "Stupie" for stupid. Even straight A's later in high school didn't change that.

During this time, Mother was spending time taking care of our brother David, but she still refused treatment for her depression. Things got worse. Nancy continued to receive regular whippings from Mother and an occasional "knuckle sandwich," but now Baby Jill began to join in as a target. From her early months, she had been slapped each time she cried longer that she was "supposed to," but now it was getting worse. I hid in the woods every day until Dad came home, and when Nancy was not at school, she stayed in her room, trying to avoid the wrath. I still had to do laundry and clean my room and theirs, so I tried to do that when she was gone to the store or to a meeting, where Mother dressed up, put on the sweet-as-pie personality and left the other one home. Regularly when she came home, it popped back out with a vengeance.

On one occasion, one of the students got hold of test answers and passed them around. I was offered a look at them, but refused. I knew everyone would get better grades cheating, and so this time I answered all the questions and got 100. The teacher read out the grades, and most of the class got 100 too. Then when all the marks were high, the inquisition started. Finally one of the girls who was left out and got a low grade shouted, "They cheated. They all had the answers before the test. I saw them."

"All who had the answers before the test, stand up." Trying to be part of the class, I stood up. We were marched to the principal's office and lectured about cheating and told to confess to our parents. Then back to class. That wasn't so bad. Since I didn't cheat, I didn't even have to confess.

The day of reckoning came later—Report cards. It stood out like a beacon—"F." I never failed a class before. I hid my card and went home. "Isn't it near report card time?" Mother asked. "Nancy has hers—all A's. Where is yours?"

RUN FOR YOUR LIFE

"I left it in my book at school, but I'll try to remember it tomorrow," I replied. Oh, no! What now? The next day at school, there were about a dozen mothers waiting to see the principal about the failing grades. Again I "forgot" the card, but this time the reminder was not an option.

"Bring it home tomorrow, or you'll *get it*." I knew what that meant, so I went to Dupont for my last day. I knew I'd be dead after Dad got home.

There was a partial reprieve that day. Because of the mothers' complaints about failing, all the grades were raised to a "D," barely passing. The cards were changed by the teacher and sent home again. I explained, "The teacher disciplined the class and gave everyone a 'D.'" I left out the cheating part. It would keep me alive for another day, but after Mother saw that the original mark was an F, she accused me of changing it. After a few calls to other moms, it was out in the open.

"Go to your room and wait till your father gets home!" The familiar sentence. The rest is history. I never cheated but the rest of the class thought it was "neat" that I took my punishment with them, without deserving it. I was now able to get better grades without being accused of being teacher's pet.

Part of my punishment was to join the mothers of the PTA raking the school lawn and planting grass seed. How embarrassing! The guys playing on the ball field that Saturday morning went out of their way to make sure I saw them laughing at my misfortune. Two weeks later, I was vindicated. My rebellion sprung up for all to see. There in the middle of the new lawn were my initials in dense rye grass, each letter three feet square. The seed I sowed had come up to show all that I had beaten the system. Even when Nancy told Mother, all I got was a scowl. From then on school went fine; I became a teenager and joined in many school and church activities.

The next three years were spent in finishing the house. The rule was *no dating until the house is finished*, except for school and church functions. By then, I had learned to tape and finish sheetrock, even the swirl finish on the ceilings. When a tropical storm blew off all the tar paper roofing one night, Dad and I even replaced it in the middle of the storm, rolling it out a few inches at a time and nailing it down by flashlight and the flashes of lightning. We built cabinets, replaced the bare light bulbs with fixtures, even modifying the ceiling for a recessed chandelier in the dining room. I learned to install plumbing, wall and floor tile, roof shingles, oak flooring, wallpaper, linoleum, glaze windows, and just about everything else needed to complete the house. Those lessons followed me in later life through construction of three new homes and remodeling of four more.

The money from Dad's sister's loan was now gone. Dad's last resource was the few hundred dollars of War Bonds I had saved in New York. He approached me and with my approval, Dad cashed in all the bonds I saved during the war and used the money buying materials for the house. Since I gave up dating and worked every day until the house was finished, Dad promised he would give me ownership of my room, but I had to do all the work finishing it, floor, walls, ceiling, doors—even the wiring.

He was not able to pay me back, but for giving up the bonds and those three years of work, he promised a good vacation each year and when the house was eventually sold, I would receive one sixth of the sale price. It was sold some twenty years later, but by then Mother had convinced him to cancel the agreement and give me the corporation he formed for part time work after his retirement. Except for a few hundred dollars worth of stock, it was useless to me. I abandoned the corporation.

The house was almost finished when Mother decided her grey Victorian wallpaper was too dull. Dad refused to replace it. Mother had chosen a small flower-filled vase design with each vase surrounded by a circular rope and a wreath. The vase in wreath design was repeated hundreds of times. The challenge was on. If no new wallpaper, then "Charles and I will paint each flower pot—flowers, wreath, rope and all." I don't remember volunteering for this duty! White pots, multi-colored flowers, and gold rope were chosen. For weeks we painted, sitting on chairs, standing and up on a ladder. It was the most boring task of the entire house.

Only two accidents marred these many months. Well, the record shows three, but the third was on purpose, but I never confessed, so it went down as an accident.

The first "accident" occurred during a game of Cowboys and Indians. I had the BB gun, so I had to be the cowboy. As Nancy circled me letting out a war whoop, I defended the wagon train by firing the gun behind her. After a few boring shots, I decided to try hitting her shoes and see if she yelped. She didn't. Next, I tried her ear lobe. Bull's eye, dead center! She yelped and jumped, and used the dreaded Indian war challenge, "I'm going to tell!" If the Indians had actually used that phrase in battle, we would still be living along the east coast and buffalo would still be roaming out west.

I couldn't let Mother know what I'd done, so we had a pow-wow. I agreed to let her shoot me twice in the fanny if she didn't tell. "No, three," she replied. "No two," "I'll tell," "Okay, three," and the negotiations were over. Unbeknownst to Nancy, during the negotiations, I had emptied every BB while pretending to reload the gun. As she fired, I jumped and hollered. Three times and she finished with a scowl. "One more or I'll tell," so one more it was. That time, I really let out a fake yell. She was satisfied. No more Cowboys and Indians after that.

The second accident actually saved me the loss of my hand or possibly my left arm. We had gone to the marshes along the Intracoastal Waterway one weekend to catch blue claw crabs. The waterway had been dredged in the 1930s, a few years before the war for commercial shipping, and the muddy marshland was a perfect spot to catch them as the tide went out. After Pearl Harbor, the waterway was used extensively to provide protection from the German subs that preyed on coastal shipping. Materials were shipped to the northeast to be loaded on ships which were then assembled into huge convoys bound for Europe. During the first six months of WWII, some 400 ships were sunk off the east coast by German U-Boats patrolling America's Atlantic coastline.

This trip, we caught a couple dozen large crabs and brought them back to the kitchen to boil and clean them. One jumped out of the bucket and scurried across the kitchen floor in its odd "running sideways" manner. "I'll get it!" I shouted and the chase was on, under the table and into a corner. As he showed his claws, I grabbed him, but he speared me in the thumb—all the way to the bone. A few days later, the thumb began to swell and ache. "Don't be a sissy; we'll just put a poultice on it to draw out the infection," Dad exclaimed. That was what Grandma Space always did. Poultices cured everything, and doctors were expensive.

After a couple weeks, the thumb was as big as a golf ball and too painful to touch, but we just had to "let the chicken liver poultice have enough time to work." That weekend, we were finally putting roof shingles on the garage, and to hold a nail, I had to use two fingers instead of using the swollen and throbbing thumb. Holding a nail that way was clumsy. I missed and hit the swollen thumb with a real whack of the hammer. I passed out and rolled toward the edge of the roof, but Dad caught me by the belt just before I fell off. Once on the ground, the blood and green ooze looked horrible, and I was rushed to Dr. Veal's office. He made me watch as he cut the thumb open, so I could see how dangerous it was to let a big infection grow without treatment. He was showing the wrong person. I had been ready to see him when it started swelling. As he removed what he called "the corruption," he removed half the flesh, and scraped the bone. He explained that it was gangrene! "A few days later, and I'd had to remove your thumb, and a week later it would have been your hand or arm. It's good that you hit it now instead of later." After filling the cavity with a pack of sulfa powder and a giving me a dose of morphine, I went home to recover. The operation was successful, although it was over a year before feeling came back to that thumb.

The third accident was after I got a new Remington.22-caliber rifle at fourteen. With the BB gun, it was "You'll shoot your eye out." With the Remington, it was "Don't shoot at any person, house, bird, animal, or yourself." At last I was "grown up." I had a gun. The Red Ryder BB gun was retired. I soon became bored with shooting at tin cans and bottles, and I went hunting. Snakes, rats, roaches, and lizards were the only exceptions to the "don't shoot" rule. While running through the woods chasing a big rat, I stubbed my toe on a piece of concrete pipe, fell down and skinned my leg. "I'll show you," I shouted at the concrete pipe, as if it could hear me. I aimed and fired. The bullet ricocheted off the pipe and into my leg, lodging in my shin bone. It was bleeding but didn't hurt at all, it was numb. I sneaked back to the house to see if the coast was clear. If I was caught, no more rifle. When I was sure no one was in the house, I went to the kitchen, got a paring knife, and dug the bullet out. There still was no pain and not too much blood. I got the hair dryer out and heated the wound until the bleeding stopped. No one ever knew.

It was now time for graduation from junior high and on to high school.

LANDON HIGH SCHOOL

September 1950 was time for my fifth school in a little over three years. Starting over was getting me down. Landon High School was about five miles from San Jose, so I had to ride the school bus each day.

At Landon, I settled into the same B grade performance I had selected at Dupont. Everything went well the first year, with little to note or remember except the school's administering an IQ test to the tenth graders as part of a new experiment to see if IQ test scores accurately reflected student intelligence. Since my parents called me "Stupie," I really needed to know if it was true. IQ results were measured in the tenth grade and then to be repeated two years later to see if the scores would be the same, as educators expected. By the time a person was in tenth grade, the IQ score was thought to be at its normal level and thereafter independent of age or education. The test results were 153, and I relaxed. I wasn't a "Stupie" after all. From then on, I would try to ignore them.

Mother's condition improved when the house approached completion after three years of work, but her outbursts didn't cease. She still suffered from migraines and depression but refused treatment, and if going to the doctor was suggested, she would go wild. Once, Dr. Manson, our doctor for several years, suggested she see a psychiatrist, and it took weeks for her to settle down. Locking us in our rooms to wait till Dad got home became less frequent, and

Dad had tried to protect Nancy and me by going with Mother into their room as soon as he got home. With glasses of Scotch, they would talk about their day. Often she would calm down, and supper was normal. Occasionally, Dad was unsuccessful and Nancy and I would feel the wrath of her anger and his frustration the next day.

The worst incidents were unnecessary and resulted in severe beatings. The first came after Mother saw me on the porch one evening. It was my junior year at Landon. She thought she was unnoticed as she watched me. I was lying on the sofa winding an electromagnetic coil for an experiment. I was always trying a new "invention." This time it was to be a remote controlled magnet. The coil consisted of fine wire wound around a steel core. I wound the wire from a larger spool on the floor, passing the almost invisible wire between my toes to keep it tight, and winding it slowly. I saw Mother watching, and I knew she couldn't see the wire in the dim light, so I slowed down my winding, then sped up to add to her mystery.

After a few minutes, she asked in a low voice, "Charles, what are you doing?"

Jokingly, I answered, "Fishing." I knew it was a mistake. She went wild. The joke had backfired! She began a low moan, followed by loud screaming.

"He's gone crazy!" she screamed as she ran through the house. Dad tried to restrain her, but she was too strong. Finally, she collapsed in sobs. In anger and frustration, Dad began beating me with his fist. As it continued, to his shouts of "Stupie! Stupie!" I tried to get away, but he held me against the wall and stopped only after he had pounded me through the wall and into the next room. I was unable to move either arm or get up from the floor. Nancy hid in her locked room, crying. Mother made seven-year-old Jill sit and watch the beating until I crashed through the wall. Every time Jill looked away Mother would force her head back to watch. When she cried, Mother slapped her. Afterwards, Dad stormed off. Mother just watched with a smile on her face.

The next day, I couldn't get out of bed. I had been unable to sleep at all, and in order to get me up, Dad grabbed both big toes and pulled me off the bed, my head crashing onto the floor. Even though it was May, I wore long sleeves to hide the bruises, which were solid from my waist to my shoulders and covered all of both arms except for my hands. I left my gym clothes home to avoid dressing out and showering. I didn't want to show the damage. For the next two weeks, I got the customary paddle swats from Coach for "forgetting," but that was better than taking my shirt off. My bruises from Coach never showed.

That summer, the family went on the annual vacation together—this time to the Ringling Museum, and on the road out of the subdivision, we saw a dragline being driven down the road. Dad had promised us a swimming pool when the house was finished, and true to his word, he had designed one out of concrete blocks, using a recommendation found in the local newspaper. Most below ground, concrete block pools were cracked by the pressure of the earth when emptied, and several empty pools just floated out of the ground during heavy rain. He decided to build a pool with four feet of the wall above ground and just three feet below. The above ground portion would be surrounded by a terrace, and be heavy enough to keep from "floating" out of the ground when empty.

He stopped the dragline, showed him the plan, and we resumed our trip to Sarasota. When we returned, the hole was perfect. That left building the pool. The concrete foundation and floor were poured, and the block delivered. We were all anticipating swimming in the pool in a couple weeks. Then came the surprise. Dad's mason had bid the job based on me mixing the mortar in a wheelbarrow and hauling the blocks to the mason! Realizing the futility of protest, I spent the summer in the pool, literally, no water, just sweat. Dad explained that I would get no pay, but to remember that when the house was sold, I would be paid with the promised one sixth of the sale price to repay me for the confiscated war bonds and for my work completing the house. In addition, Dad promised he would help me whenever I decided to build my own house.

After filling the pool just before school started, we enjoyed swimming until the cool fall breezes filled the surface with leaves. It was drained till spring. During its construction, I had discovered a small clearing in the dense woods behind the house. While the mason took breaks for lunch, I enlarged the clearing and made a small campsite to hide in after school. I was able to do homework and read without fear.

The following year, the pool was filled, and Mother thought it to be "too plain." The Atlantic Bank was renovating the lobby, and the marble floor was scheduled for replacement. Dad arranged for the family to remove the marble floor after hours, and every evening we used picks and chisels to remove the tiles. Each trip yielded about fifty unbroken tiles salvaged from the many we chipped out of the mortar. Many broke, but in the end, we had enough to finish a walkway and patio. They proved to be a safety hazard because they were slick when wet, but only a few accidents occurred.

I built a sand filter to keep the water clean and got to test the clarity one hot summer evening. I had slipped out of the house for a "skinny dip" and was quietly paddling around the pool when I heard Nancy. "Girls, come see our new pool," she squealed, and on went the porch light. Quickly, I moved to the shadow in one corner. Oh no, they were coming out! I slowly took a big breath of air and went to the bottom, holding on to a concrete block we used as a step. I could see their shadows in the water and held on for dear life. Fortunately, they left before I had to surface, but I always kept a bathing suit handy for future night swimming.

My sister Jill can also testify to the clear water, since Dad taught her to swim the same way we learned. In she went, sunk to the bottom and watched helplessly as Dad yelled, "Kick your feet!" He was dressed in a suit, and Jill remembers looking up from the bottom and wondering if he would be willing to get his suit wet to pull her out. He wasn't, but she finally paddled to the surface.

The coasting through classes with average grades abruptly stopped my junior year. I met the nemesis (an opponent that cannot be beaten or overcome) of all students at Landon High School—the dreaded Ma Perkins. No one called her that to her face, but that name still lives in the hearts of all who studied English under her watchful eye. I slid into my seat the first day and was thankful for alphabetical seating. The name Space earned the last seat in row five, a good place to hide from those eyes. If her eyes met yours, you knew she was going to call on you. The first day went by without being called to the front to recite, my greatest fear. The next day was the same, but the third day my luck ran out.

"Charles Space, come to the front of the class." This was it—the dreaded questioning in front of everybody! As I slithered to the front at the speed of a sick snake, all eyes were on me. I thought I'd die! "Sit in that empty seat in the front today—and," she added, "you are to come back after school to that seat for a seventh period." Oh, no, the dreaded seventh period!

Seventh periods were not so bad by themselves, but the punishment at home was! I had been to many the previous year, and that meant missing the school bus. There was no city bus service to our area, so it was either ride the city bus to Lakewood and walk a mile home or ride the Greyhound Bus. The Greyhound meant exposure because it was the same one Dad rode home from work. Riding the city bus meant exposure if anyone saw me and told Mother. There were no kids living in the neighborhood, so I couldn't even claim to be late from playing. I was doomed again.

The day crawled by but finally time for the seventh period came. I slumped into my seat awaiting Ma Perkins, wondering what I had done to merit this punishment. She finally arrived, and she looked at me—right into my eyes and through the back of my head, it seemed. Her eyes were a lot like Dad's when he lectured before a swat. At least the conversation didn't start with "This is going to hurt me more than you."

"Charles, I've been watching you hide in that back seat. Every time I look your way, you duck behind the person in front of you. Are you afraid to be called upon?" That was an understatement. As I nodded my head, she continued, "I have talked with your teachers from last year, and they tell me you are shy and have a low self image. I've also seen your IQ test score. You can do better, and in my class, you will not be allowed to perform at that low level ever again! When I catch you slacking off, I will call on you *every single day* until you improve.

"You will sit in the front seat permanently, but so that it doesn't appear to be a punishment, I will have the back seat of your row removed, and everyone will move one seat. I will also monitor your performance in your other classes. You may note that I announced you were assigned a seventh period in front of the class. That should keep anyone from calling you teacher's pet. If they ask, tell them I lectured you to do better." She continued by giving one of the most inspirational talks I had heard. As long as I did my best, she would not call on me unless I volunteered.

The inspiration she gave me worked. The nickname "Stupie" every day at home didn't matter anymore. Each time I heard the word, I responded silently to myself, "You should know one if you see one. Look in the mirror!" and that helped. Silent rebellion was the only way to survive. I gave up the notion of suicide that had hung over me for the past three years, and my academic grades rose to straight A's and stayed there until graduation. At home, calling me "Stupie" continued, in spite of good grades. Friendships grew, church and school activities away from home increased, and I decided to concentrate on these new opportunities and ignore my parent problems.

Mother was not pleased that she was losing control. I had made friends with Henry Cagle, who was one of the few students blessed with a car, and I no longer rode the school bus. I had many school activities as a defense and now the transportation that was refused at home. I no longer had to hide in the woods. "Knuckle sandwiches" were getting worse, but now Nancy and Jill were on their own. David was left pretty much alone. Mother's sweet-as-pie personality continued to accompany her when she left home and when she came home, it disappeared.

The next confrontation came when Nancy and I were arguing. Dad marched us both to Mother and used his "Kiss and Make Up" punishment. By now I was fifteen, and I refused, saying, "I'll never kiss that ugly face."

"If you don't, I'll knock your block off," came one of his favorite responses. I looked at Nancy, who was puckering up her lips in delight, but I still refused. Mother was smiling.

Dad picked up a four foot long piece of plasterboard and broke it across my head. Reeling from the blow, I still refused. This time, he doubled it and *Whack!* Even the double thickness broke. The room was spinning as I tried to get up off the floor. I couldn't. "Want some more?" Dad said as he doubled the plasterboard again into four thicknesses. I looked at Nancy, who was also spinning. Somehow, she didn't look as ugly as she had before. I eventually got up, gave her a peck on the cheek and went to my room locking the door behind me. That was our last big argument.

I knew I'd better make plans to "run for my life." I couldn't stand it anymore. I would have to wait till fall to leave. I would save from summer jobs and make my escape then. I knew I couldn't survive my last year of high school. My father insisted I attend college, and I nodded, but I knew I would join the Navy instead, following a dream for adventure that started during the war years and grew stronger as more war movies were produced.

I passed the Naval ROTC tests for a scholarship, and it seemed that I would be able to follow my dream. The scholarship also satisfied Dad's demand that I attend college. My good grades continued, and I was inducted into the National Honor Society. True, that Ma Perkins had inspired me to excel, but I also was given a financial incentive. I had earned $625 over the past several months, $125 for each straight-A report card. I was now a senior at Landon and planned to use the money to buy a car since Dad had told me if I wanted one I would have to pay for it myself.

I still was required to do laundry each week, but this week, cleaning her room was added to my chores for "talking back." Mother came home from a meeting just after I finished cleaning her room—dusting, making the bed, vacuuming, and taking out the laundry. When she came home, I knew it was one of her bad days. She grabbed me by one ear, pushed me into a chair, and proceeded to put on her white gloves to inspect my work. She found some dust behind a curtain on the window sill and calmly announced, "Buster, that'll cost you $125." When I exploded in protest, the fine was raised to $625, all my earnings for the year. The car money was gone in a flash. Shortly afterward, I was notified that my poor eyesight prevented the Navy scholarship.

The next day, I was really in a bad mood. Even Ma Perkins noticed. "You still can't give up," she advised after I confessed the reason for my despair. *"Life is like a four legged stool, with home, church, school, and personal strength as legs, and if the stool only has three legs, it'll still stand. Just take your weight off the broken side."* That became my motto. I still was not sure about the "run for your life" option, now that most of my savings were gone, along with the scholarship.

Instead of running, I decided to end it all and "make them sorry," but the plans were interrupted. The Mullis family with their twin daughters Joyce and Jackie moved in a few doors away. We became close friends, and they were the first to call me "Charlie." Until then, hearing "Charles" meant I was in trouble, "Stupie" meant I wasn't. Charlie was a welcome change. Sometimes the smallest event makes a huge change in our lives. Joyce and Jackie opened a door that led to restoring some of the lost self-confidence.

At the same time, Ma Perkins was at work. The class was assigned memorizing First Corinthians 13, the love chapter of the Bible, directing me to consider the verse, "When I was a child, I spoke as a child, but now I am a man, I put away childish things." She followed with a requirement to memorize Hamlet's suicide soliloquy, "to be or not to be, that is the question…" The discussion following the assignment opened my eyes and put all such thoughts behind me. It seems that every time I reached the point of giving up, God sent someone to help. It was time to look forward and put the past behind me.

Ma Perkins knew how to be a friend to her students with a level of skill that kept them close without hanging on them a "teacher's pet" label. She was available for questions, even on subjects others taught. She especially tried to instill a sense of faith and morality in students. One piece of advice she gave that stuck with me was on history classes. History was one of my favorite subjects because, like all math classes, numbers were my game. I loved them, and even tutored others. I could remember dates better than others. When bragging to Ma one day, she told me something I never considered. "Dates are of minor importance. If you want to experience history, the *When* isn't as important as the *Why*. And for you, Charles, the *Why not* is just as important for your future. Never assume anything is impossible. If you are faced with a brick wall, don't butt your head against it, go around or go over, but get past all hurdles in life. *Don't give up.*"

That advice served me well a few weeks later in trigonometry class. We were given a problem that had not been solved by any of the math students or teachers in Duval County. Anyone who solved it would get an automatic "A" for the course. After working unsuccessfully on the problem for days, I remembered Ma Perkins advice, *go around or go over, don't give up.* I sent the problem to Albert Einstein along with my trial solutions. A few days later, I received a reply, on a three by five card with tiny numbers written in ink. My solution had been close. He finished it, skipping several steps leaving them for me to fill in myself.

Twelve pages of notebook paper, filled on both sides later, I had it! I got the "A." I kept his reply in my desk, but it disappeared along with my entire coin collection while I was at Georgia Tech—losses I really regret.

My parents had insisted I select the college prep option for high school, even though I had never planned to attend college. I had concentrated so much on present problems that I never looked forward to my future. Dad hadn't gone to college and until we moved to Florida, I expected to follow in his footsteps as a banker. By this time in my life, I knew I would never follow him, but didn't know where to head. The Navy option was now out. I was adrift again.

Aptitude tests at Landon showed my strengths were in logic, inventiveness, artistic pursuits, and design. I had excelled in mechanical drawing and had even prepared several house plans for class. Wood shop gave me an interest in building, and I selected architecture for my career. At least I thought I had that choice. I was informed that I was going to Georgia Tech, study mechanical engineering, no questions asked. If I chose not to follow Dad's plan, "You can just be a ditch digger." I had to fulfill his lost dream whether it was mine or not. Even though I resented it at that time, his decision led me into a more exciting and diverse career than I could have imagined.

The acceptance letter came from Georgia Tech, and my future was sealed.

My final confrontation at home came again as the results of a prank. I may have been making all A's, but I wouldn't have if we had a grade for judgment. That day, I had come home and Mother seemed to be in a good mood. She asked about my grades, and I told her I had failed a class. Even when I told her it was a joke, it didn't help. She continued her screaming until Dad heard it. He came running, fists clenched. "Stupie, Stupie, Stupie." Wham, wham, wham! I was on the floor again. "Get to the garage!" he thundered as he took her to their room and locked the door. It was a long time before he appeared in the doorway to the garage. His beet red face made it obvious that he was frustrated and really angry.

While I had been waiting, I decided to use the table saw to cut up some tree limbs that had fallen in the latest storm. Maybe finishing a chore would lessen the length of the "big eye" lecture. Our table saw was a peculiar one. The motor had developed a short circuit and wouldn't start without lifting it to loosen the belt and spinning the pulley by hand, getting a mild shock for your effort.

The short had gotten worse with time, so I used boards to keep my bare feet off the concrete floor and a stick to lift and spin the motor to prevent electrocution. Dad came out and witnessed the procedure, and exploded! "Sissy! Stupie! Grab it!" he yelled. I explained it shocked me when I was bare foot on the concrete floor. As he balled up his fist again, I gave up and lifted the motor. I felt the shock run up my arm, but I couldn't let go. All went dim as I passed out on the floor. When I came to, he was gone and the motor was unplugged. As I got up, I was determined that if I ever got out, I would never come home to live under his roof again. He did get a new motor, though.

Christmas vacation in 1952 put a spotlight directly on me. The night before classes were to end for the holiday, I drove the family car to the Florida Theater to see a movie. I don't remember why I went alone, but that's not important. When the show let out, I returned to the car parked across Newnan Street. As I opened the door, a stranger approached me, hand in his pocket, saying, "Get in and keep quiet, I've got a gun." I got in. He told me to drive out of town. As I fumbled for the keys, I wracked my brain. What to do? He'll kill me if I drive out of town. He's got no mask, and I can identify him. I was being "carjacked" as we now call it.

I saw the parking lot in the next block, and it was on my side of the street. It had flood lights beaming and an attendant. I started slowly across the intersection, gunned the car and abruptly turned into the exit of the parking lot, slammed on the brakes and before he pushed himself back off the dashboard, I grabbed the keys and ran, leaving him to face the angry attendant. He bailed out. It's a good thing I had used the rest room before leaving the theater!

I went home and picked up Dad to go with me to the police headquarters. The detective filled out a report with my description of the carjacker, down to the scar on his cheek.

The next day was Friday, the last day of school before the holiday break. I was in—yes, Ma Perkins' class at the time. An announcement came over the loud speaker system that was piped into every classroom. "Charles Space! Go to Mr. Smith's office immediately. There are two police detectives who want to talk with you." Well, in those days, the most serious crime in school was talking in class or chewing gum. (Although my getting caught dropping BB's down the three story stairwell onto a female teacher's bald spot was a little worse. I was a good aim, though. I got five out of six "bulls eyes" before she walked off at the second floor. As I was laughing about her not even feeling the direct hits, I felt a tap on my shoulder. She had come up another stair and caught me. It was assistant principal Sam I. Smith and swats again!)

Everyone on that side of Landon had been watching the flashing lights and the officers marching me to the police car. One put me in the back seat, and we drove off, lights still flashing. I didn't return until after school was out, so by then many stories had been invented. I was infamous, and it would be after New Years before I could explain.

The next day, we received a call from the police. They had caught the robber, and I had to identify him in a line-up. We had no television in our house so I had not seen a line up before. It was kind of neat, one-way glass, spotlights on the line of men, numbers around their necks. I spotted him immediately, but was so fascinated by the procedure I waited. Each had to turn, face left, face right, step forward, step back, repeat the following: "Get into the car and keep quiet, I've got a gun." This was fun. I even had them repeat the procedure so "I could be sure." I was sure.

Oh no! I didn't believe my ears! Dad was telling the detective we weren't going to press charges, and he would not allow me to testify! The crook was going to get away! I said, "I'll press charges," but fell silent under Dad's withering scowl. I had been let down many times before, but this was the worst! My own father! We rode home in silence. He tried to explain later, but I walked out of the room. This time he let me.

The newspaper carried the story, and by time school resumed, all knew the story, except for the refusing to press charges part that I kept a deep secret. I think that was the final separation with Dad. We were now strangers.

Graduation came in June 1953. Dot Felson and I were elected the most intellectual students, a title I won only because Eddie Beardsley had been elected Best All Around. My application to Ga. Tech had been accepted, I had a summer job in Houston, Texas, and I would be leaving home for good. I had escaped! Although I visited for a few days from time to time, I never returned to live in that house.

If Ma Perkins had not entered into my life when she did, there is no guessing what my life would have been like. As I look back at the many blessings in my life, I know this lady had the greatest positive influence on those early years. She motivated me to make something of my life and to step out of the gloom that had almost swallowed me up and to become more active in school and church activities.

Ma Perkins' last words would follow me. "Remember, you are prepared, don't ever give up," she said while penning her remarks in my annual, "*And still we gaze and still our wonder grew, how one small head could carry all he knew.*" I could now obey the call to "run for your life." I was ready.

Years later, at the Little Theater in San Marco, I saw her in the lobby and had the chance to introduce my wife, Linda, to this wonderful woman. It had been at least twenty years, but she remembered me. After I expressed to her the profound influence she had on my life, she exclaimed that few of her students had come back to see her, but those who had made the long years in education worthwhile to her. She has passed on now but still lives in the hearts and memories of her many Landon students.

The harsh discipline and disappointments of those years at home turned out to be a huge benefit during the rest of my life. I was better prepared to face disappointments, more thankful for successes, and I had developed the self-confidence I lost in early years. Dad's demands for a strict work ethic gave me a great advantage over those competitors who had been given everything growing up.

THE LAST FAMILY VACATION

Graduation was over, and I had a *real* summer job. No longer thirty-five cents per hour bagging groceries and stocking shelves at the Piggly Wiggly grocery. The only thing I enjoyed there was Mrs. Alfred I. DuPont's visit in her limousine every Saturday morning. She and her chauffeur always bought one bag of groceries and let me carry them to the car. Instead of the normal nickel tip, she always had a brand new dollar bill. I made the mistake of showing the first one to Mother, and from then on, when I came home I had to empty my pockets and half of my pay and tips went for room and board.

The new job paid two dollars an hour! In 1953, that was a lot more than anyone from Landon was getting. The fall would bring enrollment at Georgia Tech, and this would be my last vacation with the family. Time to find out if Ma Perkins was right and I could make it on my own.

The job was at Eastern States Petroleum and Chemical Company in Houston, about a thousand miles from Jacksonville, and I had only been away from home once before—a week at Boy Scout camp. Eastern States had a regular summer jobs program for college students living in Houston, and Dad knew the local Eastern States rep in Jacksonville, so I was able to start before entering college. I didn't know what my job would be, but for that pay, I didn't care. Most of the summer jobs were scraping and painting oil storage tanks in the 100 degree plus heat. For two dollars an hour, I'd even brave my extreme fear of heights!

At home the previous summer, I had been scraping and painting under the roof overhang, and while hanging by my legs from a ladder rung over a clump of Spanish Bayonet plants, the rung had broken, dropping me into the sharp points. I was dazed from the pain of over fifty stab wounds but was still clutching the paint brush. After a couple weeks of fighting the infections, I couldn't even look at a ladder.

Mother and Dad and the four children left Jacksonville shortly after graduation. They decided to drive back through Houston after we took a week's vacation in Mexico. I had three years of Spanish at Landon and was eager to try out the new language. Mrs. Bryant, the Landon HS Spanish teacher, had made the subject fascinating, regularly introducing Spanish life styles, traditions, and literature to the dull conjugating verbs and memorizing new words. By the third year, we were reading novels written in Spanish, and even performing plays and dance exhibitions. I was okay with everything except Spanish dancing, and I avoided that like the plague. We even went on field trips, including a Spanish Club Convention in Tallahassee.

It was on that field trip my avoiding "the Spanish dancing thing" came to an end. Several guys snuck out of one meeting to play pool at a FSU college student hang out. We were spotted and turned in. The next Landon High All School Assembly featured several ex pool sharks dutifully dancing the Mexican Hat Dance and a folk dance to the tune of "Cielito Lindo," each dancer authentically dressed in costume—large hat, red sash and all. We were surprised that we got applause and almost no razzing. By that time, I was so captivated by Mexican culture that I resolved to move to Mexico some time in the future.

The summer trip to Mexico was a reward for graduating and being elected as Most Intellectual at Landon. With my new job located in Texas, I would be able to meet some native Mexicans who had immigrated to Houston and would have plenty of time to decide on spending more time in Mexico.

First stop—Monterrey. At the local restaurant, Nancy and I sat at a table separate from the parents, Jill, and David. I read the menu, ordered our meal, and carried on a short conversation with the waiter in Spanish. I had passed the first test with flying colors, and for the whole week, acted as the family guide to Mexico. I planned the itinerary long before leaving Florida, and until the last day in Mexico City, everything went smoothly, even the bartering in local markets.

The last day was a disaster. I had planned the final outing as the highlight of the whole trip. The "famous" Floating Gardens of Xochimilco were described in one of the Spanish novels I read as "a series of beautiful lagoons rivaling those of Venice, planted with exotic plants and flowers blooming everywhere. Mariachi bands in boats serenade the visitors." Everyone was to be escorted through the lagoons by Mexican oarsmen in ten passenger "trajineras." Mother especially was fond of flowers, as she was raised by an uncle who was the foremost landscaper in New York state until the Great Depression wiped him out. Even though her specialty was roses, this would be a treat.

After a short drive south from Mexico City, we were there. None of the spectacular flowers that were described in my Spanish novel were visible from the entrance, but I convinced Dad that we would be in for a treat once we got in the trajinera and the guide paddled us on. Grudgingly, he paid for the tickets, rented the boat and we were off! The Mexican guide pushed off through water green with algae, and around the first bend, we passed through floating sewage. A week's credibility was fading fast, and the grumbling became louder. About half way through the weeds, sewage and foul odor, a faint chant was heard by all, "My dumb son." At least the guide couldn't speak English. When we left, I was told the gardens were shut down for complete renovation. As you can imagine, our last night in Mexico City was short on conversation.

The next morning as we left, no one mentioned the gardens, and I knew if I could just make it to Houston without another problem, I'd have the whole summer to myself. It was a warm sunny day and everyone was in a good mood. We decided to drive back to the border by another route for a change of scenery and to avoid the group of armed men in khakis who had stopped us at a roadblock on the way down, claiming to be soldiers looking for banditos. They had let us pass after checking our Mexican insurance and lifting a few pesos as a passage fee, but Dad had not been impressed.

Off we went. After an hour, Dad was in a mellow mood, leaving "this ****" country" and offered to let me drive until lunch at Tamuzanchale. That was the closest Dad had seen to English, and he began to joke about Thomas and Charlie as we drove along the narrow highway.

Just south of Zimapan, disaster struck again. Oh, why did I have to be at the wheel? As I was rounding a curve, the road narrowed to one lane and there in the middle of the road was a Mexican boy about twelve riding a burro—right down the center of the road. There was no room to pass on either side.

I slowed the car to a crawl, and the burro automatically went to the side of the road to let us pass. The boy looked back at us, grinned and yanked the rope reins to block us. "El burro" walked back to the center of the road. I slowed to a crawl and followed. Dad was getting irritated and said, "Use your horn, Stupie." There was that word again! Every time I heard that nickname, it seemed that boiling water was being poured on my head. "*Run for your life*, and you'll never hear it again!" echoed in my brain, and I sounded the horn. I realized just how hard I had leaned on the horn button when the burro leaped to the side.

Again, the boy yanked the rope reins, and we were blocked. This time I drove within a couple feet of the two, hoping at least to intimidate the burro. I was getting tired of this game and so was the burro. The boy was just laughing. Dad wasn't. "Give it some gas, Stupie!" The boy's next yank on the reins did it. The burro stopped dead in his tracks. I didn't, and we met.

By this time we were near the boy's hut. He jumped off the burro onto the hood of the car, the burro manured the bumper, and they both ran off. My Spanish was good enough for me to hear the boy's father yell at him to fall down and act hurt. Dad shouted, "Step on the gas, Stupie," but I wanted to be sure he was okay. By then his whole family piled on the car. Too bad the car had running boards.

Not knowing if he was actually hurt, I offered to take him and his father to town for a checkup. We put the boy into the back seat, and he grinned all the way to Zimapan. His dad rode on the running boards since there was no room inside. I stopped as we entered town, asking a passerby, "Donde esta un abogado, por favor?" (Where is a lawyer, please?) I was directed to an office on the square. The abogado had the boy examined by a doctor and there was no injury, but we still had to fill out some paperwork.

It turned out that the abogado was also the local judge, but I didn't tell Dad that until later. We were all ushered into a room to await the local insurance representative. No one in the town spoke English, so if we were to get back on the road, my high school Spanish would be our only chance. The "room" had bars on the windows, an iron barred door, but it was "not a jail." I asked if my family could leave to have lunch while we prepared the report. He said that even though this was not a jail, no one could leave. He nodded toward the policeman with a rifle who stood outside. So, it was lunchtime, but no lunch. I wasn't hungry anyway.

As I gave the report to the judge, he complimented me on my Spanish and insisted that I translate his compliment for my family. He could see everyone was unhappy, and maybe that would soften Dad's murderous glare. My words were ignored as the chant from Xochimilco started again, "Stupie, my **** dumb son." I never did translate that for the judge, but he knew it was not a happy thought.

I was told that since we had Mexican insurance, all medical and other costs would be paid and we could be on our way as soon as the insurance man got back from plowing his field, several kilometers away. "He must clean up and change into his white uniform that is required for all official duties," the judge remarked. "I can send someone on a burro to tell him if you are willing to pay a few pesos. He has no telephone." I agreed without consulting Dad.

"As long as it isn't that boy or his father," I added in Spanish. The judge laughed loudly. Dad didn't.

Mother was quiet, but my two sisters and brother were hungry and nervous. Dad continued his chant, but now it was to some tune I didn't recognize. My apprehension died away as the judge and I chatted about my school, my new job in Houston, and my career plans. My Spanish teacher, Mrs. Bryant, would have been proud.

Near dark, I heard a burro approach. The insurance man finally arrived—bathed and shaved, with a liberal amount of grease on his hair and a generous dose of aftershave. He was in uniform—spotless white starched suit, straw hat and white shoes. With great pomp and a flourish, he signed the papers using his own "official pen," tipped his hat and bowed deeply to my mother and left us. As he bowed, I saw that the blanket he used for a saddle must have been old and worn. There on the seat of his starched white pants were several grey-brown, smudges, one shaped like a half moon. They looked like a smiling face! I was smiling, too.

The judge explained that it was getting late, and he would finish the paperwork in the morning. As I translated this for the family, panic began to set in. Where would we eat and sleep? Surely, not in this room. It had only wooden benches and no toilet. The chant stopped as Dad went speechless. At least that was one blessing. I was doing my best, but my best was not good enough to stop the insults.

The judge accompanied us out of the "not jail" room to our lodgings for the night. Surprise—*it was a small hotel owned by his brother!* No wonder that we had to spend the night. The hotel was empty of tourists, and his brother needed the money. We were almost out of pesos, but the innkeeper would exchange the dollars "for a small service charge" (50%). We had no choice.

The six of us checked in and noted the rooms were clean and tidy. We had not eaten since breakfast, so we all went immediately to the hotel restaurant for dinner. We entered a large courtyard filled with lanterns, strolling musicians and lots of greenery, just like a movie set. I picked out my own table to enjoy peace and quiet. The rest of the family sat at another table. Tensions eased, and Dad invited me to reconsider. I agreed if he would leave me alone. A few minutes later, I joined the family for a welcome meal. The food was excellent and the rooms clean and comfortable. The hotel turned out to be the nicest place we stayed during the whole trip. After getting a lunch to go at the hotel and paying the bill the next morning, we were off to finish the papers and be on our way. Dad had planned our expenses carefully, but now we were running out of pesos. Another problem had added to our difficulties. Jill had contracted Montezuma's Revenge from either the food or the water. Sick or not, Dad insisted on leaving.

The judge explained that all expenses would be covered by the insurance except for a special fee for local expenses of the court, amounting to "fill your gas tank, empty all purses and wallets and keep the equivalent of five dollars in pesos for any emergency" the rest of the pesos and all our US currency was his "fee." In the early 1950s, credit cards were rare, so traveling another 500 miles to the border on five dollars was a challenge.

I tried to lighten the mood, by offering to finish the previous day's drive to Tamuzanchale, but Dad didn't think that was funny at all. Even the Thomas and Charlie joke from the previous day was forgotten. As we headed for Brownsville with our lunch in the cooler, we all remained silent except Dad who resumed the chant, but that afternoon he stopped. By nightfall we were across the border in Brownsville and able to cash a check. I was ready to get to Houston and the new job. Only one more day to go!

ESCAPE AT LAST

Sunday afternoon we entered Houston, and after a couple wrong turns we found the YMCA building on Louisiana Street. Dad verified that rooms were available for $12 per week and that I had directions to get to Eastern States. Bus service was available, and the desk clerk had a bus schedule. Calculating that my first check would be about $70 after taxes and five days away, I would need $12 for the room and three dollars a day for food and incidentals. Confidently, I got out of the car, received $30 from Dad to tide me over until Friday and left the memories of Mexico behind. The family left for Florida a few minutes later. With my one suitcase in hand, I proudly marched away to my first taste of freedom. The clerk assigned me a room and then—reality. Two weeks' rent was due when I checked in! All of a sudden the "bankroll" was looking thin. I figured I could skimp by on a dollar a day for meals till Friday, so I skipped dinner, got unpacked, and made sure that the crackers leftover from lunch and the box of Oreo cookies were handy.

I slept well that night, and early on Monday I was off to my real job, remembering that two dollars per hour for a week would mean $80—more than I had ever earned, even in a month. The bus was early, but so was I and after passing more industrial plants than I had ever seen, I arrived at the refinery full of optimism. I had forgotten to consider the fifteen cent bus fare to and from work, and that thirty cents a day would bite deeply into my shrinking nest egg. As I considered how to ration the remaining $5.85, the bus door opened. But what was that awful smell and that burning sensation in my nostrils? It was probably just the chemical plant next to the bus stop. After the two block walk from the bus stop, I realized it was getting worse, and the smell was coming from my destination. I wondered if it was always that bad, and if scraping rust and painting storage tanks would be that smelly. I knew it was going to be hot, as it was eighty-five degrees at seven thirty in the morning, and the steam escaping from every piece of equipment added to Houston's humidity!

At 8:00, I checked in, filled out papers, and met Sam Perkins the Chief Engineer who told me, "We have a minimum age of eighteen for paint crews, and you're only seventeen, so you can't join the Texas A&M paint gang." Oh, no! What now? My dream job was gone! He then told me that the photostat and blueprint machine operator had just resigned. "Do you think you could handle that assignment instead of scraping and painting storage tanks?" The room at the Y was not air conditioned and the ninety-eight degree temperature on the previous June afternoon had convinced me I would fry while painting on a hot steel tank forty or fifty feet in the air. Also, if I worked in the office, I would not have to face my fear of heights. While waiting for my talk with Mr. Perkins, Rosie, his secretary had told me the older college kids always "let" the younger ones scrape and paint the sunny side. It was some kind of seniority program.

I told him I had studied drafting and we made our own blueprints, so I was sure I could handle the job. I wondered if they made them in a wooden frame placed out in the sun like in high school or if there was some sort of machine, but I was too shy to ask. Besides, this office was air conditioned, the smell was outside, and how hard could the job be? Mr. Perkins sent me to personnel for a badge and payroll clearance. *Problem*: payday was every two weeks not every week, and after time sheets were turned in it took a week to issue the checks. There were no computers in those days. I was looking at a one week check, but now it would be twelve days to stretch the $5.85. I didn't have to write to Einstein this time to do the math. There was little more than enough for bus fare.

I asked about a salary advance and was told that it was against company policy, but the company had a cafeteria that served breakfast and lunch, and employees could charge food against their paycheck. In addition, the refinery ran twenty-four hours a day, so a late afternoon break with snacks was available. But Cokes were from a machine, so cash only. Prayers were answered. No time to do the math, but I wasn't going to call home. I would starve first.

I was escorted to the copy center, a nine by twelve concrete block building about 100 yards away from the offices, with no air conditioning and a huge machine that had to be filled with liquid ammonia to develop the prints. It reminded me of changing my younger siblings' diapers, not one of my fondest memories. The copy center also had a darkroom to make photographic copies of correspondence, one page at a time, each taking about fifteen minutes to make the negative, then a wet copy, followed by a noisy heated dryer. The darkroom did have a fan, and it kept the temperature below 100 degrees most days, but the odors came in with the "fresh" air. I was given a short demonstration on machine operation and was ready. Aside from the odor and heat, the job was actually easy, and I found myself spending more and more time in the office volunteering for other errands.

That first day, I was given some copy work from John Chapman, a young husband who asked me about my background. When he found out I was staying at the YMCA and had no family in Texas, he offered to pick me up and take me home each evening. He and his wife drove by the Y each day, so it wouldn't be any trouble for them to pick me up. Wow! Now, over the two weeks till payday I would have an extra $2.85 for food. I only had $5.85, so that savings was significant.

That afternoon, I met his wife Kitty, and on the way back to my room she asked how I was doing in my new city. I told them all was well, and I was looking forward to a good summer. There was no way I was going to tell them about the money situation, but the next morning as I rushed to the cafeteria and wolfed down a quick egg sandwich, John guessed. I didn't know at the time, but later I realized that he checked with personnel and found out I had asked for an advance. That evening, without mentioning money, John asked if it would be inconvenient if they picked me up earlier, as he would like to start eating breakfast with me at the cafeteria.

I settled into a pretty boring routine—large breakfast, huge lunch, 3:00 snack (all charged to my next paycheck), back to the Y to read. Every night for dinner, I would go to a local cafe, order a glass of ice water and a cup of hot water. By adding ketchup to the water, I had ketchup soup and a nickel pack of crackers. After the second visit, the middle-aged waitress (at that time middle-age was somewhere in the twenties) asked if that was all I had to eat. I told her that after payday the following week, I would be a regular to make up for the ketchup. She approved and asked me to leave off the dime tip. With a smile, she said, "Just wait until after payday, and you can make it up." Friday finally arrived. I filled out my time card for my first payday a week away. I began to wonder about food for Saturday and Sunday. I had enough for a few crackers that weekend, a bottle of milk and a nickel left over.

The job was going well; I had even asked for any books I could borrow that would help me understand how oil was refined. I told Mr. Perkins that I had spare time on days that the legal department didn't send over a crate of papers to copy. It seemed that lawyers copied everything but the Sunday paper.

On the way home Friday night Kitty asked how it felt to finish my first week and get a paycheck. I had to tell them it would be another week before I got one because I was on the plant payroll, not the office payroll. I told John and Kitty that I was okay and would see them Monday morning. I was embarrassed and thought they would think my parents had dumped me without enough money. But John knew, so did Kitty. As I was getting out of the car, he also got out and told me that this might be a rough weekend and he didn't want to give me any money, because I was now on my own and with college ahead, a lot of things would get difficult. If I could make it through the weekend on my own, I would know that whatever happened to me I would be able to stand up to it. I wasn't convinced at all.

I really thought he was going to slip me a couple dollars and didn't want Kitty to see. Mother did that a lot—especially when we were angry with her. John concluded by saying he didn't want me to take on more than I was able, so if I got to the point of desperation, call him and they would come get me for dinner Sunday, but I had to at least get through Saturday on my own. I bought the bottle of milk, crawled into bed and prepared to read refinery books all weekend. By Saturday night, the milk was almost gone, and I went out for the ketchup soup, but this time without crackers. I had to save that nickel for the emergency phone call. Sunday morning I woke up. Surely this was starvation. After gulping down the last of the milk and filling up the rest of the way on water, it was back to bed and the books. I knew the ketchup soup café was closed on Sunday, so even that meager snack was impossible.

It was stifling that afternoon, and even the fan didn't seem to help. The bed was damp with perspiration, and I had enough. Hunger beat out fortitude, so I hopped out of bed, showered, took my nickel to the pay phone, and dialed John with my trembling hand. I was ready to *eat*. "I'm sorry, you have the wrong number," said the lady at the other end.

I still remember the sound of the last nickel as it rattled down into the coin box. A candy bar, a candy bar echoed through my mind. Why didn't I buy a candy bar instead of wimping out? It was back to my room and reading.

The next morning I was ready for breakfast, and as John and Kitty picked me up, they both seemed genuinely pleased that I had made it. From then on, I knew everything would be all right.

John and Kitty were Catholics and that week asked if I was also and if I went to church. When I told them I wasn't and had not looked for a church in Houston but had attended regularly in Florida, John strongly encouraged me to find a church right away. I had considered that my freedom included turning my back on everything and starting a new life with me making all the decisions on my own. But hey, he was in the driver's seat—literally. Maybe with all the recent problems melting away, John had the right idea. A lot of thanks were in order. Their encouragement and friendship were pivotal in my development.

The next week was a breeze. Breakfast and lunch at Eastern States, ketchup soup for dinner, and Friday was payday. I had never before been through a time where food was the foremost thought in my mind day and night, and I began to appreciate the agony the starving people of the world lived with. I had always been told that starving people were underfed because they were too lazy to work. They deserve more consideration.

By Friday, I had received my first paycheck, gone straight to the Rice Hotel dining room and ordered their best meal, veal cutlet, gravy, beans and rice. I followed the feast with a butterscotch sundae. I pigged out and went to sleep on a full stomach. After that first meal, I returned regularly to the ketchup soup café, caught up on my tips, and ate from the menu. Since that day, I never again have put ketchup on my food. I can boast that I have been ketchup-free for over fifty years. Even when it was accidentally put on my food, I scraped it off.

I had gotten proficient in the use of the photocopy equipment and had rigged up a way to make copies in half the normal time in order to escape the heat and the smell. I heard the mail boy had been fired for hiding several large boxes of mail rather than delivering it, so I volunteered to deliver the backlog in between copying. Sam gave me a try, and it worked out fine *and* I got my first raise—after only a few weeks, I was making an extra eight cents per hour. I had learned to measure money in terms of the amount of food it would buy, and that was equivalent to two extra meals a week.

My next challenge at Eastern States was remembering names. As the copy boy I had few names to remember, but as mail boy I had to learn dozens of names and quickly. Even though throughout school I was blessed with a near photographic memory, I had a mental block about names. It would follow me for years. I was self-conscious and avoided looking people in the eye, so matching names to faces was difficult. I made a seating chart for the office, and each day I would add the names from the envelopes to the chart.

Many of the employees had heard about the ketchup soup and the weekend of the lost nickel, and gradually everyone encouraged dropping the "Mister" and using first names. I now had a new family.

The end of the summer came quickly, and as I was leaving for Ga. Tech, Sam told me I had done well and was expected to be back each summer, and I would not be scraping and painting tanks with the Texas A&M students. His plan was to get me exposed to the lab and field employees before putting me in training for supervision after I graduated. He felt that working in the group before directing their work would make the transition easier. Many of the plant workers resented the college kids, so the plan was that

1954's summer would be spent training in the laboratory. 1955 would bring an assignment to work in refinery construction and maintenance—building scaffolding, helping boilermakers, and welding. The last summer before graduation, 1956's assignment would be in the inspection department that was responsible for the continued operation, maintenance, and repair of the equipment. He also expected me to join the staff after graduation. Wow, a new family and a job, and I wasn't even in college yet. John and Kitty's introducing me to self-confidence and my return to church formed a foundation for the rest of my career.

It was years later that I realized that my career at Eastern States was not just chance. I started too young to paint storage tanks, so I was able to meet the staff as the "copy boy." Then the mail boy quit, and I was able to perform both jobs, this time meeting top management people. My spare time reading books on how refineries operated caught the attention of supervisors, and I was given an opportunity that the other college summer help missed. The Lord had been watching over me again.

ON TO COLLEGE

I returned to Jacksonville a week before classes began at Ga. Tech in September 1953, just enough time to pack and ride to Atlanta with my dormitory roommate, Bob Smith. I had attended junior high and high school with him, and we were close friends. I was looking forward to my education, since I now knew where I was going to work and had enough basic knowledge of the refinery to concentrate on classes that would help in that career. Dad was especially happy that the summer went well and that I was going to fulfill his dream. I was just happy to be away from home.

As we entered the dormitory room on the third floor, we discovered the assignment was not a two man room, but a double with four students. Well, that was not acceptable for Bobby. Mrs. Smith marched us to Dean Griffin's office to ask for a better room. Needless to say, he was not impressed, but he was a gentleman and a diplomat, so after she finished her request, Dean explained that all rooms were full, but he would watch for an opening. Bob and I were told to let him know if the room didn't work out for us while he was looking. All Bob and I wanted to do was get out of there and never see him again. He was a legend at Tech. He was reputed to have a better memory than anyone. I never did go to his office again and never confronted him until he handed me my diploma four years later. As he shook hands and congratulated me, he whispered, "Did your roommate ever get to let go of the apron strings?" I almost dropped my diploma. He really did have a memory!

Registration the next day brought a shock. We didn't get to choose any classes as I had planned. English? I had made straight A's for two years in a row. Why English? Intermediate chemistry was next on the list. I had taken Spanish instead of chemistry at Landon because when I moved to Texas, it would be useful. The engineering drawing, math, and social studies were okay because I liked them, but then they added swimming—now that's something no engineer needs.

The swimming coach was infamous at Tech. Fred Lanoue had apparently been in charge of drown-proofing Navy sailors and airmen who attended Tech during WWII. Even though the war had been over eight years, his basic survival course remained. The class was required of all freshmen, and it began with simulating a jump into the ocean from a ship or plane. Each student was required to learn to remove clothing and convert trousers to floats by knotting the legs and inflating the trousers with lung power after jumping off the high dive platform.

One of the Cuban students in my class couldn't swim. He was thrown off the high dive when he refused to jump. A scream of "I can't sweem!" pierced the air. Everyone watched as he floundered and promptly sank to the bottom. After his rescue, Coach convinced him the importance of the drown-proofing class.

Another of his requirements was to swim the entire length of the Olympic sized pool underwater. At first we dove in to get a head start, but to pass the course, everyone had to eventually swim after jumping in feet first. This simulated what was required if you were jumping from a burning ship. The underwater swim could take you beyond burning fuel on the water. All were happy when this class was over.

The chemistry class was a bigger problem, especially when the professor announced that anyone who didn't take high school chemistry would fail, so "just drop out and save yourself a headache." I met him after class and announced I wasn't going to drop out and if he just told me what I needed to study to catch up, I was going to make it. He offered a beginners' chemistry manual and gave me two weeks to catch up or bail out. He also tutored me for five days. Thanks to this help, I made a B in the class.

We settled into the college routine and never considered moving to a new dorm room. I decided to take on the Joe College image by buying a pipe. I still remembered my cigarette episode from 1940 and Dad's near death from cigarettes, so they were never considered. With my brand new Sherlock Holmes-style pipe and a tin of Prince Albert tobacco, I lit up. It took some practice to breathe the smoke out of my nostrils without sneezing, but I mastered that technique. The pipe smoking lasted through the second tin, when I learned about pipe cleaners. I never used one. As I inhaled the nicotine and tar, or whatever the foul tasting liquid was, I choked, went to the third floor window and heaved out pipe, Prince Albert, and the matches. The pipe went out the window as Bob's record player boomed out, "Shake a hand, shake a hand, shake a hand if you can" for about the twentieth time in a row. The record followed Prince Albert, and I stomped out of the room to wash the taste out of my mouth.

Classes went well that year, except for the third quarter English class. I had failed to follow Dean Griffin's example of diplomacy. The professor assigned the first essay topic: "Why I believe that saluting the American Flag is no better than worshipping a pagan idol." I concluded my blistering essay with the statement that anyone that believed that was either mentally retarded or a communist. That was not what he was looking for—nor was I expecting the "D" I got for a final grade, along with the advice to keep my opinions to myself. I learned that some teachers were leaning a little to the left. The next year, I was assigned to another English class with a liberal professor. I had a similar encounter and an identical grade, even though this time I used "pinko" instead of communist. I now had another D to lower my average, but at least that was the end of the required English courses. Elective English courses I took later (public speaking and report writing) yielded B's. During those courses, I avoided labeling the professors.

I joined Pi Kappa Alpha fraternity that first year, settled into studies, and looked forward to summers at the refinery. The fraternity experiences were a welcome break from classes. PiKA offered fellowship, social events, meals away from Ptomaine Tavern (as the dining hall was called), and for a limited few—rooms. The traditional fall outing was the annual "Possum Hunt." Pikes and pledges alike invited dates to the exciting event. All freshmen were called "Rats" and were required to wear "Rat Caps" even to parties. After the barbecue, couples held hands as they followed the hunting dogs in the chase. Bonnie and I led the way, along with a crowd of couples. The dogs were baying and trying to outrun us as we proceeded into the woods. The chase continued, but the crowd seemed to dwindle. On we charged, determined to outlast the rest. Soon we were at the tree with a large possum glaring down at us. Gosh, there were only three couples left! The hunter quickly captured the creature, and we proudly returned to the lodge to show our prowess.

Something was wrong, though. They weren't congratulating us as the photo was snapped of Bonnie holding the possum by the tail with me looking on. They were laughing, "You actually chased a possum?"

"Sure did," I answered. Then I saw it. The laughing guys had smudges of lipstick on their faces, and the dates were smudged too. Without the benefit of a kiss, my face turned as red as some of the smiling faces.

A "Rat" Catches a Possum

The frat house on Techwood Drive was an old two-story residence with a small party room and crawl space in the basement, so parties were crowded. Fraternity hazing of pledges was minimal, but our class did get to dig out the crawl space with shovels to enlarge the party room. The work included pouring a new floor and reinforced concrete foundation wall to support the upper two stories. The fraternity had enough civil engineers to provide the design and supervision, but the labor was reserved for the pledges. The new room was opened with a great party with two beer kegs and refreshments.

The new party room was almost destroyed early in its lifetime. The next year Bob had parked his new Buick along the curb, being sure that it was far enough away from the next car that the chrome bumpers wouldn't get scratched when that car left. As several Pikes were talking on the front porch, the elderly lady living across the street began to back out of her driveway. She always backed out slowly, put it in forward and "scratched off" as the students watched. This day was a bad day, though. She scratched off before putting the car into forward. The car careened across the street "between" Bob's car and the next, stopping just short of our party room wall. The quotation marks are there because "between" meant she made a path where none existed. She even pushed one of the cars up over the curb.

As the Pike and Theta Chi fraternity houses emptied to see what happened, she panicked, put the car back in forward, sped back between the two cars and up her steep driveway into her garage. The car that had been on the curb was now back in the street. She then closed the garage door, ran into her house and pulled all her window shades down so we couldn't see her. Bob and the Theta Chi owner rushed to inspect their cars. As Bob flicked a small chip of her paint off his chrome bumper, the other owner saw his complete loss. Bob's Buick had survived as our date car.

One of the most memorable fraternity events of that year was related to my church. During high school and the first summer in Houston, church was important to me, but I began to observe that the church I attended was emphasizing many rules they added to the biblical teachings. At first, the changes seemed to be minor, but as time went by, the church rules were taught to be equal to the Bible and sometimes even more important. I visited several different churches, but all seemed to follow a similar trends whether they conflicted with the Bible or not. I was getting disenchanted and stopped attending.

During the formal dance, I invited my friend Janie from high school to join me for the festivities. She knew from talks we had at Landon how deeply some modern church changes disturbed me and gave me a book to help me in my search for a new church home. It was titled *The Searcher*, and it told of a disenchanted Christian's search for a church of the Bible. The author visited churches throughout the book, and each chapter was devoted to a different church's teachings. Eagerly, I read the book, but in the end, it was a disappointment—he never succeeded in his search. All the churches he visited had made many changes in their worship from those of the first century church. I decided to re-read the book more carefully and test the doctrine before resuming church attendance.

One evening weeks later, I lost *The Searcher* for good. It was the old prankster getting loose. I had loaned it to a date, and the following Friday night as Bob and I double dated in his Buick, we stopped at a traffic light next to a restaurant advertising *tuna burgers*. My date asked, "What's in a tuna burger?"

I replied "Tuna, what else?"

Her response, "A hamburger isn't ham."

"Oh, yes it is," I explained.

By now Bob and his date were covering their mouths to keep from laughing. Even the couple in the next car was listening. What were these college boys trying to put over on those high school girls?

"It comes from a cow," she exclaimed, this time in a louder voice. The trap was set.

"Of course it's a cow, but a pigmy cow—that's why it's called a *ham*burger. Get it? Pig is an abbreviation for a pigmy cow." As the light changed to green, we drove off. The eavesdropping driver just sat there shaking his head.

Bob changed the subject, and we went on to the movies. The next week, when I called her for a date, she told me her father listened to the pigmy cow story, and if I convinced her a pig and a cow were the same, he didn't want me talking her into anything else. She could never go out or even talk with me on the phone again. The joke cost me my *Searcher* book and my date.

During Christmas break, Janie invited me to her house, while her parents were gone. This was looking *good*! As we stretched out on the floor gazing into the roaring fire, she whispered, "Close your eyes, I've got a secret for you." *Wow*, it was looking like an early present! She leaned closer. I was ready for my kiss. "Charlie," she whispered in my ear, "I met someone and I got engaged. Isn't that wonderful?" I knew that was the end of my waiting for a kiss. I even forgot to tell her about losing *The Searcher*. So, Janie was engaged to someone else. I was now a searcher for a new girl *and* a new church.

Ga. Tech dormitory space was extremely limited, and only the freshman class stayed in campus housing. After that year, students were on their own. Many who did not stay in fraternity houses rented off-campus housing and walked to class. Cars were rare and campus parking spaces were even rarer. Students roomed in basements, converted garages, spare rooms in houses of local residents—wherever a place was available. I stayed in the fraternity house that second year, but rooms were not fancy at all. My room was shared by three students, each sleeping on the triple height bunk bed. The entire length of one wall was lined with old doors and plywood for desks, and each student had a desk chair and a goose-neck lamp for studying.

It was normal for rooms to be a "little" messy, and eating snacks was a common source of untidiness. We began to hear rats scurrying across the desk after lights out. BMac, Frank, and I would wait for the sound and as the lights were turned on, attack with baseball bats and two by fours. We were successful in seriously damaging the desk but not the rat. One night he got bolder and pushed the loose top off my peanut butter jar. Even the time it took him to climb out didn't slow him down enough for us to get him. We stopped eating from that jar, but left it there as bait for the next night. The story repeated for several nights, with no success. A couple weeks later it was over, the rat finally got the message that he was not welcome. With him gone, it was time to throw away the jar. As I picked it up, the top slipped off and there was our rat, only his beady eyes and the tip of his nose showing. We hadn't scared him off, he had drowned. It was months before we ate peanut butter again.

Our new nighttime snack was not decided, it was delivered. A delivery truck rounding a corner too fast delivered two packages for snack time, a large wheel of cheddar cheese and a case of Kellogg's Raisin Bran rolled into the street. Free food! He didn't stop, so we took the treasure to the room. Later we found out that the Raisin Bran loosened the digestive system just enough to prevent an explosion after so much cheese. Now, we had to find some other snack. Cheese and peanut butter both went to the bottom of the list—but for different reasons. After a full case of Raisin Bran, it went down on our list for a while, too.

The social highlight of every year was the Intra-Fraternity Council spring dance, a formal affair that always featured a nationally known band. This year, I had invited a new girl to the dance for our first date. The evening was going well, and she was impressed. As I was dancing, Bob came up to meet my date. I actually forgot her name, then as I stammered, she introduced herself. In my embarrassment, I also forgot Bob's name. Bob's date and future wife Edmarie just smiled. Everyone laughed, but I knew this was as bad or even worse than the pigmy cow tale. She and I were finished dating after that night. I'd tell you her name, but I still don't remember it. The search was back on again.

The Christmas holidays each year found us all migrating back to Jacksonville, but things were completely different by then. Those two weeks were so filled with activities that the difficulties at home were put aside. There were parties, dances, dating and just comparing experiences with the Landon crowd that had dispersed to many colleges.

The two principal country clubs, San Jose and Timuquana, catered more to the college crowd than high school. Each year brought another highlight, escorting the Gator Bowl Queen contestants, formal dances, debutante activities, etc. There was hardly time to go home even to sleep. During one special dance, I was going through the receiving line with my date, Kathryn, when I was introduced to Daughtry Towers, a prominent attorney. "I know you, you're Chuck Space's son," he remarked. That was the last straw! I had been "Chuck Space's son" all my life. It was time for a change. I vowed never to return to Jacksonville until I was *me*. I made my mind up to accept a job anywhere that I could develop my own reputation and no longer live in Dad's shadow.

The first two years I was able to keep my grades up in spite of going to a movie almost every week night. I studied before tests, but little more than the night before. In mechanical engineering, if you wanted to graduate in four years, the academic load was heavy. An average of twenty credit hours was required per term, and all laboratories included three hours in the lab for the one hour credit. If you failed a class, it almost always meant that you couldn't graduate on time. My worst quarter included seventeen hours of class and eighteen hours of laboratory, and one was a dreaded Saturday 8:00 AM laboratory. Saturday classes were awful. One time I went to drafting lab in my tuxedo, as the party ended only half an hour before class. There was no extra credit for dressing up for class!

By my third year, I was wearing out. The two previous years spent with minimum study was taking its toll. Having a photographic memory was no longer enough to pass a course. We were actually having to think and reason out problems. The previous term, I had taken twenty-two credit hours, and in the middle of the term had a severely impacted wisdom tooth removed by a dentist who neglected to x-ray my jaw before removing the tooth. As he struggled to remove it, he used a mallet to break the impacted bone away. It slipped, and he broke a large part of my jawbone off, revealing a large void in the remaining bone. The Novocain he gave me had worn off by then, and I slipped into unconsciousness. He packed the hole with a yard long piece of two-inch wide gauze and gave me a shot of morphine, then sent me back to the fraternity house. A few days later, after little or no sleep, I returned to have the packing removed. As an intern held me to the chair, he pulled the packing out. This time with no Novocain. Instead of gently sliding out, it unraveled and came out in a long piece, holding on the whole way. I heard the *rip!* and passed out. After I regained consciousness, he gave me a double shot of morphine, and I started walking back to the Pike house.

I never made it. One of my fraternity brothers found me lying on the sidewalk in a pool of blood. He rushed me to the Tech infirmary, where I spent several days receiving shots to control pain and bleeding. It was about six weeks before the shaking from the narcotics stopped and I was able to sleep all night. My grades suffered that term, but I passed everything.

Waking up for 8:00 classes in the winter term was especially difficult. By my third year, I was able to select some non-engineering subjects, so I decided to try an easy course, one that many of the football players selected. Business law was a memory course, required little study, and as long as you came to class it would be easy. The only problem was that classes were at 8:00 AM Tuesday, Thursday, and yes, Saturday again! The standard procedure for 8:00 AM Saturday class was: set the alarm for 7:40, dress, skip breakfast, walk the fifteen minutes to class, slip in at the last minute, doze during the lecture, and go back to bed until 11:00.

My arrival time for class had been slipping for a couple weeks, but I usually got to class by 8:10. After a few Saturdays, the professor was getting irritated. Each day he would interrupt his lecture and announce, "Class you may wish to note that Mr. Space has decided to favor us with his presence. Please applaud." Finally, his patience exhausted, one morning he changed his greeting, "Mr. Space, next Saturday is the mid term examination, and if you are late, even one second late, you will fail the course. Do you understand?" I did and took appropriate action. I went to bed early, set the clock for 7:15 instead of 7:40, and remembering the warning, reconsidered and set it at 7:05, just to be safe. Fifty minutes would be plenty. I would impress him by arriving early.

The next morning at the awful hour of 7:05, the alarm woke me up. The party the night before had lasted until three, and I was a wreck. As I groaned and turned it off, it seemed appropriate to just roll over and snooze until 7:25. I could still make it. I rolled over and closed my eyes.

I awoke with a start. The clock hand was on five minutes past. I was late already. In a panic, I put my raincoat over my pajamas, put on my slippers and ran in the rain to class. It was now twenty-five minutes after, and his quizzes only lasted for thirty minutes. If I got to class before he left, maybe I could sneak in.

My heart sank. The classroom was already empty! I slowly walked to the professor's office. I rehearsed my speech. "Professor, I know I have been late again, and I apologize. I had all good intentions, I even went to bed early, and set my clock for 7:05 to have plenty of time. I must have fallen asleep again, but I will never be late again if you let me take a make up quiz. If I fail, I'll have to stay for summer term, and without the pay from that summer job, I'll have to drop out of school." That ought to convince him—a little pity, a little apology, a little humility.

I charged into his office without knocking and began my plea. About half way through, he interrupted. "Mr. Space, you are a fool!" he thundered. "In fact, you are an idiot," he continued.

"Yes sir, I am—both, but have pity…" There was only silence. He shook his head, then laughed. Maybe I had convinced him. No, I had only given him an anecdote to share with his colleagues.

He said softly, "Look at your watch." In amazement, I looked. It was 7:30, not 8:30! I had woken up again as soon as my head hit the pillow after the alarm and thought it was an hour later! Here I was in my pajamas and slippers, in a wet raincoat looking just like the fool he described earlier.

"No time to get dressed is there? That is unless you think you can get back to your room, change and be back in time, but remember *not one second late!*" he snarled. I was first into class that day, and he delighted introducing me and asking me to remove my coat and join the class. I kept it on and was never late to his class again.

Spring breaks in the 1950s were far different than they are today. Few had enough money for that kind of entertainment. A group of four decided to spend our break in Miami, a place none of us had visited. The University of Miami had a Pike chapter, and visitors were fed and housed free. We could probably afford that, so off we went with the minimum required $25 each for gas and incidentals. We had to make the money last for several days. The trip from Jacksonville to Miami was filled with anticipation.

On arrival, we were greeted, but there were no beds available. We could sleep on lounge chairs by the pool, though. That was fine with us, and after the evening meal we left to find some excitement. We chose to visit the Jai Lai Fronton, a place where contestants threw a hard ball back and forth, similar to paddleball, but using basket-like gloves. Betting was allowed on the contests, and no one checked ID cards. After watching several matches, the novelty wore off and we decided that placing a small bet would liven up the party. After a conference to check out our cash reserves, we decided that one two dollar bet each wouldn't break the bank. Several more matches were observed to pick out the best player. None of us agreed on the best, so each picked his own.

I chose one with twenty-five to one odds. If he won, I'd have $50, twice the amount I started with. The betting line was long and by the time I got to the window, the contest was about to start. The cashier announced, "Last Bet!" I just made it! I put down my only $10 bill, picked up my ticket and waited for change. "Kid, look up," the cashier said, "This is the ten dollar window." Oh no! He was right. I was now broke and unable to get a refund. The man behind me offered to buy my ticket. I thanked him profusely and sat down to watch. My man won. If I had only kept that ticket! That was it for me—no more betting. At least my ten dollars lasted until we got back to Jacksonville, and everyone had a story to take back to college.

I planned to have a car by that summer and had announced my plan the previous Christmas vacation. Dad agreed that it was time for me to have my own car. I didn't object at all. "Let's go see Bill Massey," he exclaimed. You could hardly hold me back. As we arrived, Dad said, "You go pick out a used car, no more than $500, and then we can talk to Bill." Five hundred dollars may not seem like much, but with some new cars around $1500, it was plenty. I picked out a two-year-old Plymouth, and we went in to see Mr. Massey.

"Charles has picked out a car," Dad said.

"Good," was the reply.

"Okay, son, pay Mr. Massey." I was speechless. I had no money. "Then come back when you do," replied Dad—and we left. I thought his plan was to buy the car to replace the $625 Mother had fined me three years earlier for not cleaning her bedroom to suit her. I was wrong.

It was time for another summer in Houston, and Dad had insisted I leave a week later than usual. The whole family was to visit Gram Hilliard who was now eighty. We would travel by car to Rochester to see her for one last time. I rode back from New York to Shreveport on the railroad and rode with a fraternity brother to Houston.

That summer I worked in the carpentry department building scaffolding, concrete forms, repairing damage from fires in the refinery, and I even got to work some of the time in the welding department. I continued my second job, determined to save enough for a car. All work that summer was for maintenance and repair of old equipment and for construction of new refinery units. This was my first job where I made more than Dad, who was vice president of the Atlantic Bank. Eastern States was going through a major expansion. As new processes were developed for modern petrochemicals, some of the first full scale units were built and tested at Eastern States. The building blocks for some of the newest plastics, coatings and chemicals were first produced at the refinery. In addition, new sources of oil were arriving.

The refinery began importing cheaper crude high in sulfur to replace the Texas Sweet Crude that was so easy to refine. The denser, "Sour Crude," often with a high sulfur and salt content, was more corrosive and required major modifications to equipment and processing. New solutions had to be created on the spot, without drawings. Many pieces of equipment were made from carbon steel and were not suitable for the highly corrosive sour crude. Reconstruction of a large part of the refinery to convert to stainless steel was impossible. The interior of each tower had to be lined with stainless by welding four inch wide strips of stainless steel to the entire inside surface. No gaps, cracks, or pinholes were allowable. It was a twenty-four hour a day painstaking process of welding, grinding, inspection, and re-welding problem areas.

The hierarchy in the plant was similar to that of my childhood's Big Guys and Little Guys. The carpenters were called "wineos" and the college students "school boys." The school boys got the worst jobs, like the time a road over a dozen hot oil pipelines collapsed, and I had to lie in the middle of the hot lines and tie reinforcing rods for the replacement bridge. When concrete flowing into the forms broke through a hole, School Boy Space got to crawl into the twenty-four inch high opening and scoop it out with a bucket. They had to pull me out with a rope tied to one foot when I passed out.

Between assignments, I rode around the refinery in the back of a dump truck loading and unloading scaffolding, along with "Fats," a huge laborer. He was at least 400 pounds, over six feet tall, and just barely able to fit through a doorway. His hands were as large as a baseball players' glove. If he had been a bully, he would have been a terror, but he was a gentle person. Because of his size, he was the butt of many jokes, but none could match teasing him about his fear of snakes. Several times he had run in panic from a piece of black rope, as the gang doubled over in laughter. One day, weeks after the black rope joke had run its course, one of the carpenters brought a life-like four foot long rubber snake to work. We were all occupied pitching pennies with Fats at lunch hour, when "Fats, catch!" rang out. The fake snake landed on his neck. About fifty knew of the staged joke and crowded around the open double door, several deep to watch the panic.

Fats screamed and ran, rubber snake clutched in his huge hand. Unfortunately, those poor souls in the front row saw him coming, but those crowded around the door blocked the escape. All the laws of physics would prove no one person could get through that crowd, but just like a bowling ball, Fats did, leaving more than a dozen injured lying on the ground. The foreman shook his head as he saw his crew scattered and moaning. After that, no more snakes were allowed.

I didn't think it was very funny. Fats had saved me from a serious accident earlier in our deliveries, and we got along well together. That accident occurred on the way to build a scaffold to repair a large tower in the plant. I was thrown out of the dump truck bed as it rounded a corner at high speed. His huge hand grabbed me in mid air. "Hang on, school boy," he laughed as he pulled me to safety.

The following week, I got to test my fear of heights. Anything more than four feet off the ground was too high for me. The concrete incident from the past week had gained me a little respect, and some of the crew started calling me Charlie. I was not about to let them know I was chicken. This day's work involved climbing the outside wall of a forty-foot high furnace and replacing a thermostatic control. To scale the furnace, it was required to balance on a four inch wide angle against the wall, slowly stand and pull yourself up to the next angle five feet higher up the wall. It would take eight of these moves to reach the top. The foreman said, "You go first and we'll hand up the replacement part." I decided that avoiding looking down would be my only chance to keep my secret. The whole crew was watching.

About thirty-five feet up, one of the crew shouted, "Way to go!" He was right; it was easy. I smiled and looked down to wave. That was it. As soon as my eyes focused on the ground, my hands froze. I couldn't go up or back down. By that time, the boilermaker crew had gathered to watch. No amount of threats or coaxing would work. I planned to stay there with my eyes closed until my body decayed away. At least then I wouldn't have to face them.

I felt a boot kick my hard hat. One of the boilermakers, a huge man of at least 300 pounds, had climbed above me and hollered, "Grab my foot!" I tried to force my hand open to obey. It didn't work anymore! It was frozen. This time, he said in a low voice, "If you don't grab it, I'm going to kick you off this heater!" I grabbed it. It's amazing how a little bit of encouragement works.

He climbed to the top of the furnace onto a work platform, dragging me up with him. At the top, I let go as he grinned, "That's some grip you've got there, school boy." Then I saw it. Leading down from the platform was a ladder. I could have gotten up that way instead of scaling the wall. It had all been a joke. I didn't think it was funny. As I sat down, he told me they all knew of my fear of heights, and that most of them had to get over their fear before they got hurt, so they thought this would be the best way to cure me. The crowd looking at us all knew and was there to see the school boy go on to the paint gang with the rest of the students.

"Now," he said, "you have two choices: down the ladder and off the crew, or back down the side. If you take the ladder, I'm going to be at the bottom and beat you to a pulp for almost wringing my foot off. Grab the steel the way you grabbed my ankle, and you'll never fall." I took the coward's way—I went back down the way I came up. It actually was easier than I thought possible. From then on, I would climb without endangering myself or any of the crew. After work, we all went out and each had a Lone Star Beer. That night, I became the latest "Wineo." The paint gang would have to wait for reinforcements.

"Wineo" on the Furnace Model

Later during the same shutdown of the unit for maintenance, platinum cata-lyst regeneration, and acid cleaning to remove build-up of scale, carbon, and sulfur accumulations, I had my next close call, this time with potentially fatal consequences.

In the 1950s environmental awareness was in its infancy in Houston. Even though the Houston Ship Channel was used as a dumping place and had caught fire more than once, Big Oil was slow to accept changes. The standard procedure for a quick turnaround was to prevent the hydrogen and sulfur fumes from leaking during maintenance. The hydrogen was explosive and the hydrogen sulfide deadly. All were dumped into the storm sewer system leading into the Ship Channel where they dissipated, as the solids and floating waste oil washed into Galveston Bay. Years later President Kennedy would echo what most in industry believed during the '50s, "The solution to pollution is dilution."

To protect the workers from fumes, all the sewer gratings had to be sealed, which was done by covering each opening with canvas covered by a foot of clay. This also prevented welding sparks from igniting the fumes in the sewer.

During this particular "turnaround," asbestos insulation was being torn off a pipe about ten feet above the ground, and I stopped to allow the asbestos dust to settle. Little was known of the cancer-producing properties of asbestos then, but experience told me to wait. Dozens of times I had nose bleeds from inhaling the particles, and frequently a bloody nose and sore throat. As I waited, I watched a welder cutting pipe next to the asbestos demolition. To see better, I stood on top of the clay covering of a four foot square sewer grating. Only five feet below flowed a mixture of sulfur fumes, water, solvents, and gasoline. It was then I saw it—a small drain pipe that was right below the welder. It had not been sealed, and the sparks were dancing all around it!

Before I could react, I heard a dull rumble, like loud thunder, but it wasn't in the distance! It was right under my feet! In what seemed to be slow motion I began to rise up off the ground, still standing on the sewer grating. Flames, smoke, and fumes poured out in all directions. My shoulders hit something, and I instinctively caught hold of the pipes I had hit. I was now hanging, ten feet in the air, with my head between two pipes. I hadn't even lost my safety helmet. I watched as everyone ran from the explosion. A couple of the pipefitters passed out from the fumes and were being dragged away. I was alone, hanging above the cloud of deadly fumes. The sewer grate I was standing upon had blocked the flames as I was blasted into the air.

There was no fire after the explosion, but there also was no wind to blow the fumes away.

I started to let go, but they yelled, "Hang on, the fumes may kill you! We'll get you down when all is clear!" I looked down. I was now hanging not only ten feet up, but directly above the four foot square sewer opening. The grating that had propelled me into my perch had fallen to the side, and if I let go, I'd drop down into the sewer and its poisonous "soup."

It seemed longer, but actually it was less than ten minutes before the "all clear" sounded and I was safe on the ground. Then I looked to see if I had lost the quarters I kept in my upper pocket of my coveralls. I had won them at lunch playing "far away," a contest to see whose Coke bottle had the name of the city farthest from Houston. As I proudly showed them to the rest of the crew, I saw they all were blackened. The toxic fumes had come within a foot of my nostrils! I shuddered to think that I had come so close to being overcome and dropping into the sewer with its toxic mess. Surely the Lord was looking after me that day.

After that encounter, the summer went by quickly. I had begun a second job, wiring houses for John Chapman, and was helping with the construction of John and Kitty's house in Hunter's Creek, a village west of Houston. I was determined that the next trip to Mr. Massey's dealership would be more successful than the last. It was. When I returned home that fall, I bought a three-year-old Dodge for $500 and proudly drove it to Atlanta.

That third year at Tech year was a good one, although my success in class was not matched in social activities. Sure, we had parties every weekend at the frat house. Even if you didn't have a date, there were always plenty of chances to break in on a brother and dance with his date. I had dated several young ladies, and none had resulted in any lasting involvement. Some had been close but never worked out. One evening long after the pigmy cow episode, I was at my customary seat in the phone booth (actually a converted closet in the fraternity house) when a large hand reached in, grabbed my shirt and pulled me out. Carl Sweet was about to change my life forever.

"You've got a date," he announced. "I have a date with Jeanne, and she can't go unless we double date. Your date is Linda League, a Druid Hills High School sophomore."

"Hey," I protested, "I was calling someone else!"

"Too bad!" came the reply with a grin. "Besides, I'll drive—you won't have to rent a car."

I met Linda and her parents at her home. It was not proper to date a girl without going to the door and meeting the family those days, and even after meeting them, you always went to the door, never sat at the street and just blew the horn. They were pleasant, but I was five years older and I didn't think they were enthusiastic. She didn't seem to be either.

We made the best of it for a while, but conversation was sparse in Carl's car as we made our way to Snapfinger Farm, southeast of Atlanta. There PiKA had a picnic, then dancing. She was a good dancer, and I gradually warmed up. By the end of the evening, I knew she was the one I had been searching for. My task was to convince her, but maybe I should hold off on pranks for a while. I didn't want to blow this chance.

My job that last summer before graduation was in the inspection department, which was to be my assignment when I graduated. The group of five men inspected new construction, as well as recommended and supervised repairs when refinery sections were shut down for routine maintenance. The pay was better than Ga. Tech graduates were making, especially with overtime. I had never been paid overtime before, and I wondered if I would have to take a pay cut after college. With two incomes, the savings were mounting up. To help even more, the Chapmans gave me free room and board for the help I had been on their house construction the previous two summers.

The '53 Dodge was cheap transportation, but showed signs of old age. During the summer in Houston, it was parked every day next to Consolidated Chemical, and the acid rain ruined the paint. Standing pools of acid in the potholes splashed the undercarriage, and it was badly corroded. The wiring had shorted out to the rear half of the car, and I replaced it with left over house wire from my second job that summer.

I left Houston for the fall term after work at 3:00 PM the Friday before the last day of registration. It was to be a long drive, sixteen hours non-stop, leaving time to shower and make the noon deadline. I packed sandwiches so my only stops would be for gas. I had a pack of No-Doz to keep me awake. All went well until I reached Hammond, Louisiana, when the engine blew a head gasket and a mixture of oil and water covered the windshield. I coasted into a local garage that was still open, even though it was almost 9:00 PM.

After explaining that I would miss registration if they couldn't work on it, the mechanic, who had a son in college agreed to stay late and get me back on the road by midnight. I had a full tank of gas and fifty-five dollars—no checkbook. I had a gasoline credit card, but the shop didn't accept it. He shook his head, alarming me that that might not be enough. Slowly, in his Cajun drawl he responded. "I guess if I charge you fifty that will leave you five for emergencies. You sack out in the back seat, and I'll get to work. I've got the right gasket in stock."

I didn't get any sleep, but I did get a break from driving. Just before twelve, he finished, shook my hand and sent me on my way. "Stay awake and be careful, and good luck, son." I thanked him and was on my way.

Before I left the lowlands of the Gulf Coast, a huge puff of steam erupted from the hood, and I stopped the car along a deserted section of the highway. I was on a back road in the middle of a swampy area, having taken back roads to avoid patrolmen who might not appreciate my need to travel eighty miles per hour. Fortunately, I had a Sears set of tools including a flashlight. The radiator hose was fine. The clamp was loose, and I quickly tightened it. But I needed to refill the radiator to continue. The swamp was only ten feet below the roadway, and a quick search with the flashlight showed many frogs but no water moccasins. All I needed now was a bucket, but that was a problem. A thorough search failed even to turn up a cup or empty bottle. I finally resorted to filling my steel-toe work shoes. It took 132 shoes full of water to fill up! I was lucky that all the water hadn't drained out. By the time I finished I was exhausted.

A swig of water from a hose at a closed gas station in the next town washed down two No-Doz tablets, and I was on my way with no time to spare. By dawn, I was in Alabama. The windows were open half way to let in cold air, the radio at full blast and the windshield wipers turned on to keep me awake, but just barely. After dozing at the wheel and hitting my ear on the window glass, I woke with a start to see I had crossed the centerline and a large truck was bearing down on me. He missed me, but from then on I needed no pills. The adrenaline kept me wide awake all the way to Atlanta!

I registered with fifteen minutes to spare, went to my rental room at the Holders' house, and collapsed. Sleep at last! I woke hours later, realizing I was supposed to pick Linda up for a date, and I was late! She patiently forgave me.

My senior year at Tech flew by. Linda was slowly coming around to the realization that I might be the one for her, and we dated every weekend. I even taught her to drive my Dodge. Any couple that could put up with the pressure of driving lessons had a good chance together!

During the cold winter in Atlanta, the only heat was from a can of burning Sterno on the floor of the back seat. With one hand on the wheel and one wiping the condensing water off the windshield, driving at night was a little hazardous. Most guys had their arm around their date, but constantly drying the windshield prevented that. I would have to wait for warmer weather. There was no danger of carbon monoxide fumes because the floorboards were rusted through, and I had replaced them with the sides of an old apple crate. There was plenty of ventilation!

One wintry night, Linda and I were returning from the movies when a group of teenagers pulled alongside our car and motioned for us to pull over. I ignored them, fearing a mugging or worse. They continued, and it was then I noticed them pointing to the ground under the car. As I looked to the left to find a place to turn off, I saw the reflection of the car in the snow. We were on fire! The emergency brake spring had broken and the friction of the brakes had set grease on fire and the apple crate floor was burning! I pulled off and threw snow on the fire, which went out quickly now that the breeze from driving quit. A new can of Sterno and a new apple crate, and the Dodge was back in service. The Dodge only lasted until Christmas vacation 1956. My father's 1956 Plymouth was replaced with a brand new 1957 model, and I was able to trade up to his old car with a heater and floorboards for a modest sum.

Linda and I both fell in love and planned to marry, but I had to wait until she graduated from Druid Hills High School a year later.

I only got three D's during the four Tech years, the two English classes and in one lab. The Air Conditioning Lab D resulted from a final grade of 90, the minimum score to pass for our lab group of six. That would seem to be harsh grading had it not been for the prank. Yes, one did emerge from time to time, but this was the only one that affected my grades. I didn't count calling two English professors communists as pranks; I was deadly serious then.

It was about 4:00 that Friday evening, just before a big dance. We all watched the thermometers on a huge air conditioning unit (we had to read about a dozen every five minutes to calculate and graph the performance under numerous conditions). Three hours of watching thermometers, turning a few valves and recording the results was pretty boring. The dance later that night, the beauty of our dates and shopping for beverages filled the conversation in between measurements.

The next experiment on the agenda was to spray water mist into the air conditioning unit to simulate performance in warm, foggy weather—then measure how long the unit took to remove the extra water. "What if we sprayed Crème de Menthe instead of water?" I asked. Well, it was a boring afternoon and the professor had left at four, so, why not? I slipped out, bought two bottles, one for the test and one for the dance, along with a spray bottle to produce the "fog." I had avoided all alcohol until my third summer in Houston, when we celebrated my acceptance into the carpentry gang. I still refused to drink Scotch, remembering all the times it was forced on me as "medicine."

It was time for the mist. As we all took positions, each took a sip to be sure it was top quality test material. It was. One rule in lab was to be sure sub-standard test materials were eliminated, so technically the sips were part of the experiment. The mist was quickly sucked into the unit, and as it disappeared, we began taking the readings. Well, another five minutes to go, so let's sip again. About three sips later there was a loud knock on the door. We ignored it. Then a banging! The next sound we heard was a key in the lock. A red faced professor entered the room demanding an explanation. The unit we had been testing supplied the Department Head's office and conference room, and the Friday staff meeting had been in progress when the smell of mint entered the room. After being threatened with expulsion, the D grade seemed mild.

As graduation neared, it was time for job interviews. There was a short-age of engineers that year, so interviews were abundant. I traveled to several job interviews during the last few months of my senior year, in case the Eastern States job fell through. There were trips to refineries at Mobil, Conoco, and Phillips 66, all resulting in job offers far in excess of the average that year. The four summers' experience at Eastern States was paying off.

Only one of the other interviews was memorable—the trip to Pratt and Whitney. P&W was constructing a plant in Florida and needed many new graduates. They flew hundreds of candidates for plant tours and interviews in Hartford, Connecticut. My trip was much more unusual than any other interview. We arrived at the plant and were divided into groups of about ten, each led through the plant by a recent college graduate dressed in the P&W standard uniform—starched white shirt, dark pants and narrow striped tie.

On our visit to a jet engine test stand, we were allowed to view the entire test from start-up to full power and back to idle. Our guide proudly explained the advanced features of P&W's state-of-the-art test facility, one that would even be outdone by the ones we could expect to man in Florida. As he explained the procedure, he reached behind him for the start button. While he continued to talk, there was a warning siren and the window rapidly turned white. The engineer had pressed the fire suppression button, and foam was flooding into the room. We were ushered out quickly by the red-faced guide and escorted to the engineering department where we saw what seemed to be an ocean of white shirts. Engineers were bending over drafting tables with their adjustable fluorescent lights. The only sign of individuality was the haircut and the color of the tie. That was it for me. That was not my ambition. I decided to limit future interviews to the oil industry.

The other adventure came on the return trip. The flight was delayed, and as we sat in the lounge at the airport, we decided to down one shot of booze every ten minutes of the delay. "Shot" was an accurate description of each traveler by flight time. I just dimly remember slumping into my seat and looking for the seat belt. It wasn't there! I called the stewardess (oops, flight attendant) for help. She found the belt. I was sitting on it. I smiled—she didn't. As we began to taxi, one of my friends patted the attendant on the fanny and asked to be tucked in. Her glare was his only answer, and as we taxied down the runway, we all promptly "went to sleep."

A gentle shake on my shoulder woke me up. "Boys, we've landed," she cooed. *Wow, she sure is friendly*, I thought as I walked down the steps.

"Welcome to Houston" the pilot announced.

"We were booked to Atlanta," the fanny patter exclaimed.

"I know, but you looked so cute sleeping there, I couldn't bring myself to wake you, *smart alec!*"

What language to use on a customer. The other passengers cheered the flight attendant! The noise hurt our swollen heads. We caught the next flight back and all behaved that time.

Sam Perkins and Chester Strunk flew to Atlanta to discuss my future at Eastern States in April. I took Linda to the interview dinner to meet them at Aunt Fannie's Cabin, one of my favorite restaurants. I introduced Linda to both men, and she added glamour to the discussions. After the meal, their offer was discussed, and it was exactly the same salary as that offered by Mobil Oil Company. Conoco and Phillips 66 offers were slightly lower, but still above average. The Mobil job had a training period of several months, the Eastern States job was to enter as an equal to the existing employees, giving me a head start on advancement. I agreed to let them know my decision in two weeks. The following day Sam called to announce a $25 per month increase in the offer. I chose Eastern States, not just for the money, but because they were installing new technology faster, and I had already been accepted by many of the people I would work with. After starting over so many times I was eager to retain the stability I had built in Houston.

Graduation day came, and after receiving my diploma, all I wanted to do is get away from Tech. The schedule had been brutal, and I was glad it was over. I had not graduated with very high marks, but just enough to enter Pi Tau Sigma, the mechanical engineering honorary society. It was a shock when I was notified of acceptance because my average was only a B+.

After saying goodbye to my friends, it was time to pack the car and leave. I was a little depressed because that would mean leaving Linda in Atlanta for a year, until her graduation from high school. If what we felt for each other was real, it would last. After the family dinner and a final date, I was off to Houston. I was ready to take on the world.

A BUMPY START

June 1957, and I was on my own at last. The choice to return to Eastern States had been made, and I drove to Houston in my 1956 Plymouth. That set of wheels was plenty large to move all my worldly possessions—a phonograph, a box of records, my clothing and diploma. On arrival, I found a furnished apartment to rent and moved in—all before Sunday lunch.

Monday morning I was on the job in the inspection department. The schedule was hectic, with renovations and new construction constantly demanding attention. I was on call twenty-four hours a day, seven days a week. I had been right in choosing to return to Eastern States. The four summers had given me a huge advantage. I enrolled in a correspondence course on refinery operations and kept up with the newest installations. My favorite units were the new Platforming Unit, the Desulfurizing Unit, and some of the newest plastics processes.

Early on, during the scheduled routine maintenance (called a turnaround) of the Platforming Unit, I had my first chance at innovation. I was watching the regeneration of the platinum catalyst, the heart of the operation. The extremely expensive platinum not only changed the feedstock to a valuable chemical building block, it reduced the temperature required for the change, saving energy. As heated oil feedstock was passed through the reactors, the oil molecules were modified and carbon and hydrogen were released. The carbon coated the platinum and gradually reduced its effectiveness. The hydrogen was burned during the initial operation, but later was used to remove sulfur from oil products. To remove the build-up, the platinum would need reheating in the presence of oxygen to burn off the carbon. Temperatures were carefully controlled to prevent destroying the catalyst. All the catalyst would then be dumped, screened to remove ash, then re-loaded into the reactors, a process that took several hours. During this operation, the refinery lost production amounting to over $100,000 per day, so it was critical that the regeneration process be successful the first time.

This time it wasn't. The screens inside the reactor failed, and the entire load of platinum catalyst was dumped out revealing most of the carbon still in place. If we waited for repairs to the reactor and had to repeat the regeneration cycle, the unit would be out of service for several days. Ordering new catalyst would be too costly, and even if it was purchased, it would take over a week to manufacture and ship to the refinery. The refinery was facing a serious loss of income.

I proposed building the first out-of-reactor regenerator and designed the crude unit in two hours. We used a junked tower about thirty feet tall, cut open the top, installed a manway, then filled the tower with the useless catalyst. To provide hot oxygen for the carbon burn-off, we installed a compressor with piping that recirculated compressed air through a gas fired furnace built that afternoon. By nightfall, we were ready. We had no instrumentation available to check the temperature. If the temperature was too low, no carbon would burn; too high, and the catalyst would melt and be useless. I proposed the burn for nighttime. We could measure temperatures by climbing the ladder and marking the rusty tower steel with Templstiks, special crayons that melted at a specific temperature. One crayon was used for too hot, one for too cool. Just for safety, the process would start at dark and continue until daybreak. We could then see the dull glow on the thin steel tower wall as the fire proceeded up the inside of the tower. If the fire got too hot, we would add nitrogen to reduce the oxygen and slow the burn. If too cool, we would add more compressed air.

It worked like a charm, but climbing the glowing hot tower while the fire burned inside was a treacherous job. The only safety equipment consisted of as-bestos gloves, goggles, and white coveralls that reflected some of the heat. We didn't even have safety harnesses, so one slip and it would be a trip to the hospital or worse. There were no OSHA regulations in the 1950s. A short time into the process, watching the reactor turn the dull red color turned out to work, so the tower climbing to check the crayon melting was suspended. By morning, the reactor screens were replaced, the catalyst was regenerated, and only about fifty pounds was ruined. The unit was back in operation with no lost time, resulting in a savings of over a million dollars. I got a pat on the back and a $25 per month raise. That made the car payments.

It was shortly after that I was approached by my supervisor, Jack Dahlberg. Eastern States was planning to build and operate a new oil refinery in Cuba, and I was on the list of supervisors for that plant. I would be moving to Cienfuegos on the south coast of Cuba if I accepted the assignment. It was a tempting opportunity, with a significant raise and fringe benefits. My adventure in Mexico five years earlier had proved I was proficient in Spanish, which was a big plus. After our wedding, Linda and I would move to Cuba in 1959 as construction began.

As negotiations for the refinery proceeded in 1958, a cloud appeared on the horizon. A communist rebel, Fidel Castro, was gaining a foothold against the Batista regime since their landing on Cuban soil in a yacht that sailed from Mexico in 1956. Although Batista shrugged them off as "just a small nuisance," they were now attacking government outposts on the eastern end of the island. Negotiations ended and the job vanished before I was able to discuss the assignment with Linda.

That project's cancellation was a disappointment at the time, but in 1961, I knew how fortunate we were. The Cienfuegos refinery site was only forty miles from the catastrophic Bay of Pigs invasion, and had we been there, government reprisals would have been severe. Castro overthrew Batista in 1959, and he was not known for treating enemies with compassion.

January was to begin with the biggest turnaround of the refinery. The catalytic cracking unit and the entire gasoline production section of the refinery was scheduled to be shut down for cleaning, repair, and replacement of worn out parts. The work was always scheduled during that time because gasoline demand dropped after Christmas travelers returned home.

Just before the scheduled "turnaround," I had found a large leak in the thirty-six inch diameter hot gasoline vapor line. A mixture of hot gasoline fumes and catalyst were pouring out and in danger of exploding into a huge fireball. The leak blocked our escape, but the unit operator who had accompanied us was still next to the elevator. He rushed down to spread the alarm. There were no cell phones then, and he didn't want to stay in the danger zone long enough to use the telephone on the other side of the elevator. He bounded down the stairs much faster than he could on the elevator. Besides, he was in no mood to wait for an elevator. The pipefitter and I grabbed live steam hoses and directed steam on the leaking gasoline to prevent a fire. The steam, even at over 200 degrees was cooler than the gasoline vapor, so it cooled it below the flash point. As long as we kept the steam blowing into the fumes, they didn't catch fire. We were both holding tightly to the steam lines. We had asbestos gloves to prevent burns, but when you are over a hundred feet up in the air and on the open side of the unit, burns were not your greatest fear.

The alarm was spread, and we saw Sam Perkins and Chester, the plant engineers, running toward the base of the unit. As I looked down, I realized the unit was not being shut down! Keeping the unit on line during the pre-Christmas weeks was critical to meet sales commitments. I realized they were trying to see how to keep it running and still patch the leak! If we stopped the steam to try to escape through the fumes, the unit would have exploded. If it had exploded, we would have either been blown off, falling over 100 feet onto the road or burned up in the fireball.

Sam told me later that he heard my shout even above the noise that always was present in the refinery. *"Shut the oil off! This damn thing is going to blow! The leak is getting larger!"* He was polite to call it a shout; it was a scream!

After a few minutes, the operators were able to shut off the gasoline going into the unit, but draining the unit took longer. The hot catalyst recirculation was continued. That meant the unit could be re-started quickly as soon as the leak was patched. The welders repaired the leak wearing hoods and goggles to keep the leaking catalyst from damaging their eyes. Welding the patch on the leak revealed the entire line would have to be replaced, *but not until after Christmas.* The patch would have to last that long.

As we both descended to the ground, we were met by cheers and pats on the back. The cold shower felt good! It was after the ordeal was over that I began to shake as I realized just how close a call that had been. The Lord was watching over us that day.

I returned to Jacksonville for Christmas that year to spend Christmas with Linda, who was visiting my parents. We rescheduled our wedding from August to June, and we both spent the rest of the holiday in Jacksonville before returning to work and school.

The shutdown began in January 1958, five months before Linda and I were to be married. Because the unexpected replacement of the line would take longer than the schedule allowed, we began preparations before the unit was completely shut down. It was a dangerous procedure, but one chosen by the management. As I inspected the damaged area, a boilermaker loosened some bolts to see if the unit was clear and ready for the replacement. There was a loud noise. My goggles were blown off, and the hot catalyst blasted my face before I could even shut my eyes. Everything went dark.

I woke up in the hospital with my head wrapped in bandages, with only openings to breathe and take liquids through a straw. There was little pain. I seemed to be numb all over. The doctor explained that I had been burned and there was some eye damage they thought would heal in a few weeks. My contact lenses had been destroyed, but the plastic had been removed from my eyes. I was led to a phone to call Linda and inform her of the accident, leaving out the fact that the nurse had to dial the phone.

Later, when the bandages were removed, I opened my eyes. I could not even see the flashlight shining into my eyes. The doctor could not explain the blindness. He replaced the bandages, and once more I was alone in my room, in complete darkness. That was a bad day for me. I panicked—less than six months to my wedding. Linda would never marry a blind person who couldn't work. Were all the years of preparation for my life going down the drain? The second time the bandages came off, still nothing. This was getting serious. The doctors (I now had three) could suggest no treatment.

I began to recall how my sister Nancy and I as children used to close our eyes and pretend to be blind. With our outstretched hands, we would see who could walk the farthest without bumping into furniture. We both peeked a little, and then laughed as we bumbled around the room. But then we could always open our eyes and see. It was really frightening when I opened my eyes and couldn't.

I was discharged when the burns healed and driven to my apartment by the company nurse. Cooking became my next challenge. I lived alone and learned to choose different size cans to open. That assured me I'd at least have two different things to eat. Later, I was able to pick out some by listening to the sound as I shook the can. Every Monday and Thursday the company nurse picked me up for eye examinations and grocery shopping. She arranged the cans in the cabinets by type of food, so I was getting a balanced diet.

I had a lot of spare time to reflect on the incident. Many others had been injured and some even killed in the rush for maximum production. I began to consider another career, but unless my eyesight returned, that was out of the question.

After two months, I was able to see light and dark, and another month later dim shadows. One day as a neighbor read my mail to me, I was shocked. The letter was a Draft Board notice to report for my pre-induction physical. I was being drafted! What next? The refinery safety officer made several calls to request cancellation of the physical, but the answer came back, "Show up or go to jail."

I don't know if it was a first, but when I showed up being led by a nurse, they were not impressed at all. "Get in line! Drop your drawers like everyone else, Goldbrick!" I was probed, pushed, poked, and stuck and never knew what direction it was coming from. After it was over, I was scheduled for an eye examination by an Army eye specialist and driven home by the nurse. At that exam, I was told, "I agree with the diagnosis, you are permanently blind and will never see enough for Army service or even to drive or work again." At that moment, I would have enlisted for the rest of my life if I could just see.

By now, Linda was aware of the situation, but she didn't want to cancel the wedding. We both prayed for improvement, and it came very slowly. I was fitted with eyeglasses to replace the contact lenses I could no longer wear. Twice each week the company nurse drove me to the eye doctor for examination. Each trip I received new prescription lenses as the scars changed my vision.

I knew it would be best to find a new place to live before the wedding, as my apartment was near the airport, right under a flight path. Well, the fact it was in an apartment complex where dozens of flight attendants lived had some bearing on the decision, too. There was no dating though. They knew I was blind and some would bring the mail. During one such delivery, Linda's ring was spotted on the coffee table, and I was "off limits" by choice. Theirs and mine.

By Easter, my eyes were healed enough for daylight driving only. I was able to drive back east to give Linda her engagement ring, and the wedding plans were still on schedule.

Shortly after I returned to the apartment, my timing for moving was accelerated. While I was watching TV one Friday night I heard a loud bang, then another. I answered the knock on the door, and there stood two of the girls from across the hall, wearing frightened looks. "Someone's shooting in the apartment downstairs, and we could get hit if a bullet comes through the floor." Several more shots rang out. I let them in and bolted the door. The man living in that apartment was a strange person. He never spoke to anyone and kept strange hours. No one even knew his name. There was now screaming as more shots rang out. I peeked out the window and saw two pink Cadillacs surrounded by several men, who stood over our neighbor who was lying on the ground in a pool of blood. No police were in sight, so we got away from the window, fast!

The cars left just before the police arrived along with an ambulance that carried our neighbor away. The police also left without interviewing anyone, but they returned the next day. About thirty minutes before they arrived, here came the Cadillacs again, this time the men were armed with axes and a chain saw. As the bullets were chopped and sawn out of the walls, the apartment manager watched. Her initial complaints were silenced by a handful of cash. We were briefly interviewed by detectives that morning and found out our neighbor had double crossed some gamblers, but he wasn't dead. He was "an example." He had been shot in his hands, feet, knees, elbows, and some other "painful spots." He was now "retired" to a wheelchair. I found a garage apartment and moved the next weekend!

The wedding was June 1, 1958, and after a honeymoon in the Smoky Mountains, we returned to Houston. I still was unable to see 20/20, but life looked good. After settling in and almost blowing the garage apartment down by using too much gasoline to burn the wedding gift wrappings we settled in to married life. A few months later, Linda and I became homeowners. We purchased a small three bedroom home south of the airport and moved out of the furnished garage apartment. My four prized possessions—TV, nine by twelve rug, stereo record player, and gooseneck lamp weren't enough to set up housekeeping, so we went furniture shopping.

We bought almost everything at Joske's at Gulfgate, but when we went to pay, the newly hired clerk needed help. She had never sold that much furniture for cash and didn't know how to write it up! Needless to say, she got help—quick. We moved in and set up house, and Linda started classes at Massey Business College.

During a lull in inspection department activities, I grew restless. The old saying "Engineers don't idle well" fit me. I was always looking for something new to try. This time Chuck, another refinery acquaintance, and I decided to become entrepreneurs. A coin laundry on Telephone Road was for sale, and we bought it, agreeing to alternate days cleaning the facility and collecting the receipts. We also alternated repairing the machines. The first night we both met at The Wash Tub to check on a wiring problem that cropped up that afternoon. In came some armed thugs to break open the machine coin boxes. Chuck and I locked ourselves in the boiler room to hide, and after they left, replaced the empty coin boxes into the washers. Our new venture started off with a bad omen.

The operation was moderately successful, but required far more work that we planned. Receipts were erratic with daily receipts on days I collected far greater than Chuck's days. Chuck explained that there were fewer customers on his days. When we changed collection days, the customers changed too, according to Chuck. It was obvious that this deal wasn't working out, and I sold my interest to him. It was an expensive price for "not idling well."

Eastern States was at that time a leading importer of foreign oil. The demand for specialty petrochemicals was expanding world wide, and we bartered crude oil for refined products. The federal government was attempting to limit imports because the less than two dollars a barrel price was having a negative effect on domestic production. Voluntary limits were imposed to reduce the impact on domestic wells, which at that time were regulated to allow pumping less than thirty percent of the time. In order to meet contract commitments, we headed the list of violators of the voluntary limits every month. The refinery was booming, and I was on call twenty-four hours a day, which placed a strain on married life.

A typical after-hours assignment came when Eastern States' president contracted with D.K. Ludwig, owner of some sixty supertankers and bulk carriers. His first supertanker to enter the Houston Ship Channel brought a load of Saudi oil to the refinery. The tanker just barely made it to our terminal, its hull sliding part way on the silt in the Houston Ship Channel. Our task was to precede the tanker to the dock at high tide, in an aluminum fishing boat. Using a fishing line and heavy sinker we probed the depth of the soft mud on the channel bottom to be sure the ship would not run aground. It was not as fancy as modern instruments, but it worked! It would be some fourteen years later that I would meet Mr. Ludwig and become an engineering consultant for one of his projects.

Linda and I became friends with another young couple, Jere and Martha Ruff, shortly after we returned from our honeymoon. Jere and I worked at the refinery, and we decided one fall day just before Christmas to try our luck at duck hunting. He knew of a place in the middle of a rice field, and we were eager to shoot a duck and have the girls cook it for a holiday meal. I had been duck hunting once before, but I didn't let Jere know all the details.

It had been three years earlier, during a long weekend at Tech. One of my fraternity brothers, Phil Laney was the son of the former Arkansas governor.

Phil's family owned a large farm in Conway, just a short drive from Stuttgart, the "best duck hunting place in the world." He invited me to go with him to try our skill at being "great white hunters." After driving all night, we arrived early in the morning. Following a huge breakfast, his dad suggested we pick up hunting licenses and go on a practice shoot before the Stuttgart hunt the following day. Phil's dad loaned me his shotgun and showed me how it worked. That first day was not good hunting weather. By the time we got our licenses and shells it was late afternoon, the sun was bright, the sky was blue, and it was hard to keep from being spotted by the ducks in those conditions. Phil and I made it worse by driving to the middle of a plowed field, parking in plain sight and walking to the marsh nearby, jabbering all the time. Just as we reached a group of trees, the sound of a flock of ducks reached us. I fired the borrowed pump shotgun three times, getting only a couple feathers for my effort. Phil fired once and yelled, "It's jammed!" He had forgotten to pump it to reload! A fine couple hunters we were! After deciding never to tell this part of the adventure, we slogged on into the swamp. I should explain this part is in my book only because the statute of limitations on hunting promises has expired!

It was now getting dark and starting to rain. We could hear quacking ducks flying low to find a spot to land for the night. After Phil's dad's remark that we better bring home some ducks, I was determined to do just that. The rain was coming down harder now, and we couldn't have seen a duck ten feet away. We decided to go back and face the scorn. In frustration, I fired one last shot at the quacking sound and heard *splat*. I had hit one, but where was it? I gave Phil the shotgun and as he headed for dry land, I headed for the sound of the duck hitting the mud. I stood up on a beaver hut to see, and it collapsed, propelling me spread eagled in the mud. My hand landed on something warm. It was the muddy mallard. We had our catch! I splashed toward the shore and found Phil up to his chest in mud, slowly sinking and yelling for help. Both shotguns were raised above his head to keep them dry. I rescued him and covered with mud and slime, we both arrived at the back door proudly displaying the prize. "Is that all you got?" Phil's dad exclaimed, chuckling at the sight of two muddy hunters. Even our faces were covered.

"Go shower, and tomorrow we'll get some *real* ducks." The rest of the trip was not very exciting. We hunted from a duck blind, watched the sky darken as countless thousands of ducks took flight at the first shot. We both had respectable success and went back to Tech as "experienced" duck hunters.

In preparation for this latest duck hunt, Jere took me to a sporting goods store where I bought a complete outfit, Winchester Model 12 shotgun, hat, boots, gloves, jacket, and waders, all appropriately camouflage colored. We were ready for the adventure. Before dawn in below freezing weather, we set out, arriving at the hunting pond in dark, windy conditions. We had been told that the hunting blind was just across the pond, a few minute's trip in the rowboat we could use. With the wind howling in our faces, we rowed across to the blind. We had all the gear necessary except for a flashlight. We rowed on and on and on. How far was it anyway? Finally we arrived at the blind, exhausted. Jere and I crouched down to avoid the biting wind and waited for daylight. We could hear faint quacking from across the pond, so we knew they were there.

Dawn broke, and we saw that the dock we had spent so much time rowing from was only twenty yards away. We could have walked there in a few minutes if we had a flashlight! Here came the ducks, though. About twenty landed at the far end of the pond and, ignoring our duck calls, they refused to budge. It was even too cold for the ducks. I fired to stir them up, but no luck. They fluttered up a few feet and landed again—still out of range. Jere crawled to the ducks' end of the pond to scare them up, and I ducked as he fired into the air, showering me with pellets as they descended. The ducks flew half way to me and plopped down, still out of range. We were determined not to shoot them while they were on the water. After taking turns showering each other with pellets, a lone mallard got too close. *Bam!* We had our duck. I don't even remember who fired the successful shot, but our wives prepared the feast a few days later, and we celebrated our hunting skills. Their baby son Jay pulled over our Christmas tree, a diversion that kept us from telling the whole story.

My hunting record was now perfect, one duck in Arkansas and one in Texas. It was time to try something new. I chose geese. If I was only going to get one bird per hunt, at least a goose would be big enough for leftovers. Goose hunting required more gear, though. Hunting for geese in the Houston area meant finding a open grain field, buying or making your own goose decoys (usually crumpled newspapers with a fake goose head), getting to the field early enough to set out the decoys before the geese flew over, silently hiding under a tarpaulin so they wouldn't hear voices or see movement, and waiting, and waiting and *waiting*. The last part was the hardest for "Engineers that don't idle well." I couldn't find a private field to hunt, so I selected a "day hunting farm," a place open to anyone with $5 who wanted to hunt. Success depended on all the hunters cooperating and staying still until the geese arrived. Then it was every man for himself. The greatest risk (other than getting shot) was that someone opened fire before the geese got into range.

I was set. Decoys out, tarp in place, dawn breaking. I peeked out to see if all the other hunters were ready, too. They were. Just as a large flock started circling, in came a brand new white Cadillac convertible with large bull horns attached to the grille, top down, and driven by a huge man wearing a cowboy hat. I was sure he had one of those huge belt buckles, too, but I couldn't see that far. Oh, no a novice, barreling through the middle of the field. We all saw him slam on the brakes, jump out and take the wrappings off his brand new shotgun. He had just wrestled it out of the box, loaded it as the geese began to circle. I thought, *I bet they're getting a better look at that idiot!* Not waiting for the geese to fly into range, he opened fire. Hunting laws required installing a plug in the magazine to limit it to three shells at a time, but not him. As he blasted away six or seven times, all the flock flew off except one lone goose that had been unlucky enough to be flying a little low. A few feathers flew off, and the nut hollered "*Whoopee!* I got him!" Well, the rest of us were tempted to shoot him in the butt. He had ruined a perfectly good $5 hunt, but he was now providing entertainment.

He reloaded and emptied his shotgun again, and a few more pellets had hit the goose. It was now landing in the muddy field, about fifty yards ahead of him. He charged; the goose ran. He stopped and reloaded, the goose stopped too, just out of range. On he charged, blasting away. The goose fell over. As a sign of his hunting prowess, he came within ten feet of the poor goose and unloaded several shots. Then, he picked up the bloody mass, swung it over his head and yelled, "Hey, look y'all, I got mine," threw it in the back seat and roared off. Hunting was over for that day, and I never again went to a "day hunting" farm.

I continued my amateur hunting, but now was concentrating on doves. Mr. King, the antique store owner who had sold us The Wash Tub, owned acreage off Fellows Road in the prairie south of Houston and allowed me to hunt dove there. He even offered to sell the five acre lot to me. One day I was considering his offer and walking along the boundary fence when I saw a crew surveying across his land. As I shared my six-pack with them, they explained they were surveying for the future Houston south loop road. It crossed the southern tip of Mr. King's land and would be near a new north-south major highway. I accepted Mr. King's offer and purchased the tract. I didn't get any doves that day, but I now had my own hunting parcel. Mr. King even threw in a 1930s Ford tractor—something new to tinker with. Some day when the highways were built, I could pocket a large profit for my corner parcel.

During the boom times of imported oil of less than two dollars a barrel, maintenance at the refinery was deferred, and fires occurred regularly—more often than any other refinery. Several employees had been injured or killed. One afternoon, I was called to inspect a hot spot in a furnace heating oil and hydrogen gas to remove the sulfur. Upon arrival, I looked in and saw one of the steel tubes beginning to swell at the hot spot. I sounded the alarm to shut down the unit and evacuate. One last look at the tube showed it to be ballooning out like bubble gum. I ran for my life! Burning hydrogen is far more deadly than an oil fire. About ten yards into my escape, the furnace exploded, and the ball of fire engulfed me.

Safety training saved me that time. I had learned if a fire is imminent, inhale deeply and, just like the title of this book, *run for your life*. If the flame catches up, close your eyes and *don't breathe*—the flames will burn your lungs. I followed these instructions and those observing the fire saw me blasted out of the flame by the force of the explosion. As I came down to earth, I was still running—faster than they had seen anyone run before. My sight had returned to near normal from the blinding accident, and I was able to wear contact lenses again. One contact lens had warped from circular to egg shaped and was stuck in my eye, but the emergency shower and eyewash fountain nearby loosened the lens enough for me to remove it before the eye was damaged. I had dozens of blisters from the hot rivets fastening the pockets to my coveralls, but young guys heal fast, so I lost no time at work.

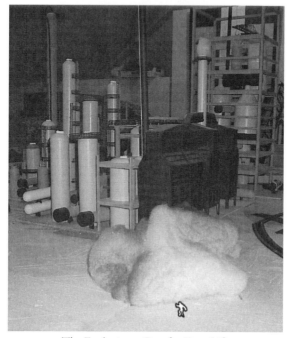

The Explosion—Run for Your Life

Several other near misses occurred. Late one night, I was inspecting work on the vacuum tower in the rain. I was soaked to the skin and cold. I borrowed a pair of dry coveralls from Lyle O'Connor, who outweighed me by at least 150 pounds. Just after returning to the top of the forty foot tower, a gust of wind caught me. I was flat on my back, sliding toward the edge! I rolled over onto my stomach just as I slipped over the side. I grabbed a piece of wire hanging nearby, but it only held for a few seconds and I was falling! Fortunately, the oversized coveralls saved me. The belt caught on an angle iron just feet from the ground. I was bruised and scraped but okay.

A few weeks later, several tons of steel boiler tubes fell in a furnace I was inspecting but missed me by a few inches. An acid leak burned through my arm all the way to the bone. Regularly, I had to knock asbestos insulation with a hammer to inspect piping, resulting in breathing in so much asbestos dust that I often had sore throats and nose bleeds. It was standard procedure to inspect furnaces still 400 degrees Fahrenheit with no protective gear other than being sprayed with water when you got out. The damage to the skin on my face from those burns never healed completely. When my eyes were damaged again by catalyst, the excitement and high pay of those early adventurous days was fading away. I began to realize that now I was a married man, it was time to move on to a safer job. It was about that time I coined the motto: "It's better to be a Christian than a cat. Cats only get nine lives."

The decision was made for me. I hated leaving my Houston family, but in 1959, the federal voluntary import quotas were made mandatory, and the refinery slowly shut down operations. Storage tanks were filling and all the foreign sales for products in exchange for crude went away. We limped along on domestic sales, but Eastern States was dying.

DEATH
OF A FRIEND

The last attempt to salvage the refinery came in a lawsuit. The suit claimed Eastern States should be exempt from the federal mandatory oil import quotas on the grounds that we were exporting more refined product than we were importing, and therefore not importing to compete with American oil companies. As the suit proceeded slowly, some of the office furniture was sold to make payroll. Employees regularly brought restroom tissue and towels from home after they disappeared at work. Even so, I was hesitant to leave to find another job because I enjoyed the people I worked with and I had never applied for a job before. Dad had arranged the summer job here when I was in high school.

The answer on my career choice came from a friend I had met at Eastern States. Bernie Johnson was a valve salesman who knew of several openings at Reed Roller Bit, a competitor of Hughes Tool Co. Reed was developing its version of the tri-cone bit. I applied and was hired. By this time, Massey Business School notified Linda of a job opening, and after a successful interview, she accepted a job with Hughes Tool. Both Hughes and Reed plants were near each other, and Linda had the same work schedule, so transportation was simplified. Each day we rode to and from work together, discussing our jobs. I knew little about oil well drill bits manufactured at Hughes. If I had remained at Eastern States, long hours would have made commuting together difficult.

Drilling wells before Howard Hughes Sr. invented the roller bit was crude. Initially, a chisel–like steel bit was suspended on a cable and literally dropped into the well, chipping the rock. After a few blows, the cable and bit were removed, the bit sharpened, and the rock chips bailed out of the hole. Later improvements included using a drill pipe instead of the cable and pumping drilling mud through the pipe to flush cuttings out of the hole. As the well got deeper, a lot of time was spent raising and lowering the drill string (pipes and bits). Each lift also meant unscrewing every section of drill pipe and storing the pipe for reassembly after the bit was sharpened or replaced.

Howard Hughes Sr. realized that if many small chisel shapes could be set around a roller they would do the same thing as the dropping bit, and the bit could be moved around by rolling, and pushed into the rock by the weight drill string. Many more teeth would be possible on a roller, and if the teeth were rolled instead of dropped, the teeth could be sharper. Less wear and breakage would result, and much of the time for removal and re-sharpening would be eliminated.

His first design was patented in 1909. It consisted of two interlocking cone shaped bits, and was an immediate success. In 1933, two Hughes engineers invented the tri-cone bit, which has been the standard of the industry ever since. This bit has three wheels and is more stable in drilling a straight hole. The Hughes patent for the tri-cone bit lasted until 1951, after which other companies started making similar bits. Later versions were furnished with a jet nozzle to help dislodge the rock cuttings.

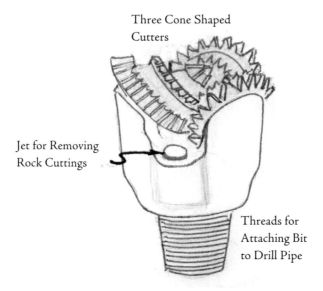

Three Cone Shaped
Cutters

Jet for Removing
Rock Cuttings

Threads for
Attaching Bit
to Drill Pipe

Sketch of Tri-cone Oil Well Drilling Bit

Design in the 1950s was far different than design today. The slide rule and Monroe Calculating Adding Machine were about all we had. Development was as much trial and error as anything. We designed the bits by drawing them to scale on plastic film to be sure the teeth missed teeth on the adjacent cones. Full size models were made to select the number of teeth, and each tooth was individually cut on a milling machine. The criteria required that all cutter teeth land on a different place each time the bit was rotated, complicating the design.

The cones were hardened in a furnace. The assembled bit was tested in a laboratory drill rig, first on cast iron then on rock. The tooth design was then modified to optimize cutting speed in different materials. One of the challenges of the job was to estimate which milling tool to use for the teeth. At that time, there was no program for this function, so engineers used trial and error or "guesstimates." I decided to tackle the problem to eliminate the lost time.

Reed had an IBM650 computer for accounting and some engineering functions, but it bore no resemblance to today's computers. The console unit and rotating drum memory were about the size of two twin beds lying on their sides.

To support the console were many other pieces of equipment—disk unit, card punch, power supply, card reader, control unit, auxiliary unit, magnetic tape unit, and an inquiry station, all occupying two rooms. A large air conditioning system was required to cool the equipment, and miles of wire under the floor connected the components. Today's laptop has hundreds of times the capacity of that computer.

Programs were crude. We used a stack of punch cards called a Bell Deck, a system designed by Bell Labs. But even with the deck, it was like trying to wrestle an elephant. Here are the steps to be followed:

1. Write an input form containing each mathematical step in order of execution.
2. Another engineer checked the input form.
3. Have a "patch board" (wiring panel) assigned for the calculation.
4. Each engineer had to wire the board for his project, usually installing dozens of wires and connections.
5. A third engineer checked the wiring.
6. Install the patch board into the 650.
7. Obtain the Bell Deck from the safe.
8. Pick up the Bell Deck after it slid off the console onto the floor.
9. Wait for a turn on the sorter.
10. Re-sort the Bell Deck.
11. Load it in the computer.
12. Run the program.
13. Figure out what went wrong.
14. Wait in line for another turn.

The program worked and was used thereafter for quickly selecting tooth milling cutters and tilt angles. I was promoted to lead the company's program for a new line of exploration bits. Reed planned a series of smaller diameter bits for use in exploration for oil, coal, iron ore, and other minerals.

RUN FOR YOUR LIFE

We were settled in the new house, and I had even begun two additions, one for an enlarged master bedroom and one for a workshop. Remember, "Engineers don't idle well." One of my prize accomplishments was our yard. The house was located in a "cookie cutter" neighborhood. Most floor plans were the same, one car garage, 60x100 foot lot, one three-foot tall tree, six shrubs, and the exteriors all similar except for paint color. I tackled the midget tree first. By installing a four-inch diameter stove pipe in the ground next to the tree and heavily fertilizing and watering the roots through the pipe, our tree grew to twelve feet in a little over a year. The grass was fertilized so heavily that it needed cutting three times a week. I had used 300 pounds of sheep manure to encourage its growth, then topped it with ammonium nitrate. The first week after the manure was put out, all the young mothers kept checking diapers for the source of the odor. The shrubs didn't respond and grow as fast. I had a novel approach for them, too.

Just before I left the refinery, the department was treated to Brown and Root's private fishing retreat for a weekend of fishing. The water was low in the pond, and the bass were plentiful. I brought a washtub full home to Linda. She was not impressed with that much fish. "We'll have to eat bass every day for a month." There were few home freezers at that time.

The problem of where to store the bass was solved the first night. Because the pond was so low, the bass I fried tasted like the mud in the pond. Even though I tried to fake it, they were not edible. I buried the rest under our shrubs. The shrubs loved the bass, but so did the neighbor's cat—at least until they got too ripe even for him. At least we had the biggest shrubs in the neighborhood and the only tree more than ten feet tall now.

In 1959, I was offered a dealership importing used Mercedes Benz automobiles directly from a dealer in Germany. There was a greater demand for these vehicles than could be met by trade-ins from current dealers, but financing was not available, and the offer could not be accepted.

It was now time for the first visit from Linda's parents. The visit was in July 1959 and coincided with the arrival of Hurricane Debra. The skies were darkening the day they arrived, and by that evening, the rain began to pound the house. The road was now under water. By morning, the full fury of Debra hit. Linda's mother was panicky, and her dad just stared quietly. "We're going to die!" Edith repeated every few minutes in between moans and tears. It was worse inside the house than out. When the eye of the storm hit, the sun came out, and Edith was determined to get out, too. No sooner had she opened the door when the other wall of the storm hit. It took all four of us to close the door against the 85 MPH winds. As she looked out the window, she exclaimed, "Oh, look someone is losing their roof!" I didn't have the heart to tell her it was us. I could hear the water dripping in the attic. By then all the trees in the neighborhood had been blown down, except one—ours with the three-foot deep roots fed by the stovepipe. It had lost all its leaves, and about half of its bark had been blown off. The storm was over quickly, but we had three feet of water in the street, half of our roof shingles were gone, and Edith wanted to *"Get out of here right now!"* When the water drained away, they left with their basket of peanut butter sandwiches, vowing never to visit Houston again. A few years later, after our daughter, Suzanne was born they did venture to Texas, but by then we lived seventy miles inland, and the desire to see their granddaughter overcame the memory of the storm.

A month after my promotion at Reed, I was invited to lunch with my friend from the days at the refinery, Bernie Johnson. He was interested to see how his suggestion that I try Reed was turning out. Bernie made small talk and then unloaded his proposition. He had been hired by an Illinois company to relocate their two plants and manage the new manufacturing facility in Conroe, fifty miles north of Houston. Even though I was only twenty-four, would I consider being the chief engineer? It would be more money but require longer hours and some travel.

SPARKLER

It didn't take long for us to decide to accept the chief engineer offer. Linda and I decided to sell our house, and as I was putting the "for sale" sign in the yard, we received an offer, at the price we asked. I was speechless. Maybe we had asked too little. I raised the price, our offer disappeared, and I began the long task of commuting from twenty miles south of Houston to fifty miles north, through downtown. Linda continued at Hughes Tool, car pooling with a neighbor and contributing $1.50 per week for half the cost of gas.

I started at Sparkler in January 1960, and the first engineering department employee I hired was Jim Reneau who rose to be president of the company years after I left. My next assignment was to travel to the home office to get familiar with the designs, products, and the manufacturing process, leaving Jim to work in Conroe. I was responsible for supervising the closing of the Illinois Engineering Department, packing all the records, and seeing that the transition to Texas did not unnecessarily interrupt shipping. Most of the employees were not moving, so there were only a few experienced personnel to make the transition.

I was ready for the assignment but not for Chicago's weather in January. I had no time to shop before leaving, and as soon as I stepped out of the plane at O'Hare, a frigid blast from the North Pole hit me. I ran across the tarmac with only a sweater and windbreaker to keep me warm. I rushed up the stairway to meet the Sparkler people, who took me to the Karcher Hotel in North Chicago, which was to be my home for the next several weeks. Don Cooper graciously loaned me his extra overcoat (five sizes too big but warm and welcome), and I was loaned a car to use during the stay. Sparkler operated two plants, one in North Chicago and one in Mundelein. I was hesitant to accept a lesson on driving in snow, but my driving coach, Stan, insisted. I skidded a little at first, but soon gained confidence, starting, stopping, and making turns slowly in the six inches of new snow. Then came the driving on hills part. I slowly coasted down a long hill toward a T–style intersection. About half way down, Stan suggested I start braking slowly. I hesitated. It was still a long way to the cross street. "That was not a suggestion, Charlie, *start braking now.*" I must have pushed on the pedal too hard because the car went faster, but now in circles down toward the intersection. We spun around several times before sliding off the road into a large snow bank, which then collapsed and buried us completely. The tow truck driver who rescued us just laughed, shook his head, pocketed the cash and drove off. I had now graduated from Stan's driving school. I now knew to brake carefully when in snow.

Shutting down the operation and preparing to move was a boring task because most of the time during this orientation period, the information I needed had just been packed. Special attention was given to the "Red Book" the record of all filters manufactured during the past twenty-five years, with replacement parts identified for each unit. The loss of this book would be devastating. None of the engineering employees were slated to move to Texas, so they did as little as possible to earn their pay, and cooperation was minimal. Fortunately, my refinery experience included design and inspection of pressure vessels, gaskets, and seals, all key to the Sparkler operation.

I returned to Conroe as the last of the records were packed, and returned to recruit an engineering staff. One draftsman I hired proved to be a bad choice. A few weeks after he joined the department, he began starting arguments with the staff, even complaining to the shop employees about the incompetence of the whole department.

It was time for an employee counseling session. I received plenty growing up, but I had never reprimanded anyone before. I decided it would be best to do so after work because our parents reprimanded the kids in front of others, and I knew how embarrassing that could be. After everyone had left the office, he began by declaring, "You're going to fire me aren't you?"

"No," I replied, "I just want to know why you are so belligerent, and maybe we can work through the problem."

"You SOB" he shouted, "You're going to fire me!" and he swung at me with his fist. I ducked and flipped back out of my chair onto the floor. He convinced me—I *was* going to fire him. I did, and he cleaned out his drafting table drawer and left that day.

I thought that was the end of that but the next morning I received a call from his wife, demanding I tell her why he was fired. Refusing to discuss it over the phone, I suggested she ask him. "I did and he wouldn't tell me, even after I whipped his butt." I began to understand his attitude now.

"He's been fired before and never told me why. I'm going to meet you in the parking lot after work, and if you don't tell me, I'm going to whip you, too."

Bernie advised me to ignore her. "She's just blowing off steam. She'll never show up." I agreed and the day went on. But at closing time, there she was—waiting outside the door. She was *big*. I considered calling the police, but Conroe was a small town of 8,000 and we didn't need publicity. I called home to tell Linda I would be late for supper, and I just stayed in the office. She finally gave up and slowly pulled out of the parking lot. I waited to be sure she wasn't coming back then drove home, taking a different route and watching to make sure I was not being followed. The next day, she called and apologized.

As we unpacked the records, the "Red Book" was missing. The box it was packed in was empty. We never found it. For the next year, it was necessary to visit factories and measure worn out parts of older filters to manufacture and ship new parts. The records were eventually rebuilt enough to continue smoothly.

Before coming to Sparkler, my job had been a nine to five schedule, something I hadn't experienced at the refinery. The old "Engineers don't idle well" saying bit me again just before I left. Since the early days of hunger at the YMCA, I always had food stored up and prided myself in buying by the case to save money. I had been introduced to home made pizza and found out the cousin of one of the Reed engineers owned a meat market in Pasadena, Texas. "He could probably get Appian Way Pizza mix by the case," I was told. I contacted him, and he not only offered to get the pizza mix but also a case of LeSeur peas, and by the way, would I like to invest in his meat market? I could get meat wholesale and share in the profits. That seemed great. Even though his cousin warned me to be careful, I threw caution to the winds and "invested" $1000 to become his partner.

That venture lasted only a few weeks when I found out the $1000 was not to expand his business, but for a more comfortable place to "entertain" his female customers. The husband of one of her customers caught up with him, and the market closed for good. I was out my investment, but the calamity had occurred so quickly that the partnership agreement was never recorded, and I was not responsible for his debts. I never told Linda of the "investment" and the "bargain" pizza and peas for $1000. But like all secrets, somehow the worst ones get found out first.

I struggled at Sparkler for several months as my new engineering staff and the shop employees were being trained. Our house in Houston still had not been sold, and it was difficult to become close to the employees while we lived seventy miles away. Linda had met only a handful of Sparkler people. Few of those who moved from Illinois had time to visit us in Houston during the time they were settling in, but Don and Debbie Cooper were the exception. They accepted our invitation for a grilled steak dinner. As the fire was starting on the patio, Don and I were sitting in the living room, talking. I heard Linda tell Debbie how much we appreciated Don's coat keeping me from freezing while I was up north. Then Debbie dropped the bombshell, "I bet it's nice to have your own meat market. I wish we did. Don loves steak." I jumped up to interrupt, but it was too late. The dead silence told me Linda had heard. Then I heard, "Meat market? *Charlie.*" I was cleaning up the glue from the tube I stepped on in my rush to the kitchen. Now, even my nine by twelve rug was ruined. It was not my day. The confession was short and so was conversation during the meal.

Linda left Hughes Tool, and we moved to a rental house in Conroe the summer of that first year, even though the Houston house had not been sold. With the loss of Linda's income and the Houston house payments continuing, there was no way we could buy another house. Eventually, we returned the house to the previous owner and were able to buy a newly completed house in Conroe.

At Sparkler, two new lines of filters were developed, the HRC and MCRO. Standardized price lists were prepared to speed up response to prospects, and the company's financial condition improved. Several new designs were patented, and Sparkler developed more advanced industrial process filters. New materials were used, expanding the market to meet the needs of more clients. New ASME welding procedures were approved to meet the pressure vessel code, and Sparkler was beginning to prosper.

Two significant field installation trips followed—one to work with a unionized customer in Michigan and another to Tokyo and a customer trying to prevent unionization in Japan. Sparkler was now entering the world of automation.

By this time, Linda and I were expecting our first child. In those days, you had to wait until delivery to find out if you had a boy or girl, so we were ready for either. I observed Mother's pregnancy with Jill and David, so I was somewhat prepared for the morning sickness and the moody times, but it's different when it's your wife going through difficult times. One of the unexpected challenges was Linda's driving, seated further back from the steering wheel each week. I had just purchased a set of butyl rubber tires for the car tires, the newest type. "Guaranteed to never skid!" I was told. Soon afterward, black tire marks appeared on the garage floor of our new house. Linda seemed to be weaving back and forth as she backed out. This was wearing the tires, and it needed to stop! I still hadn't grown out of my bossy phase.

"The garage doors are too narrow, and I have to turn to miss the center post," she explained.

"I never have to," I responded. "Just get in, look out the back window and back straight out. It's simple if you know what you're doing!" (I could tell she was not convinced.)

"Charlie, I have a hard time driving out. I still need to steer a little." It would take a demonstration.

I hopped into the car, cranked it up and gave it the gas, straight back. She watched my skillful maneuver. *Bam!* I turned to see where the noise came from. The engine stalled as I braked. The entire front facing of the garage slowly tipped over onto the hood. The car wouldn't crank to get out of the way! I finally nonchalantly got out, pushed the shattered wood off the car and back up against the garage. I heard some loud laughter. Linda was sitting on the ground, rolling back and forth like a Buddha doll. She was laughing so hard she couldn't even say, "I told you the doorway was too narrow." But I now knew she was right! That was my last driving lesson. After that, some of the black marks on the floor were mine.

Conroe was one of the nicest places we lived during our almost fifty years together. It was a small town of about eight thousand friendly and hospitable East Texans. Just about everyone knew each other, and social life revolved around church, families and friends. If you needed help, someone was always ready to volunteer. Clyde Ledbetter was one example. When we bought the investment property along the proposed new beltway in Houston, Mr. King included me his pre-WWII Ford tractor he kept stored on the lot, a purchase Linda questioned. "What do we need with a tractor?"

"It'll be fun to drive and clear the land." By then we had purchased property on the shores of "future Lake Conroe," but for then, it was just woods and underbrush. But my new tractor was still south of Houston, and we had no trailer to bring it the seventy miles to Conroe.

Early the next Saturday, Clyde showed up with his trailer and a friend to help, but the trailer had no ramps to drive the tractor up onto the deck. "Just disconnect the trailer, and we'll hold up one end up so the back hits the ground. Drive on and stop as soon as you are balanced in the middle," suggested Clyde. I forgot the tractor had no brakes until I hit center and continued down the other side almost flattening Clyde and his buddy. The next try, we put a four by four crossways to stop the front tires. I cut the ignition and coasted into the timber. Quickly we chained my prize down and set off for Conroe.

Six miles up the freeway we passed Gulfgate Mall. There in the center of the median was a truck, boat and trailer. The trailer had a flat tire, and two women were looking at it helplessly. We were too heavy to pull off on the soft shoulder to help. As we passed Clyde's friend shouted, "What's wrong ladies, run out of water? Ha! Ha!" We paid for that remark because no sooner than he finished his taunt, we heard *bam!*

Our blowout happened so close to the ladies, we heard them laughing! As we waited for the service truck, theirs arrived, and as they passed us I heard, "What's the matter, guys, run out of field to plow?" They had the last laugh. After buying a new tire for Clyde's trailer, we pulled into Conroe, several hours behind schedule.

The tractor remained in one side of the two-car garage while I repaired the brakes, tuned it up, and gave it a glossy new coat of paint. The finishing touch was a golden seat. As I drove it proudly to the new lot, the rear tire sidewall split open, but the tube inside kept it from going flat. Linda followed me back home in our car. Each time the split part went to the bottom, I bounced up off my golden seat a little, and the tube bulged a little farther out of the tire. The split was on the inside of the tire and soon the tube was bulging so far out it began rubbing the fender. Just before entering the town, the tube developed a leak. By then the sight was so comical, Linda dropped way behind so no one would recognize us. I looked like I was riding a bucking bronco. With each revolution of the tire, I would bounce about a foot above the golden seat and had to hold tight to the steering wheel to keep from being thrown off. The leak was now forming a ring of water along my right side, just like a cowboy's lasso. I did reach home before the water all ran out but not before friends got to see the sight. "Ride 'em, cowboy!" and "Hang onto the gold seat" were some of the comments I heard for months.

WILDCAT STRIKE!

Auto manufacturers were no stranger to Sparkler filters. We had furnished filters for use in removing impurities during chrome plating of bumpers, headlights and other chrome accessories that were so popular on cars in the 1950s and 1960s. These horizontal plate filters had a serious drawback. Even though they performed flawlessly, cleaning and replacing filter media required more labor than desired. Sparkler was contracted to design a new filter that could be cleaned and media replaced without even opening the cover, and to furnish automatic controls for the cleaning and recoating process. Two HRC filters along with automatic controls were ordered for the General Motors Technical Center.

The HRC filter had been invented by the firm's founder, A.C. Kracklauer and developed by Sparkler to combine the best features of two styles of filters:

> The horizontal plate filter, which was extremely stable in operation and highly efficient was labor intensive. It could be started and stopped many times without losing efficiency. These filters had to be cleaned by opening the tank, removing and disassembling the plates, cleaning them, and replacing the filter paper.

> The vertical plate filter could be cleaned without opening the tank and by flushing out the waste to the plant's waste treatment plant or the city sewer system if permitted. Concern over water pollution led to it being more desirable to remove the wastes in a dry cake. In plants where this

was desired, air could be passed through the filter to dry the wastes, a vibrating mechanism shook the plates to remove the waste materials, and a screw conveyor in the bottom of the tank removed the wastes in dry form for landfill disposal. This type of design overcame the vertical plate design's disadvantage—whenever the flow was interrupted, and often during drying the filter cake fell to the bottom and the unit had to be opened, cleaned, and recoated with filter aid material.

The new HRC design allowed filtering in the stable horizontal position, and after filtration was complete, the waste material could be dried without falling to the bottom. The waste was removed by rotating the plates to vertical position for cleaning. The vibrating mechanism shook the plates to remove the waste materials, and a conveyor carried them out of the tank for disposal. This design allowed the option to automate the entire operation.

One hurdle I faced in designing these automated units was in contracting with a Professional Engineer to design the automatic control equipment. I was told that the unions at GM would never allow automation equipment for a process that was normally run by a licensed operator. Besides, there was plenty of work in the oil industry to keep them busy. We had the contract, but no one would design the controls. Even though I was the chief engineer at Sparkler, I was a mechanical engineer, not an electrical engineer.

I decided to learn how to design the system myself. I moonlighted during college, wiring houses for John Chapman, and had a limited knowledge of electricity. My electrical engineering courses at Ga. Tech were little help, as they concentrated in fundamentals, not applications. Since the process steps were all controlled by time and each step had to have independently adjustable time cycles, it was easy to research the types of timers available. I selected the Taylor Instruments Flex-O-Timer, a multiple wheel mechanical timer. It allowed field adjusting the time of every step of the process, without rewiring—a critical requirement since we could not do any wiring in a GM facility. Union personnel would be doing all the work installing and adjusting the system.

The filters along with the controls were shipped and the piping connected to the unit. The start up was scheduled just after the Memorial Day weekend, and I was required to be at the plant to be sure the start-up and operation went smoothly. Apparently they did not know "smoothly" was missing from my dictionary. Three days before the holiday, we went to the Tech Center to inspect the installation and be sure the filters, controls and pumps were all in place and functioning. I was in for a surprise. Our representative Bill Mullen told me the controls had not been connected because of a problem with the electricians. None of the wiring from the control panel to the equipment had been installed! *And* no one was willing to touch it except me, but I was non-union and couldn't. All the equipment was working except the automatic controls. We were told that the unit would have to be run by an operator.

The weather in Detroit had been miserable for weeks, but the prediction for Memorial Day was clear and warm. It was going to be a great weekend, one that would be much better if an extra day off was added. If the impasse on the controls was not resolved, we could still get the filters working and I could return to Conroe until the use of automation was resolved. Late in the afternoon two days before the holiday, I was in the plant, preparing for start-up when a pipe wrench fell from above, almost hitting me. I looked up to see the pipe fitter looking down at me, apologizing for the near miss. "Please hand me the wrench," he said. "I'll be more careful." I did, and less than a minute later, a police whistle sounded. Wildcat strike! Just in time to add that extra day to the holiday. My heart sank! I had caused a strike by handling the wrench. "Minimum fine is $25,000, for you or your company!" I was told.

I went back to Bill's house and spent the long weekend in Detroit with his family, and it was far less fun than the plant employees were having on their extended weekend. I dreaded the return to Conroe to report my wildcat strike and the fine. Bill suggested we delay telling management until after the issue was resolved.

The morning after the holiday, Bill and I went to the Tech Center to start up the filters—without the automation and discovered the entire basement room containing the filters was underwater. When the walkout occurred, the pipe fitter who almost crowned me with the wrench left a hose running and the multi-million dollar section of the center was flooded. And guess what? Our filter station had the only pumps hooked up and ready to run. Until GM accepted the filters, they were ours, and they would have to get our permission to use them! After a few minutes of quick negotiation, it was agreed that the $25,000 fine was imposed in haste, and if we let them use the pumps, it would be forgotten. We turned them on and immediately one quit. An electrician had dropped a small fitting into one pump's inlet and bent the impeller. It had to be replaced. The other pump successfully removed the water before the flooded custom, acid proof tile floor was damaged. Bill agreed to repair the broken pump at no cost if the cooperation continued.

The following day after the area was completely dry, discussions were held on the automation installation. I offered to do the connections and testing, but I was non-union. A compromise was reached. I could do the adjustments if a union electrician sat and observed. The observer would be paid by GM. That seemed to be a reasonable compromise, so I began. Midway into my wiring, another police whistle sounded! What had I done now? The steward rushed over and announced. "You're working too fast. Our observer can't keep up with what you are doing." A second observer was added, and the project was completed. I returned to Conroe exhausted.

LAND OF THE
RISING SUN

In the summer of 1961, Sparkler delivered two automated HRC filters to Nippon Fats and Oils in Tokyo. This installation was to be the first custom designed filter installation for use in the refining of animal fats and cooking oils in Japan. The design was very similar to the system sold to General Motors for installation in their GM Tech Center, for use in chrome plating for auto parts. However, they were the first HRCs used with standard filter aid plus activated carbon to purify the oils.

After installation and startup, we received a frantic call from our agents in Tokyo. The filters processed the oils as designed, but when they were rotated to clean, they broke down completely. The cake fell off all at one time and jammed everything, even damaging the units. The Japanese were having to open the unit and shovel the cake out and were not happy. After a couple weeks, the unhappiness turned to anger, and by August to threats of court action. They needed someone *immediately*!

Our sales personnel had passports and could leave immediately, but I was "volunteered" to go to the plant as the Japanese insisted on the chief engineer. I applied for a passport and visa. I was required to take a series of Cholera immunizations shots, usually given over a longer period of time than was available, so they were given over a few days. I don't recommend that procedure. I got a high fever and was weak and miserable, but by the time I received a passport and visa, I was feeling better. Major Hurricane "Carla" was headed towards Houston, and I left two days before it hit, leaving Linda and Suzanne, our infant daughter, behind. Conroe was almost 100 miles from the Gulf, so no one expected much damage that far inland.

The trip to Tokyo was far from uneventful. In Dallas, the flight was delayed due to a malfunction in the water injection that provided additional thrust to the jet engines. All passengers were told the plane would take off as soon as the engineers at the factory checked whether it could take off safely without the added thrust. About half the passengers decided "not me." I decided to stay on and wait for the answer. After all at twenty-five, I was confident that it would be safe. Engineers know what they are doing.

Very late that evening we were cleared to fly, and we taxied to the runway, then waited for a "tug" to reach the plane and push it backward to the very beginning of the runway. I began to get nervous. If we needed that few feet more to make it, maybe this was a bad decision. Fasten seat belts! We began to move. I had been on many flights before, and this one wasn't moving very fast. By mid runway, the pilot gave the engines full throttle, but still we seemed to be going too slow. I don't know if there is a setting past full throttle, but we lurched forward and just after we left the pavement, we clipped some branches off several trees and rose into the air. The pilot announced that we were on the first and last flight to take off under those conditions, and "free drinks for all."

It was just the beginning though. As we approached the West Coast, a huge fog bank descended on California, Oregon, and Washington. We had used so much fuel during takeoff the pilot couldn't divert or turn back. We would land using military radar approach control on the nearby field. The pilot made it more exciting by turning on the landing lights long before we reached the coast. Everyone watched out the windows waiting for a mountain to come out of the clouds and get us.

When we finally landed, there was a cheer, and all were ready to get to the terminal. In 1961, the Jetways we now enjoy were not available, so we had to use the stairs and walk to the terminal. The fog was so heavy we couldn't see the terminal clearly and ropes were stretched from the aircraft stairs to the door, so that no one would stray.

On to Anchorage and then south to Tokyo. Just as I was about to doze, the seat belt light came on with the announcement, "Ladies and gentlemen, we have strayed off course into Russian air space and are being chased out by two MIG fighters. We are in contact with the Russians on the ground and are in no danger. Please remain seated and calm until we are back on course." One look at the wide awake passengers told that no one was calm.

Landing was at about 2:00 AM, and I was exhausted. I knew someone representing our Japanese agent was to meet me, but I didn't know who. I disembarked and no one was there, and I didn't have any way to contact them. So, I sat and sat and sat. The lobby was almost deserted, with only two other men there, both reading. After an hour wait, I was getting nervous. Where were they? Finally, the two men who had been sitting across from me for the entire time approached and asked, "Are you Mr. Space? We've been waiting for two months for someone from Sparkler, and just couldn't believe someone finally came. Welcome to Japan." They both smiled.

This was not a good sign. They were making a point. I had to pay for their two-month wait. We got to the Imperial Hotel, I checked in, and they followed me to the room to explain the situation at the Nippon Fats plant. The plant officials were angry and would not welcome me without letting out their frustration, and a meeting was set up in three hours at 8:00. I was too upset to sleep, even though I had been awake for over thirty-three hours. The morning television news showed the widespread damage as Carla ripped ashore in Texas. I was worried about Linda and Suzanne. I tried to call Linda, but all lines were out, adding to my stress.

I showered, changed, felt a little better, then dozed for an hour. After a light breakfast, off we went. I was prepared to meet the manager, get chewed out, and then get to work. No such thing. I entered a large conference room where about twenty-five engineers, operators and managers sat. As I stood at attention at the head of the table, each proceeded in turn to chew me out in Japanese, followed by a translator repeating the insults. I was expected to apologize to each at the end of the translation, then listen to the translation into Japanese.

About ten o'clock, I asked to be excused to use the men's room. At least I could escape for a few minutes. I left the room amid loud chuckling. "What's so funny about going to the men's room?" I asked, as I was shown the way. I soon found out. I looked for the plumbing fixtures, but there were none—only round holes in the floor with footprints painted on the floor, one on each side. It didn't take a college degree to figure it out. But even worse, it was a co-ed room. Two Japanese women squatted right next to me and started giggling. It didn't take me long to get back to the meeting. The laughter ended as soon as I entered the room, and their scowling faces returned.

By lunch, we were only half-way around the table, and I was worn out. Only one hour of sleep in the past fifty hours, and this! Another try to contact home was unsuccessful, and I wasn't able to reach the office either. My stress was building up fast.

After lunch, the rest of the table's occupants got their turn, each speaking a little longer, and now each was nodding in approval even to the translation. My apologies got shorter. They finished around the table about 7:00 PM. I remembered the stories of brutal interrogations during WWII. At least they had not pushed bamboo splinters under my fingernails or torn them out. The first day was over, I could finally get some sleep, and we could get to work the next day.

No such luck. For the next two days, the procedure was repeated, except the managers were absent, replaced by other employees. To the delight of all (except me) I stood there and took it. I was expected to remain standing the whole time.

At the start of the fourth day, I still had no news from home. I reached my breaking point. I apologized for the last time, announcing that I deeply regretted their inconvenience, and I was humbly going to admit defeat. They could return the equipment for a full refund, and I would return to Conroe the next day. Super Typhoon Nancy was approaching Japan, and I wanted to leave before its Category 5 winds struck. To my amazement, I heard comments like, "We can't do that, we will lose face for recommending this equipment." "You must help us get it to work." "What can we do to assist you?" *They all spoke English!* The whole three days had been brainwashing! I was furious and told them I would reconsider leaving only if they really wanted to get to work. I would give them my reply in the morning.

By morning, the typhoon was just offshore, and after a short meeting at the plant, it was agreed that they would cooperate if I stayed. All left to prepare for the storm. I rode it out in the Imperial Hotel, one of Frank Lloyd Wright's most famous works. It was a magnificent structure, but as was common in his works, magnificent style was not always accompanied by magnificent engineering and construction. The drainage was sub-standard as the site was in a low area, and the waterproofing leaked under the onslaught of Nancy, the sixth-deadliest typhoon to hit Japan at the time. Outside in the street, the water was over three feet deep. The entire hotel was surrounded by thousands of sandbags, which reduced flooding inside to a minimum, but only because the staff mopped up the leaks in the dike continuously. Phone service was restored in Texas, but now we were without electricity or phones. I still hadn't reached my family.

Typhoon Nancy, renamed "Second Muroto Typhoon" by the Japanese, destroyed over 11,000 houses and damaged or flooded about 300,000 others. Over 300 ships were sunk or blown ashore, and many more were damaged. One hundred and ninety persons were killed or missing, and over 3,000 people were injured. I even got to see one freighter that had been washed two blocks into an industrial area. Fortunately, the Nippon plant had not been significantly damaged.

Two days, and back to work. The damage was significant, but phones were restored, and I was able to reach Linda. There was severe flooding in Texas, but our house was not affected, other than a large tree falling behind the house. Mother and daughter both were fine, and friends were taking care of them.

The attitude at the plant had significantly improved. I redesigned the damaged filter parts on the spot. The new filter parts were manufactured locally in one day and reinstalled. The first trial run after the repairs pinpointed the problem. The large chunks of activated carbon and filter aid used with the lard in the process jammed the conveyor and caused the breakdown. I designed motorized "cake breakers" to break the large chunks that blocked the discharge, and the lower part of the filters were lined with stainless steel to prevent sticking. It was interesting that "lard" was hard for Japanese to pronounce, so the filters were named "hog grease filters."

Disassembling both units, cleaning out the "hog grease," sandblasting, and welding all took several days, and during those hours, the plant engineers asked me to teach fundamentals of mechanical engineering to the staff, which I did gladly—"provided I could sit down," I explained. I was greeted with laughter and applause, the first sign that the attitude change was genuine. Those plant engineers were starving for new knowledge and soaked up the discussions like a sponge. I was even able to solve several equipment problems in other areas of the plant. We all learned from each other.

One of the first questions I asked was, "How can you justify spending this much for automation equipment when many plant workers were earning 400 Yen (about $1.12) per day?" They explained that companies in Japan looked beyond the immediate investment to the future of their industries. In Japan, management had a good relationship with employees, and at that time most employees worked their entire career for the same company. As the industries expanded, they would have to import foreign workers if every job was done manually, and soon Japanese culture would be diluted. Foreign workers would not have the loyalty to the company and soon, there might even be labor strikes like in America. If every plant used the latest equipment, they could keep Japanese workers employed and compete in the world markets. An example they gave was the hog grease filters. Because of the automation I was installing, they could import lard from America, refine it and ship it back to the states cheaper than American refined lard.

I was asked to join them on a visit to a local stainless steel rolling mill to select the stainless type for the lining of our filters. The mill was a prime example of Japanese industrial planning for the future. Stainless steel slabs were shipped from the US to the plant. There, they were unloaded onto a moving conveyor, submerged in a large tank for acid cleaning, rinsed, dried, heated and run through several rollers until the slab was the correct thickness. Then they were put through large sanding machines and finally polished and cut to size. During all these steps, not one human hand touched the steel. All work was done by automated machinery. This opened my eyes to the competition we could expect in later years. Crating and loading the finished products was the only work done manually, and most of the output was shipped back to America. Remember, this was 1961.

The next week, all the modifications needed by my redesign were completed and the filters were ready for a trial run. The managers reappeared to witness the test. I had been told that if this didn't work on the first try, I would be "losing face," the Japanese words for disgrace. I really didn't care much about that, I just wanted to get back home and clean up the mess left by Hurricane Carla. A friend had arranged for the tree to be removed, but the rest of the clean-up was up to me.

The filter run went perfectly on the first try, and we were all pleased. I planned to leave the next day, but the management insisted I stay to celebrate the success. Because I had let the Japanese do all the modifications under my supervision, the victory was shared.

The celebration lasted two days. The first was a trip to the ancient capitol of Kamakura with a tour of the Buddha Temple and a private banquet with a performance by the local Japanese dancers. The next day included a surprise trip to the warehouse of Mikimoto, a well-known jewelry distributor of pearls. The trading company that represented Sparkler also represented Mikimoto, and I was ushered into a large room containing thousands of pearl necklaces, hanging in bundles containing hundreds each. I was allowed to choose one for Linda, since she had been alone with our first child for weeks. "It was the least we can do for such an inconvenience," they explained. I chose a necklace containing a matched set of graduated top-of-the line pearls. I insisted on paying for them because it was enough of an honor for me to serve them in their need. They bowed and accepted the forty dollars they claimed to be the value.

Next was the presentation of a movie camera to film my family and new child. That night featured another banquet and a trip to a Japanese night club where I was presented with a gift—a beautiful Japanese porcelain figurine in traditional dress. The next day was goodbye. I was escorted to the airport where I was given a letter of personal thanks from the plant manager along with an order for three more HRC filters with the specific instructions to make them just like the ones we had rebuilt together. When they agreed the success was a joint effort, I knew the strain of the first few days was forgotten. After that bumpy start, it turned out to be a wonderful experience.

HOME AGAIN

The trip home from Tokyo was another unexpected adventure. The send-off party the night before put me in a good mood for the long trip home. I was sure the frightening trip to Japan would not be repeated. That was a once in a lifetime experience—I thought.

I boarded the Japan Air Lines jet and settled down in my seat. It was my first flight on JAL, and as I climbed the stairway, I noticed the name of the plane was *City of Kamakura*—the site of my visit to the temple two days before. I always selected a seat next to a window and the emergency exit. Just before takeoff, the flight attendants started through the standard seat belt instructions and demonstrated use of the life jackets, first in Japanese, next in English, finally in Spanish, as there were several Philippines onboard. The seat belt demo went fine, but by the time it was repeated in the three languages, we were airborne. As the flight attendant put on the life jacket, and began instructions in Japanese, an elderly Philippine lady misunderstood the rapid speech to be an emergency. When the pilot raised the landing gear with a loud *thud*, she was sure we were going down. She began squealing, put on the life vest, and pulled the inflation tabs. I'm sure it was not as amusing to her as it was to the rest of the passengers.

She couldn't have gotten out of the plane, even if we had been going down. The inflated life jacket had her firmly pinned in her seat, unable to move. Even the fold-up arm on one side refused to budge. As the flight attendant tried to pull her loose, her cries got louder. Finally, it was obvious she could be released only by deflating the vest, but as the flight attendant pulled out a nail file to puncture the vest, the passenger went wild—she thought she was being stabbed. Another Philippine lady came to the rescue, calming her, and earning all the passengers' applause. After a free round of drinks for everyone, we settled down for the trip to San Francisco.

Midway between Tokyo and Hawaii, the seat belt light and chimes went on, and I woke up to see the inboard engine on my side of the plane was trailing smoke and flames. We were on fire! The flames were extinguished in less than a minute, but the smoke continued. The pilot calmed everyone by explaining that a hydraulic hose had burst and there was no danger. The engine was shut down, we would be stopping in Honolulu for temporary repairs and would be a couple hours late arriving in San Francisco. That was enough for me! I changed flights in Hawaii and decided to spend two days as a tourist, visiting Pearl Harbor, the city, and the beach. While there, I took the $40 necklace to a jeweler, who appraised it at $400 wholesale. I'm sure they were smiling in Tokyo, knowing that it was a surprise gift, and they had allowed me to "save face."

I was anxious to get home to Linda and Suzanne as I climbed the stairway for the flight home. I glanced at the name of the plane and was shocked to see *City of Kamakura* painted on the fuselage. It was the same aircraft! I had selected the same seat for this leg of the trip, and sat down with a feeling of déjà vu. At least the Philippine woman was not there. We took off without incident and about an hour out of San Francisco, the same engine began to smoke, but this time there was no fire. Again the announcement of the broken hydraulic hose came over the speaker. I wondered if the line had been replaced or just taped, but didn't ask. When we landed, I said a prayer of thanks, boarded the flight to Houston, and relaxed—this engine was not smoking. That adventure was over.

The following year saw many improvements. The HRC filter was expanded to several different sizes, and manufacturing in high alloy metals continued. I received patents for two filter plate designs, redesigned another filter line to eliminate an "O" ring seal design that had proved difficult to assemble on larger horizontal tanks. It was a similar design that NASA would use later on the doomed Space Shuttle *Challenger*. The redesign also allowed for simpler automation and eliminated bulky supports that were difficult to keep clean. Both the HRC and the MCRO lines remain in production at Sparkler, forty years later. Automation of units continued and was gradually being accepted in unionized plants.

One spring day, I received a post card notifying me of an upcoming international convention on automation. I was interested but far too busy to attend. There was no time to adjust schedules because the meeting was in two weeks. I sent my regrets. Three days later, I received a frantic call from San Antonio.

"You have to be here; you are on the program," the conference director exclaimed. I was floored.

"I never agreed to give a speech; who accepted the assignment?"

After a pause, he replied, "A Mr. Bernard Johnson."

"Are you sure? He never mentioned it to me, and I have nothing prepared."

"I'm sure. I have his signature before me."

"I'll check it out and call back."

With a sheepish grin, Bernie admitted he had signed me up without asking.

"Why?" I asked.

"Would you have agreed?" he responded.

"No," I replied.

"Well, that's why I didn't ask."

I was furious, but after my blood stopped "boiling," I realized it wasn't anger, it was panic. A survey was taken years ago, asking individuals to list their greatest fear. Speaking in public was first on the list; death was second.

"What is the subject of my speech, and how many will attend?" I asked Bernie.

"*Automation Progress in the Filter Industry*, and only a few will attend, it's no big deal. Just draw a couple twenty-four by thirty-six charts and wing it."

I was all right talking to a group of a dozen or so, but larger groups were a different matter. The twenty to thirty in meetings in Tokyo had been my limit.

Memories of the first several days' harassment by Nippon managers made me wary of large groups. When I called the conference director back, he explained that he would rearrange the schedule and put my presentation last. "By the last talk, most attendees will be packing to go home, and there should be only a handful left," I was assured. I agreed and prepared my three charts.

When I arrived the first day to observe the talks in the auditorium, I was apprehensive. Several hundred watched talks that included professionally prepared colored charts and photos, projected on a movie theater size screen. My small charts would not be visible beyond the first two rows!

"Don't worry, you're last," echoed in my brain, but I didn't believe the message. The final day arrived, and so did the speaker I was to follow. Again, a setback. He was the internationally acclaimed Taylor Instruments design and applications chief, and he would include in his presentation the Taylor equipment I had used as the basis of my talk. *Everyone stayed*. I was looking at a sea of strange faces, and my exhibits were so small, I couldn't even hide behind them!

Somehow, I got through without passing out, and even though I got applause and many questions later, I was sure Sparkler would be permanently out of the automation business. I was surprised, though; our sales picked up.

I believe the success of designs at Sparkler was directly attributed to the ingenuity of the firm's founder, A.C. Kracklauer and the company's field service. If a client had a problem, we would dispatch a sales engineer to help solve it. If necessary, a pilot plant test unit was loaned to a client and the process was tailored to his needs. If the sales engineer was unable to succeed, one of the engineering staff was sent to assist. The difficulty in the Tokyo installation had been caused by eliminating the pilot plant test.

Friction within Sparkler had escalated during the first months of 1963. In spite of long hours and re-checking designs, unexplained problems plagued me. Stress was mounting, and I ended up hospitalized with an ulcer. One afternoon, the president's secretary called me to her office and asked me to do something strange. "Would you please take my trash can and dump it out for me?" she asked.

"I don't understand," I replied.

"You will if you empty it slowly and observe what falls out."

Mystified, I left with the trash, and as I dumped it out, I understood.

There lay three memos to me from another officer. All were originals and all were signed. Each informed me of an immediate problem that could be avoided if I took prompt action. Copies to the president were noted on each, but the originals had been thrown away so that I could not foresee the problem and take action. For weeks, I had been under fire for ignoring problems I was supposed to know existed. Copies of warning memos were always produced. So, this was why.

"How long has this been going on—the destruction of memos?" I asked.

"Several weeks. You can't win. *Run for your life*, or you'll be destroyed."

There it was again—*run for your life*. I knew she was right. This dream was over, too. I was twenty-seven, we were expecting our second child, and now my job was in jeopardy. One afternoon, the company vice president had even threatened to beat me up in front of my employees when I disagreed with him.

A few days later in the spring of 1963, the answer to our prayers came via a call from Jacksonville. The space program called me to a new frontier, provided I could report for the new job in two weeks. Moving would be reimbursed, and I would be making the same salary, even though my job would no longer be as chief engineer. I said goodbye to friends and left Conroe two weeks before Steve was born. Linda followed as soon as they could travel. The house was listed with a realtor, but we couldn't wait for it to be sold.

TO THE SPACE PROGRAM

In February 1963, I received a phone call from Jacksonville. A new engineering company had opened an office for work on the space program and was recruiting engineers for the design effort. Mason-Rust was a joint venture between Mason & Hanger and Rust Engineering of Pittsburgh. Their Jacksonville office had been hired by Thiokol Corporation to design and construct a manufacturing and test facility for their design for a solid fuel rocket for one stage of the Saturn IB, predecessor to the moon-landing rocket. I applied for the job. It had been ten years since I left Jacksonville to establish my independence, and I was confident that my career had moved well enough that could return as Charlie Space, not "Chuck Space's Son." Whatever came out of the venture would not be because of his influence.

The need for help was so critical that Mason Rust insisted I be in Jacksonville immediately. I could not delay beyond the two weeks notice I gave at Sparkler, even though our second child was due two weeks later. Mother went to Conroe to take care of Suzanne during Linda's delivery and recovery period and to help with packing for moving our furniture before traveling to Jacksonville with them. I moved to Jacksonville, found a house to rent and reported to work. A few days later, I received the call. Steven David Space had been born on March 18. Mother and son were doing well, and my expanded family was looking forward to joining me soon. They arrived in Jacksonville two weeks later.

I had opted not to file for Professional Engineer Registration while in Texas, because the program was new and qualifications were less stringent than other states. PE Registration was not necessary for most engineering work. The situation was different in Florida. Registration was a must, and each applicant was required to demonstrate engineering experience, including being in charge of projects. A written examination was also necessary. Most took the examination four years after graduation, but it had been seven years for me. Many of the engineers I knew doubted I could pass on the first try, given the length of time I had been away from Ga. Tech.

The examinations for Florida and Georgia were scheduled only a week apart, so I decided to apply in both states. That way, if I passed only one of the examinations, I could be accepted in both. Time was short, and I was able to do little review for preparation. Calculators were not allowed in either exam, so I would have to leave my Monroe at home and dust off my slide rule. The first exam was Florida's, which allowed the applicant to choose questions from a large selection. I was able to select most from my field of experience, but not all. As I left, I was not sure I had passed, but I knew that Georgia had a reputation for being less stringent in its standards. I would surely be able to find easier questions there.

The next weekend, I drove to Atlanta, confident of success. I opened the exam and almost passed out. Instead of a selection of all the questions, 25% of the score was based on a problem that all applicants had to answer. With the minimum score of 75%, miss that one and everything else had to be perfect. That problem was addressed to the many aircraft designers and engineers in the Atlanta area. I had no idea or plan to solve the problem. I attacked it using everything I knew, including dimensional analysis that often worked on difficult problems. After over ninety minutes, I had made no headway and gave up. I completed the rest of the test without difficulty. Before handing in my work, I wrote across the test paper, "This first problem is limited to those with very specialized experience, and I have elected to avoid solving it. In its place I have selected two, hoping you will consider them. Both are in my field of practice. If this is acceptable, I promise never to design an inertial guidance system." Weeks later, I was notified that I passed both state exams.

During this phase of our lives, another challenge appeared on the horizon. Suzanne was starting to show signs of serious health problems. Just before leaving Texas for the new job in Florida, she began having problems with balance and coordination. For a while, we thought it to be a temporary ear infection, but it turned out to be far more serious. The Lord was watching over us then because the first doctor that examined her was familiar with the rare disease she had contracted. It was diagnosed as cerebellum ataxia, and Dr. Skinner believed it was triggered by the excessive use of a drug by our pediatrician in Conroe. Suzanne had developed a boil on her seat, and he used the new drug to prevent a scar from lancing.

By the time Dr. Skinner diagnosed the disease, Suzanne had lost motor skills and coordination. In the beginning, she began weaving side to side when she walked, then she stopped walking at all. Soon she could no longer feed herself or sit up. She was two years old—too young to understand the changes her body was going through. She gave up trying. Most waking hours were spent crying. We were desperate for a cure.

Dr. Skinner had several tests performed at the hospital, including a spinal tap that went wrong. During her thrashing from panic and pain, the orderlies lost grip, and she fell on the tile floor, injuring her head, further frightening us. I was working every day and often late at night. Linda was at the hospital as long as possible, but with an infant at home, she could not spend all her time with Suzanne. When she left, Suzanne was left to scream in her crib until she passed out from exhaustion. A net was placed over the top to keep her from falling out. For years afterward, it was an ordeal to put her to bed. The terror of the disease and the net set her to screaming as soon as she was put down.

The diagnosis was confirmed, and the doctor informed us that up to that time, the disease was incurable, and that most patients deteriorated to a vegetable-like state and were institutionalized. Her case had some promise, though. It had been diagnosed early. All others patients' ataxias were far advanced before being diagnosed. He proposed an experimental treatment that might help, but the decision was ours because it had high risks. The treatment required use of a drug that virtually eliminated the body's immune defenses, but might slow down the progress of the ataxia. Something as minor as a common cold might kill her. We would have to keep her in isolation during the treatment.

After serious prayer, we decided to go ahead. If we didn't, she would continue to deteriorate, and she was constantly in terror. For weeks, Suzanne and Linda spent all their time at home, no visitors, no fresh air, no progress. Even baby Steve was separated from his sister. I was able to go to work, but have limited contact at home. Slowly, the screaming and decline stopped. The treatment was working! The months of unsuccessful trying to control her body had damaged her will as much as the disease had injured her body. She gave up trying to do anything—she just sat and stared.

It was then that Dr. Skinner proposed beginning therapy to rebuild brain paths that had been injured and rebuild her self-confidence. The program required one-on-one therapy for hours every day without parents or observers. The therapist forced her to pay attention and strictly obey every instruction, often repeating the order many times. Constant eye contact was required. The therapy involved what we considered to be brutal treatment, but we had no other options. We were not allowed to attend or observe. It was extremely expensive for a full-time therapist, but Dr. Skinner paid the entire cost! We reimbursed him for the materials used in the retraining, but he paid the rest out of his own pocket. He felt doctors should take responsibility for side effects of drugs, even though he had not been the doctor who prescribed the culprit medicine.

Suzanne slowly returned to normal, and she was taken to a medical symposium to demonstrate the success of the treatment. Dr. Skinner continued to follow her progress as she successfully completed grammar, middle, and high school. He was one of the true professionals we ever met, and we give thanks that our prayers led us to him.

During this hectic period, I was immersed in the Thiokol solid rocket project. At that time, the space program consisted of two separate views on the proper type of booster. One camp had its roots in the WWII German V2 program. Supporters insisted that liquid propelled rockets were superior and had far more successes. The liquid booster had several points in its favor. The thrust could be controlled by reducing the fuel flow, the fuel had consistent quality and had a high thrust-to-weight ratio, and there was far more experience in the hardware. The thrust pressure occurred outside the fuel tanks—in the nozzle, so the fuel storage tanks could be low pressure. The negative points included the expense and complexity of the thousands of components. Failure of any component could spell disaster. The fuels were also more hazardous to handle, particularly hydrogen.

The proponents of solid-fuelled rockets favored the simplicity of design (just light it and let it go), the stability of the solid fuel, safety in handling, and their low cost. Negatives included the combustion pressures occurred in the fuel tanks, so the thick walls had to be designed for high pressures, making them heavier than tanks on liquid fuel boosters. The rocket thrust could not be adjusted after it was ignited because the thrust was determined by the shape of the central cavity. The fuel, usually a rubber-like material, had to be mixed with granular oxidizers and adhesives to stabilize the mixture. After mixing, these fuel components were and transported for casting into the steel shell. The shell was filled with the shell in a vertical position. The propellant was cast around a star-shaped hollow center core that ran the entire length of the rocket. The booster would have to burn along the entire length of the core to develop maximum thrust. The star-shaped hollow center provided more burning surface and thrust than a cylindrical core. The mix had to be consistent, with no air pockets to cause uneven burning or breaking off of unburned propellant. After casting, a tent-like cover was installed to maintain even temperatures and humidity during curing and to protect the booster from the weather during curing and installation of the nozzle.

It was an easy task to build small rockets and success on small solid fuel rockets was good. Often the fuel could be mixed in a single batch, reducing the chance of uneven batches. On a small unit, controlling the cure temperature and humidity was also uncomplicated. There was limited experience in building larger boosters, so NASA selected Thiokol and Aerojet General Corp. from among several contestants to build two manufacturing, casting, and curing and testing facilities. Each company was contracted to build and test fire a single 260-inch (21'-8") diameter motor, "Winner take all" as I was told. The successful company's solid booster was to be used as the first stage of the Saturn IB, the test vehicle for the Apollo Saturn V moon rocket components. If the Thiokol design won the Aerojet-Thiokol race, NASA was considering an even larger solid booster for the first stage of the final Saturn V vehicle headed for the moon. The stakes were high for both companies.

This stage had to be so large that a casting, cure, and test pit fifty-two feet in diameter and over 120 feet deep had to be designed and constructed. The pit was designed with load cells installed in the bottom to measure the weight, and for the first one constructed, to measure the thrust during test firing in the pit. In addition, the production rockets had to be removed from the pit, turned from vertical to horizontal, and then loaded on a barge to be shipped to Cape Canaveral ("the Cape"). The adhesives in the mixture had to keep the star shaped points of the fuel from breaking off during vibrations from burning and the liftoff. It also had to be strong enough to keep its shape during handling, transporting, unloading, and assembly at the Cape. Since this stage was so large, location along the Intra Coastal Waterway was necessary. Building a 120-foot deep pit that close to the water would mean almost all of the excavation was done underwater. It was a huge engineering challenge, one I gladly joined in March 1963.

The construction of a single, large booster was a risky venture for NASA and both competitors, especially Thiokol. It was not just the financial risk on this project because the government was paying much of the cost under its contract. Thiokol was firmly entrenched in the small rocket market, and if this venture failed, it might impact that market.

The Air Force was selected by NASA to co-manage the initial phases of the 260-inch booster program. A contract was already underway between United Technologies and the Air Force for the development of the Titan segmented boosters, which were 156 inches in diameter, and both agencies shared technology.

Design and manufacture of the steel shell to contain the propellant and to withstand the high pressures and temperatures during firing was a challenge in itself. To give the reader something to compare the size of this effort, the shell diameter would almost two thirds as large as a Polaris submarine hull. This was no "tin can." The Air Force had a large influence in the shell design, requiring both competitors to use a steel alloy that had limited previous use. The proposed Air Force design included heat treating the steel for additional strength. The increase from 156-inch to 260-inch diameter more than doubled stress levels.

One of my first assignments was to review the shell design drawings. As chief engineer at Sparkler, I had been very active in use of new materials and developing approved welding techniques, all for ASME Pressure vessel approval. One specific project involved design of a pressure vessel for nuclear reactor coolant, a design that required critical welding and heat treating of the steel shell. During my review of the Thiokol design, I found the proposed shell design did not meet criteria I considered to be safe, given the limited experience with the material, the welding proposed, and the heat treating. The design seriously compromised the industry accepted safety factor. The Air Force and Thiokol disagreed. My comments were not accepted, and I was assigned another task.

The competitor's engineers were more successful in convincing Aerojet management of the design's risk. They opted for a larger safety factor than that dictated by the Air Force. It was proven later that the decision was a wise one. The Thiokol test unit ruptured during its first hydraulic pressure test, one of the factors that eventually eliminated them from the competition for the large booster.

The Air Force preferred a segmented rocket to the large, single piece booster, largely because the Air Force facilities at Vandenberg were not accessible by barge. The Air Force boosters also were limited to about thirteen-feet diameter, the limit for rail transportation.

A rocket made up of several shorter segments would eliminate much of the cost of the huge one-piece boosters but that design required sealing each joint, a seal that would have to resist changing temperatures and high pressure. The Air Force Titan boosters were segmented and had been successful. Thiokol was considering a modified Titan "O" ring design for their segmented booster design that would eventually be used on the space shuttle boosters. I was now reviewing a preliminary design for this application after the rejection of my initial assignment recommendations. An important difference between the Titan design and the Thiokol proposal was that Titan segments were assembled vertically and the Thiokol booster would be assembled in a horizontal position.

At both the refinery and Sparkler, gaskets and seals were a critical component of our pressure vessels, and I had tested hundreds of combinations of materials and configurations. For a time, the "O" ring seals that Thiokol engineers proposed were used on Sparkler filters, with little success. We found that materials advertised as "good to 400 degrees" did resist those temperatures in many applications, but "O" rings lost their shape even though they did not melt. Our experience also taught us that vertical assembly was much easier than horizontal assembly. As the design was applied to larger diameter horizontal vessels, the difficulty of assembly without pinching or rolling the "O" rings in the groove grew. Excessive grease needed to assemble without pinching or rolling sometimes temporarily sealed damaged O rings, only to begin leaking when the grease leaked out as temperatures rose. Following my recommendation, Sparkler abandoned the design. I advised the Mason Rust and Thiokol management of that experience and designed a more conventional seal—a stainless steel ring joint seal used in high temperature, high pressure oil refinery applications. It was rejected—too heavy. Years later, as I watched the explosion of the *Challenger*, I knew the "O" rings were at fault before the fragments reached the ground.

They say, "the third time is a charm." I hoped it was true because both my first two assignments ended in rejection. I designed the fuel mixing and handling process during the time the 120-foot deep cast, cure, and test pit was under construction. A short section of the fifty-two-foot diameter caisson was constructed with an open bottom and water jets around the edge. It was then placed on the spot for the pit. The pumps supplying the jets were turned on and the force of the water washed away the sand and the shell slowly descended. It was just like my pushing a water hose down into the yard as a kid. As the shell sunk into the sand and shell, new lengths were welded in place, and reinforced concrete poured between the inner and outer steel shells. It worked like a charm! As the hole got deeper, a dragline dug the soil out of the center. Over half way down, and still going great. Then it stuck!

The jets had been turned off during the easy part, but when they were started again, they were full of sand that would not budge. A diver discovered that some limestone had blocked the descent. A few explosive charges removed the limestone and the descent continued to within a few feet of the desired depth. Then it stopped, this time it was stuck solid. After several days of blasting there was no progress. The pit could not be left shallower and still function, so contract negotiations began to bring more fill to the site to raise level of the top. In the middle of negotiations, it began to sink on its own! It slowly settled for what seemed an eternity. Down it went a few inches at a time, finally settling near the design depth. We were lucky, plain and simple. No engineering, just luck.

A diver was lowered to inspect before the concrete plug was poured in the bottom to keep it from settling more. Part way down, he stopped.

"What's wrong?"

"I'm hung up on a piece of steel."

"There's no steel in the middle of the pit!"

"Don't tell me that, I'm a'sittin on some. It's a rebar from the side. Thar's a hole in the side. Musta been the dynamite."

"How bigga hole?" The Thiokol engineers were frantic.

"Wal, I done grabbed the steel and swung all the way around without hittin' anything. Didn't even hit the side. Hole must be at least ten feet wide."

After the initial panic and consultation with structural engineers, the open bottom was plugged, and the large hole in the side was repaired, so on went the project.

The plans for the final construction contract were a week from completion in the fall of 1963 when the Chief Engineer sent an unsigned mimeographed memo to all but three of the design and drafting staff essentially stating: "As of next Friday you are terminated. There will be no severance pay, and please do not leave the office during working hours to apply for another job. We still have a little over week to finish the contract plans, so we expect every employee to continue at full speed. Thank you for making this project a success."

Even the Rust Engineering employees who had moved from Pittsburgh were given only a week to sell their Florida homes and return. As the employees neared riot stage, the Chief Engineer hid in his office. Three engineers had not received the notice of termination. We were left to supervise the project completion. Ray Grehofsky and I begged draftsmen to make corrections, but we were told where to go. Those were the longest hours we spent on any project. Day and night for eleven days, we did the drafting, checking drawings, writing specifications, and occasionally eating at our tables, while the terminated employees glared at us. At least after eight hours a day they were gone.

The final contract design was delivered to Thiokol, and we wondered what was next for the handful of remaining employees. My answer came a few days later. The Mason Rust joint venture was dissolved. Ray and I were transferred to a project in Greeneville, Tennessee. It was a research and development project to design textile machinery. The fabrics were to be sold for a newly invented process that promised to revolutionize the paper making industry. Paper and textiles were new fields for me, but I was ready to try. We arranged for storage of our furniture and headed to Tennessee.

DETOUR TO TENNESSEE

It had been less than a year in Jacksonville, and we were now moving to design the textile equipment for Formex, the company we were being loaned to in Greeneville, Tennessee. It was only the previous year that President Kennedy gave what came to be known as the "Moon Speech," where he assured the crowd that America would "go to the moon in this decade." It appeared that my dreams of helping to put a man on the moon were gone.

The family loaded up our luggage into the car and headed for Atlanta on Friday, November 22, 1963. I was to drive to Greeneville to find a furnished place to live while Linda and the kids stayed in Atlanta for Thanksgiving. As we drove north, the news blared out "Assassination attempt! President Kennedy has been shot in Dallas." We were in shock like the rest of the country. By the time we got to Atlanta, we knew he was gone. What would happen to the Apollo Program? Little did I know then that months later I would return to Jacksonville to work on that very program.

Ray and I found furnished apartments two doors apart in a second floor above a flower shop, and the two families moved in. It was cramped quarters for a family of four in each unit, and the heating system was a mess. Early December in the mountains was a new experience. The apartment would get cold, and when the heat came on, it was like a blast furnace. Shortly after arriving, we were transferred to the Formex payroll.

Our assignment was to complete the design of a large textile coating and finishing machine and to design a modification to weaving machines that would provide superior paper machine textiles. The company, Formex, had developed in the laboratory a polyester fabric which would reduce the amount of heat needed for making paper. When coated with a sealant, the fabric would outlast conventional felt and reduce maintenance on paper machines. Tests on small samples were successful.

Our task was to take those lab tests and build a coating machine that would handle one-piece fabrics forty feet wide and over one-fifth of a mile long.

The fabric coating process was done in seven steps:

1. Weave the fabric to customer's specifications.
2. Load the fabric on the lead roll.
3. Thread it through the tension control rollers, coating vat, heat set section, and attach it to the end roll.
4. Fill the treating vat with sealant.
5. Start the heat set radiant heaters.
6. Start the rollers. The speed of both rolls was varied to keep a constant speed through the heaters.
7. Roll the entire fabric through the heat set section.
8. Package and ship.

The first customer's fabric had been woven days before, and it was waiting for sealing as soon as the finishing machine was operational. Testing of the machine had not been completed, but the customer was pressing for immediate delivery. All the components had passed their individual tests, but we had no fabric large enough to test the entire machine in operation. Management decided to use the customer's fabric for the test, over our objections. "We hired you to make it work, and it better. This fabric is worth about $100,000! Get to it!"

Ray and I were most apprehensive about the tension roller controls, which were a novel design of Ray's. If the tension got too tight, the coating would not be uniform, but if it was too loose, the fabric would droop down on the radiant heaters and burn through, ruining it. At each turn of the fabric rolls, the diameter changed and the speed of the motors had to adjust slightly to keep the fabric at a constant speed in the coating vat and over the radiant heat section. If not, the coating would be uneven and the fabric ruined. There were no computers then, so pneumatic controllers were used.

We attached a scrap fabric to lead the good fabric through, crossed our fingers and hit the start button. Our baby woke up, began the process flawlessly. As the fabric reached mid point we congratulated each other—prematurely. Our baby burped and the fabric slowly sank toward the heaters. In a panic, I dove off the top of the machine onto the fabric just ahead of the heaters. I sunk to the floor, and my weight pulled it just barely tight enough. The fabric had not yet hit the heaters. The controls caught up and raised me gently. The fabric was saved.

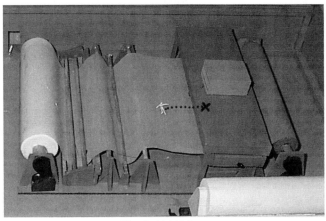

The $100,000 Leap

"You should have jumped onto the other side! The cloth could have dragged you into the heater and fried you!" yelled Ray.

"Thanks a lot," I responded, "Do you want to try it again?" He laughed. It wasn't necessary. The machine was adjusted and worked fine.

We were told later, "That one fabric sold for enough to pay for the construction of the entire finishing machine."

Greeneville was a small mountain town in the 1960s and had few amenities or facilities for outsiders. The countryside was beautiful, living was informal (it was said that dressing up meant clean bib overalls, and going formal meant starched overalls). The only restaurant was the coffee shop at the motel, and before our families arrived Ray and I had eaten there too often. Before Linda and the kids arrived in Greeneville, Ray and I took Rosalee (Ray's wife) to the fanciest place in town—the Elks Club—where we feasted on frozen lobster and melted oleomargarine. To celebrate my family's arrival, we took our wives on a trip across the Smokies for a fancy meal in Asheville. That one trip was all we mustered, since Linda got car sick riding on crooked roads. We pretty much stayed in the rental apartment, especially when the snow came down.

From early December on, we were marooned. Even getting to the office in the snow was difficult. The US highway through town was kept clear, but other roads weren't plowed. Local folk sometimes even walked down the center of the snow covered roads, slowing all traffic to their speed. Christmas Eve was particularly bad. Ray had waited to buy their family tree until that evening and left work early but the lot was closed. Luckily, a sign was left offering trees free, and he got home just before the ice hit.

I was not so lucky. By the time I was ready to leave, ice covered the roads, and I was not even able to drive out of the parking lot. Our flower shop apartment was only two blocks away, and I decided to walk. The problem was that a high ridge had to be crossed on foot. The road crossing the ridge was too icy, so I climbed using the ditch for a path. Enough weeds were still poking through the ice to grab and pull myself up the ridge. Sweating, I reached the top and started down. Out went both feet and I slid down on my seat, gaining speed as I went. The traffic light at the bottom of the hill turned just as I slid across the main highway on the seat of my pants, I waved to the lone car stopped at the red light. Instead of waving back, he just stared.

Christmas was cozy with presents bunched under our two-foot high tree perched on top of the TV set. We knew this was not the place for us to settle and made plans to return to Jacksonville. Shortly before the assignment was completed, Linda went back to Jacksonville to find a rental house for the move.

It had now been just over a year since leaving Texas, and our house there had not yet sold, so money was getting short. I began traveling to Jacksonville on weekends to move boxes of belongings in order to reduce the final moving cost. I removed the rear cushion and seat back to make more room and loaded the car until it was almost sitting on the axles. About 2:00 AM Saturday morning, as I was passing through Hoboken, Georgia, I heard a siren and saw flashing lights. What now? I had carefully slowed below the speed limit because I had been warned of speed traps in small south Georgia towns. He pulled me over, and I rolled down the window.

"You didn't fool me by slowing down, Tennessee," he snarled, "I know what you mountain boys bring through here, moonshine! Get out of the car, slowly."

He pulled out his pistol. Seat belts were not common at that time, but I just had to have the latest gadgets and had installed my own. As I clicked the latch to release the belt, he thought I was cocking a weapon! He raised his pistol and pushed the barrel into my face.

"*Seat belt!*" I hollered. He cocked the hammer.

"Look, both hands!" I continued.

He shined the flashlight in my face and said, "Git out, and keep both hands in plain sight. I'll open the door." He did. "I guess you don't have a pistol. I'm sure glad I didn't shoot you!" I was glad, too.

I unlatched the seat belt the rest of the way, got out, and showed him the car was full of boxes and small furniture. "I'm moving, not hauling 'shine." He was still shaking as he apologized and let me continue on to Florida. I was still shaking, too. I found a rest room before I left town—just in time. The incident did keep me from getting drowsy for the rest of the trip. That night I gave thanks that I was still alive. God was still watching over us.

The next Monday while I was at work for my last week, the moving van arrived, five days early! We were renting houses in Tennessee and Florida, had an unsold home in Texas, and the movers arrived early. That meant a motel for a week. I refused. I just wasn't going to pay for a fourth place. I kept three chair cushions, one pillow, two pans, enough dishes for meals, a blanket, and an ice chest. The stove stayed with the house, so I had a way to cook. The movers took everything else. I camped in the empty house for the week.

The first night, I found that cushions on a hardwood floor didn't stay together. Every time I moved they slid and I hit the floor. That was solved by sleeping in a closet where the walls kept the cushions together. Besides, it was warmer in the closet. Saturday's trip after settling the utility bills put me back into Hoboken again after midnight. This time the officer blew his horn and waved. I waved back. A shiver went down my spine as I recalled how close a call I had.

With the new job in Jacksonville, this would be three moves and five employers in the fifteen months since leaving Texas. I was glad that Suzanne and Steve were one and three, so they didn't have to go through the moving transitions I struggled with as a teen. I was now headed for the most rewarding job of my career, the architectural and engineering firm, Reynolds Smith and Hills, one of the largest A&E firms in the south. My first assignment was in the advanced projects division.

APOLLO
AND THE MOON

The previous year, before leaving for Tennessee, I applied for a job at Reynolds Smith and Hills, the Jacksonville based architect-engineering firm designing the three Saturn V Mobile Launchers for the Apollo moon landing. Three launch umbilical towers were designed by RS&H and the structures were under construction. Design of the mechanical and electrical systems was in process, and RS&H was searching for engineers in the advanced projects division. After a successful interview with Hoyt Broward, the division manager, and Ralph Heim, the partner in charge, we went back to Hoyt's office to discuss salary.

"You're making more than I am!" Hoyt exclaimed.

"I don't see how I can consider a pay cut," I replied. "I'm leaving for Tennessee for an assignment in a textile research facility, and my income is going to increase."

Hoyt went on to explain the many benefits of the state-of-the-art work done in his division, and the great opportunity for advancement. I decided to inquire about fringe benefits. They had a medical plan, vacations, and sick leave were comparable and so were holidays.

"Do you have a profit sharing or retirement program?" I asked.

"We expect engineers to save for their own future, and our pay is adequate for you to do that," he replied. No help there.

The cordial interview ended with my suggestion, "Why don't you call when you get a raise? I'm interested if the pay is right. I'll keep in touch."

Several months later, Hoyt called me in Tennessee. He had gotten his raise. The job was mine if I accepted. I did, and that brought us back to Jacksonville. The furniture arrived in Jacksonville while I was "camping in the closet" in Tennessee, so by the time I arrived, the house was all set up and most everything unpacked. I was ready for the new assignment.

Monday morning, I completed the employment documents and was assigned my office. I was disappointed when I found I was not starting on the space program. A new project had been awarded to RS&H by the Navy. During WWII, sonar research and development was conducted in Orlando, Florida, in Lake Gem Mary, a small fresh water lake south of town. The Navy was planning to conduct future research, development and testing of advanced sonar arrays to be located deep in the ocean. They desired to perform future work in salt water, and at pressures of up to 5,000 pounds per square inch (psi), many times more than the 17 psi in the current lake. This pressure far exceeded the maximum pressure on the deepest operational submarine, and the desired fifty-foot diameter exceeded steel mills' capacity to make steel plate thick enough. Our task was to prepare the conceptual design to prove feasibility and the funding request to be presented to Congress.

Hoyt drove us to Orlando to meet Captain Owsley and his staff, and after a full day's review of their requirements, we returned to Jacksonville that evening. On the way, I was exposed to his driving. He insisted on always driving and had to look at you as he talked. It was common for someone to sit in the front seat with his back to the windshield to encourage him to look forward. I was doing just that when I turned around and saw a sign in the median. "Mr. Broward, there's a sign ahead," I warned. He looked back at the road, heading straight for the sign. "It says *keep right!*" I shouted. Just in time, he cut the wheels to the right and the rear tire hit the curb, partially straightening us out, but now we were off the road on the shoulder. Hoyt stopped the car less than five feet from the shore of Lake Monroe. If the curb hadn't knocked us back, we would both have gone for a swim. I got back home late and slept poorly that night.

Just as in the Thiokol booster shell, the Navy project required stretching the limits of design and manufacturing. Pressure vessel and seals experience was again needed, but this time the military was not dictating the design. We could design a test facility without compromising safety. Using Southwest Research as a consultant, we proposed two spherical tanks, one inside the other, each capable of withstanding 2500 psi. With the water-filled chamber between the two tanks at 2500 psi the outer tank would operate at 2500 psi. The inner tank could be pressurized to 5000 psi because the 2500 psi on its exterior would compensate for half the pressure. With the proper controls, it would work. Following is the conceptual model of the facility. The front wall is removed to expose the interior. For the model, I used pieces sawn from a burned out computer main board to simulate the electronics.

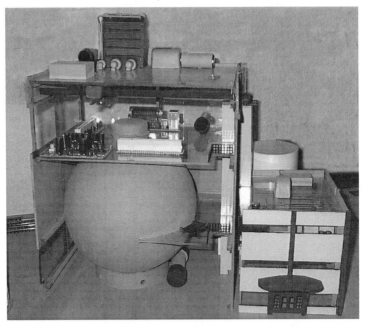

Concept Model of Underwater Sound Research Laboratory

The facility we designed had two drawbacks. It was proposed during the time Lyndon Johnson was stretching the nation's financial capacity by fighting the

Vietnam War and funding the Great Society welfare programs. Military funding was stalled. Further, the proposed site in Orlando was seeing Disney World in its future. Lake Gem Mary would no longer be in a rural area.

Eventually a scaled-down facility was constructed closer to Washington. It was a disappointment that my first project at RSH was only partly successful, but it gave me the opportunity to meet my first Navy captain, Captain Owsley, the facility's officer in charge. For a highly ranked military officer, I found him to be exceptionally cordial, cooperative, and friendly. The project served as a foundation for many future successful projects for the Navy.

Shortly after completing this project, I finally got to work on the space program. By this time, construction of the three launch umbilical towers (LUT) was well underway, and the crawler-transporter had driven under one of the towers. This was to be the first test to lift the LUT and drive it a short distance and return to the construction site. It was much lighter than final weight because none of the equipment was installed, and it carried no rocket, but it was the heaviest of the three.

As in many first tests, lessons were learned. The lift went fine, and the crawler began to move. Then came the first attempt to turn. As the hydraulic cylinders tried to move, the crawler treads tried to turn sideways. Then, everyone heard the sound *pop, pop, pop*. The friction was too great, the bearings flew out of the crawler. The LUT was returned to the mounts and let down, and the head scratching began. How to reduce the friction? Simple—a thicker layer of river gravel was placed over the paving, and it moved with the tracks. No computer needed, just common sense.

My responsibility was to design and test the gas piping systems serving every level of the tower. The piping included nitrogen piped to every electrical device. A possibility of fuel spills or vapor leaks was ever-present with the fuelled rocket on the launcher. To prevent explosions, each cabinet was pressurized with nitrogen and furnished with a bleed device to let a small amount escape. This assured the cabinet was constantly purged and safe. In addition, the elevator machine room at the top of the LUT was pressurized and purged. After completing the design for the tower, it was time to present the proposed construction contract, design drawings, and specifications to NASA for approval prior to bidding. The roll of drawings was almost a foot in diameter and the book containing the bidding package almost two inches thick. The model I built of the LUT with a Saturn V on the deck and the VAB in the background is shown below. In this photo, the LUT has been turned around to show the Saturn V better.

Scale Model of the Mobile Launcher Carrying the Saturn V Moon Rocket in front of the Vehicle Assembly Building

In the 1960s, word processing was unknown, and all contracts and specifications were typed by secretaries. Any changes meant hours of retyping. The drawings were all manually completed on Mylar film—each sheet almost three feet high and three and a half feet wide. For the review, two sets of drawings and four books containing the contract and specifications were delivered to NASA, in preparation for the formal approval meeting. RS&H's

Partner in Charge, Ralph Heim insisted that everything be done perfectly, without exception.

Two years earlier in Texas, I learned to operate an offset printing press after convincing Sparkler's management that we could produce our own brochures, technical bulletins, and price lists for our sales representatives. I had expanded the task by adding color illustrations to increase their appeal. By printing in house, turnaround time was minimized, and we had the ability to customize sales data for specific prospects—all at a reasonable cost. I learned to prepare the printing plates, ink the press, print all the materials, and clean the ink drum after the run was complete. Cleaning up my hands was a different matter. I often went through the day my hands stained by several colors of ink.

I proposed a similar approach for this NASA project. Instead of the customary black and white covers of our competitors, we now had the red, white and blue NASA logo on the cover of this submittal. It was added prominently—next to the official name of the NASA group: Launch Operations Center (LOC). Ralph was delighted! This surely would be a feather in his cap. The printing was complete and the package ready to hand deliver for the formal meeting the next day. The four books with the special cover were wrapped separately. Ralph would personally present them to "Buck" Buchanan at the start of the meeting.

But like many well-intentioned projects, a huge obstacle appeared the day before the submittal. NASA informed us that management had decided that all projects would now use "Kennedy Space Center" instead of LOC. Since the new cover design was to be a surprise, Ralph did not want to ask for a delay in the meeting. "Charlie, you have overnight to redesign and reprint those covers. We will be ready, won't we?" It was obvious that it was an order, not a question!

The NASA Merrit Island facility was renamed Kennedy Space Center by Lyndon Johnson the previous year, 1963. I was not at all enthusiastic about the change. President Eisenhower had signed the bill creating NASA in 1958, and he was my hero growing up. To me, it seemed that Kennedy had been taking all the credit. In addition, I was adamantly opposed to JFK's casual approach to water and air pollution. His quote, "Dilution is the solution to pollution" was a lie! I had almost lost my life four times at the refinery, and three of those accidents were directly related to dumping wastes into the air or the water. His simplistic approach was unacceptable to me. But Ma Perkins' advice from high school came back to me: "If you are faced with a brick wall, don't butt your head against it, go around or go over, but get past all hurdles in life. Don't give up."

I realized that this was not the time or place to take a stand. JFK was now the "hero" of the day, after his assassination the previous year. It was inevitable, and looking back on those days, I believe that Congress might not have appropriated the funds for the moon landing program if JFK had not become the fallen hero.

It was an all night task, but in the lull while the covers were being reprinted, a prank slowly took shape in my brain. The new covers were printed, the ink was dry, and it was time to place them into the spiral binding. What if I put the old covers on top of the new ones, and as soon as it was noticed, I would simply tear the obsolete cover off, revealing the corrected version? The package containing the four books had the new cover attached, so it should be a surprise. Ralph was too stiff anyway. Buck would have a good laugh when it was over. I decided to make some additions to the obsolete cover to make the joke better, and sealed the package.

During the two-hour drive to the Cape (name change and all, it was still the Cape to me!), I worried that the prank might backfire, but it was too late.

The conference room chairs were all full, and the meeting was brought to order. Ralph made some introductory remarks, unrolled the drawings and then began to tear the paper off the four books. *I better be ready to leave if this backfires,* I thought to myself.

Without looking at his copy, Ralph slid a book with the color logo down the long conference table to Buck. As Ralph smiled, Buck read slowly, "*Kennedy Space Center, formerly* Launch Operations Center, *Formerly the Alabama Boon Docks!*" (referring to the original team's location in Huntsville). I had typed the words shown in italics onto the original covers. "Ralph, what in h——- is this, some joke?" I looked at Ralph whose face was now purple, and his eyes bore through me just like my dad's did during the "big eye glares" I got as a kid. I slowly stood up walked up to Buck, reached for his book and tore off the fake cover. Underneath was the brand new cover with the new name!

The room was completely silent for a minute, then Buck smiled, then laughed out loud. The rest of the room followed his lead. It turned out to be a welcome break in the tension we all felt after months of sixty- to eighty-hour weeks without a break. "You took a big chance, young man," Ralph whispered to me, but after NASA's acceptance of the design, we all celebrated that evening. Even Buck relaxed with us.

I designed the corresponding systems on the VAB and the mobile service structure, used to install the explosive devices at the launch pad. Designs for some launch pad interfaces were added to our contract later.

It was at that time Linda and I began searching for a place to build a permanent home, a project that is described in the next chapter.

In the early days at the Cape, there was little or no security. I even drove Linda to see the work. As I drove under the LUT, there were dozens of children and adults climbing the 450 foot structure like it was a jungle gym. The word got out quickly and the security forces stopped the weekend "fun."

I was leaving Complex 39 one afternoon in a blinding rainstorm and gusty wind. Suddenly, I realized that I had a flat tire and pulled off on the shoulder. I had no raincoat and the storm continued, so I took off my suit coat and tie (yes, in those days casual dress for engineers was not appreciated) and got out the jack. The car was up in a jiffy, and the wheel removed. Just then a large truck went through a pond of water on the road, soaking me to the skin. As I wiped away the water, I saw the car had also been hit by the same wave, and it was off the jack and on the ground—with the spare wheel still in the trunk! I used the tire iron to dig a hole in the oyster shell and finally got the car up and the spare in place. By then, I was covered in sand, shell and mud. I took off my shirt and muddy pants, used the shirt to wipe as much mud as possible and threw the soggy mess in the trunk. I could drive to the motel in my under shorts, wait for the coast to clear, and sneak in to get my dry clothes. I was cold, so on went the heater. As I drove north, I saw the new security gate. I had forgotten about that. I reached for my badge and realized it was on my shirt in the trunk—*oops*. I stopped, ran to the trunk and found my badge. "Nice polka dots," the guard commented, as he waved me through. Someone must have told, because the next day I found new under shorts on my desk with a note: "No polka dots, sorry."

Work those years never stopped with a forty-hour week. It was common to work sixty or seventy hours to keep up with the workload. Engineers were classified as "supervisory personnel," so overtime or comp time was not allowed. The brutal schedule was aggravated by assignment to other projects in parallel with the NASA project. My long workweeks ended abruptly in March 1966. Linda's father passed away, and we took three days off for the services and family matters. On my return, I was informed that my paycheck would be docked three days pay! After my protest was denied, it was a forty-hour week—no more, no less. I had been at RS&H for two years without a raise, and this was the last straw.

It turned out to be a good decision. We were building our first house. I was contractor, plumber, electrician, and every other job I couldn't afford to hire out. Months later, the policy was revised and straight time pay and comp time were authorized for extra hours, but by then the house was almost complete.

The long hours resumed, and everyone was getting worn out, especially Hoyt, my boss. He had a difficult time with delegating responsibility and reviewed every detail of work performed by dozens of engineers. He checked every drawing after it was approved by the design engineer. He even proofread every single document including thousands of pages of specifications. He once confided to me that he never read the newspaper without having a red pencil ready to correct errors. He even practiced rewriting articles to improve them. Nothing was ever good enough for him, and he constantly changed engineers' work. This extreme concentration on work led Hoyt to be the most distracted and dangerous driver I ever met. His close calls while driving were legendary.

One morning he entered the office with his necktie over his shoulder. Jim Hutchinson said, "Wait, Mr. Broward, your tie is crooked," and reached to straighten it. Hoyt swung his fist at him but missed.

Embarrassed by his reaction, he explained, "On the way to work I ran into a man at an intersection, and he grabbed my tie and tried to hit me, but the policeman stopped him. I guess I'm not over that." He never explained more about the incident, but the next week, he confided another near miss to me.

"Some fool in khaki pants and shirt was standing in the road waving at me last night, and I almost hit him. It would serve him right!"

"That's strange," I replied "Did you see anything else?"

"Well there was a car with blue flashing lights there."

"That was a highway patrolman!"

"No, they have red lights."

"They did several years ago, but now they're blue."

"He should be more careful!" That ended the discussion. Hoyt never lost a debate.

During an especially trying period, Hoyt drove to the Cape for a meeting with NASA. I protested riding with him after Gordon Priday reported the previous trip results. Gordon insisted on driving, but Hoyt refused, compromising only by saying jokingly, "Gordon, I'll drive until I drive into a ditch, then you drive." Hoyt was in a ditch before leaving Gordon's subdivision.

We left Jacksonville at midmorning and arrived at the vehicle assembly building for lunch. I was designing piping systems in the VAB, piping that would connect to the launchers. After lunch, he instructed me to wait in an exhibit room while he visited the men's room. Fifteen minutes later, I was still waiting. I went to the men's room to check for trouble. He had been working to his endurance limit and might need help.

On entering, there was no sign of Hoyt. I even checked each stall. Another thirty minutes waiting in the exhibit room, and I decided to check the parking lot. No sign of Hoyt, but the car was there. This time I returned to the room and called the office. They had not heard from him, so I left word and waited there until five. By then his car was gone. I was on foot, miles from the office! Fortunately, I was having dinner with one of the men from the office, and he drove to the VAB and picked me up. No one had seen Hoyt or his car.

We arrived at the office at dark, just as Hoyt did. "Where have you been?" he demanded. I was speechless!

"You left me all afternoon at the VAB," I finally replied.

"No such thing," he responded. "You drove down yesterday. Now, we have to work. Just skip dinner. And, Dick, you go and eat, we've got lots to do since Charlie has been goofing off all afternoon." Dick left, and we began work. After a few minutes, he said, "I'm hungry, let's get a bite to eat."

As he got into the car, he realized the office was unlocked. He handed me the key and waited in the car. When I got back, he was *gone*. For the second time that day he left me. This time I was locked out of the building, at night and with no car, two miles from the nearest phone. Dick had recognized Hoyt's strange behavior and returned to the office, then we went to dinner. On our return to the office, there was no sign of Hoyt or his car, so I went to the motel. Gordon Priday, our lead electrical engineer, met me at my room. Hoyt had just left, and Gordon was worried. In the middle of a conversation, Hoyt got a blank look on his face and began running across the parking lot, out onto the highway and disappeared into the night. We followed, but by then he was nowhere to be found.

The next morning he was at breakfast, acting as nothing had happened. He had no recollection of the previous day. He was required to take a two-week vacation to settle down, and returned in fine shape, red pencil sharpened and ready for work.

A night launch was scheduled for one evening when we had no work planned at the office. There were no visitors allowed for that launch, but I was determined to drive as close as possible to see the Titan solid fuelled rocket lift off. Ever since my experience with the Thiokol solid rocket project, I had looked forward to seeing one in operation. It was an Air Force launch, and the pad was located some distance from NASA's Complex 39. I had no road map for the Air Force launch area, so I drove close enough to see the complex in the distance. As darkness fell, I began to drive toward the launch site along a sandy trail through the palmettos, stopping in an area surrounded by sand dunes. I couldn't see the launch tower, but I was sure it was closer than watching from the main road.

Suddenly, I saw a blinding light followed by the loudest roar I ever heard. There to my left, just a short distance away was the Titan, lifting slowly into the darkness. I was too close! A hot blast rocked the car, and I had to cover my ears and close my eyes because the heat and light was so intense. I dove for the floor. When it was over, the inside of the car was as hot as a summer afternoon. High in the distance was a small glow from the Titan. I had missed seeing the rest of the launch. I didn't care. I was happy that I hadn't been roasted like a Thanksgiving turkey.

I got out to check for damage. One headlight didn't work, and the car was covered with a light coating of sand. I started to leave, but the door handle was still too hot to touch. I got in the passenger side and quickly returned to the motel. It was a long time before I got to sleep that night.

The next major task I undertook on the MLs (The LUTs had been renamed mobile launchers by then) was the worst assignment of my career. RSH had been selected to write ten operations and maintenance manuals for all major systems of the MLs—the structure, plumbing, quench water systems to protect equipment from heat during a launch, air conditioning, electrical, elevators, crane, heat and blast shields, and some I don't even remember. The work included thousands of components, required expanded diagrams, parts lists, and lots of information I considered bookkeeping, not engineering. It was pure drudgery, interrupted occasionally by a new project, usually for another client. It did have one future benefit, though. When I began constructing scale models for my model railroad, I had no drawings of the ML details to guide me. After a couple weeks search of photos on the Internet, I actually found part of the manual I wrote showing details of the structure. The scale model I constructed is based on that manual. I realized the Internet version was the very one I wrote when I noticed a couple typos, and that it was in a typewriter font used only on the manuals I wrote.

I was assigned one other project for NASA, the design and testing of the emergency alarm systems. Concerns for accidents and fires was uppermost in the minds of NASA management, and I was to tackle the fire and emergency alarm design, installation observation, and testing. The system was specified to include standard fire alarm hardware, with a back-up system to test and report the operating status of all components. In addition, a third system monitored the back-up system. It was interesting, but it included the writing of another operations and maintenance manual, which was completed during the installation of the system.

The manual was done, the equipment installed, and it was time for the final testing. Equipped with access to NASA's communication system, we would be able to station personnel in every location and complete the test in two days. The first day, January 26, went smoothly, and we should have been able to finish by quitting time on Friday. I had a new project waiting for Monday.

Shortly after lunch, problems cropped up. Not in the tests, but in the communications system. We were disconnected several times and quitting time was approaching. At about 5:30, NASA informed us that a problem with communications on an adjacent complex required canceling the balance of our test. We could leave and resume Monday. I left for Jacksonville and a quiet weekend.

It turned out that the "*problem*" was not just a problem, it was the catastrophe everyone feared, the Apollo 204 capsule fire that cost the lives of Gus Grissom, Roger Chaffee, and Edward White. Every time I look at the photo in my file of the open hatch and the charred interior, I shudder. It was a horrible mistake.

Testing was resumed and the ML fire and emergency system was approved, but only after NASA was convinced that the system I designed was superior to the system on Complex 37 where the three astronauts lost their lives.

Later, I was able to inspect the ML after the first Saturn 5 unmanned test launch. The damage to the ML was minimal, in spite of problems with the deck quench water. There were no computer programs for predicting the effect of the flame from the first stage booster, but during my final year at Ga. Tech, we used a procedure for estimating the impact. It was a graphical method to be used in future computer analysis, but very time consuming. Buck Buchanan, our NASA liaison, asked me to try it on the ML, assuming the 50,000 gallon deck quench water system failed. The analysis showed the only negative effect would be a small amount of paint would burn off. The extra heat and blast shields would be needed only in a booster failure. The biggest damage I recall was to the engine service platform, which was tied to the ground several hundred feet away from the launch tower. It had been lifted from its anchors and blown several yards away. It looked like the program was on course, and we would make it to the moon before 1970.

My new project proved to be a real letdown and my last at the Cape. It was another operations and maintenance manual! I couldn't believe it! At least this project was interesting. The manual was to include all the ordinance systems on the Saturn V moon rocket—the capsule escape tower, stage separation explosives, and dozens of other devices that removed components in flight. Normally, the manufacturer would provide the manual, but each stage and major component had a different supplier. NASA wanted a single manual covering all. Everyone desired the job, but none wanted a competitor to inspect their equipment. It was a compromise for RS&H to write the documentation, as we neither designed nor supplied any of the components. I was able to complete most of the work from information on components furnished by each supplier, but photos of the assembled parts would make the manuals more useful. The photographs would also identify components we were not allowed to copy for the needed illustrations.

None of the ordinance was installed in the VAB for safety reasons. All had to be installed at the launch pad, using the MSS (mobile service structure—originally named arming tower). My security badge allowed access to the assembly areas, but not the launch pad or the MSS and not to inspect the assembled Saturn V. The contractor for the launch pad security refused me a badge, hoping that RS&H could not complete our contract. Many suppliers felt we were too close to NASA anyway. Keeping me from meeting the deadline would fix us.

In spite of numerous requests by NASA, my badge was bogged down in red tape. I was told, "You're a bright engineer, find a way." I did. The chance came during a huge fuel spill at the launch pad during test fuelling the first stage. This Saturn was not to fly; it was only on the pad for the fuelling test. I had been unsuccessfully trying to find a way to sneak in with a photographer (he had a

RUN FOR YOUR LIFE

badge). My chance came as the evacuation alarm sounded and people rushed out of the gate, I ran to the guard and asked, "Which way to the spill, I've got a photographer to take pictures." Without even looking at my badge, he pointed the way. We rushed onto the MSS and up to the access platforms. Using tools I brought along, I removed the access panels, took the photos, and replaced the covers. The removal and replacement had been reviewed and approved by NASA and none of the devices were armed, so the risk was minimal. Many successful photos were taken until we opened the door to the S-IV platform, where the lunar landing module was located. There stood a guard who had not evacuated. Before we could back out, he grabbed me. He saw my badge did not allow me on the vehicle, and confiscated it, along with the camera. The stack of Polaroids was in my pocket, but he missed them.

"Charles *Space?*" he exclaimed. "This badge has to be a fake. No one is named Space." After I showed my driver's license and American Express card to him, he accepted the name as genuine, but now my badge was gone! A phone call to NASA released me from custody, and I went back to Jacksonville to complete the manual. After congratulating me for ingenuity, I was told my badge had to be permanently revoked. Even though my efforts were successful, the word that an unauthorized person breached security demanded severe action. The sacrifice turned out to be worthwhile. The manual was completed, and I was assigned to other projects, but never another manual.

The new project was one that would prove to be just as exciting as NASA. I was assigned to develop a command/communications center for defense of the Panama Canal, in the event of nuclear attack.

Over 27,000 workers had died building this vital link between the Pacific Ocean and the Caribbean. Over 20,000 died during the French attempt starting in the 1880s and almost 6,000 during the American program from 1904 to 1914. The Panama Canal had been completed in 1914, the year that World War I began. The United States was neutral during the early years, and the Canal was not considered a likely target of German Naval vessels. After the armistice of 1918, military planners convinced Congress to appropriate funds for the defense of this strategic asset. In the 1920s, attack by sea seemed to be the only credible danger.

Between WWI and WWII defenses against naval attack and bombardment were installed, including many Battleship "Rifles" (14" and 16" bore guns). Some were fixed in fortified bunkers, others mounted on railroad cars, capable of moving to another position if spotted from the attacking battleships. An extensive system of rail lines was installed and many fire control batteries constructed to spot enemy ships and direct fire of the mobile guns. In the 1940s, defenses against attack by air were added. The lesson from Pearl Harbor proved that bombing could also be deadly.

The fire control batteries constructed in the 1920s were constructed of thick reinforced concrete walls and roofs to withstand naval bombardment, but in the shadow of the Cuban Missile Crisis of 1962, more was needed. A near hit with a nuclear weapon would leave the Canal defenseless, and without communications to the outside world.

The project included a redesign and reconstruction of one of the batteries constructed in the 1920s for controlling firing of the large naval defense guns. The reconstructed battery would have to survive a nuclear attack and serve as the communications center to coordinate Canal defenses after an A-bomb hit. It was not capable of surviving a direct hit on the facility, but one on the canal itself. Installation of automatic blast gates, reinforced doors similar to those used for bank vaults, air purification to eliminate fallout contamination, and many more critical components were included in the project.

Even though I no longer had my NASA badge, my security clearance was intact. I was not allowed to discuss the Canal project with anyone, and the work was done in a separate, locked room, with access denied even to corporate officers. I could not even let the staff copy drawings for the Corps of Engineers. I was required to make the prints myself and immediately keep them locked up.

As I was recently preparing the scale models of my projects for my model railroad, I had to determine if this could now be discussed, since President Carter had given the Canal away. I found the facility description and photos posted on the Internet by a former guard at the Canal. The "secret" was out, but I'm not adding any more information than is already published.

From this point, our lives entered a new phase, one that brought new projects, new challenges and new rewards. My career evolved from single project assignments to many activities occurring at the same time.

THE DO-IT-YOURSELF HOUSE

Shortly after we settled in following the move from Tennessee, the work at RS&H was going well, and we were ready to put down permanent roots again by building our own house. Steve was now two and Suzanne four. The house we were renting was located at a busy intersection, and with growing children, we preferred a safer location. We had fenced in the back yard to protect the kids from the traffic. One afternoon, there was a knock at the front door. A stranger had Steve by the hand. "Is he yours?" he asked. "I found this youngster wandering along the busy street and brought him back. I thought you might miss him." Steve had climbed over the four-foot fence and crossed the busy street. I was supposed to be babysitting while Linda was at a meeting. I was startled that he got out while I wasn't watching. I thanked the stranger, and we decided that evening to start looking in earnest for a new place to live. From then on, we hired more competent sitters when we went out.

One evening as I was driving our sitter home, I asked her where she went to school. "Terry Parker," she answered. "Did you go to Parker too?"

"No, I went to Landon, and there were only three high schools then."

"Wow, Mr. Space! Did you go to school in the *olden days?*" I mumbled something or other in response, but from then on, we hired another teenager, and I kept my mouth shut taking her home. Imagine, olden days! I was only thirty!

We were hoping to find a riverfront lot close to the office. The few that were available were too expensive. We soon discovered a 100-foot wide lot that had only ten feet of solid land on Pottsburg Creek, a tributary of the St. Johns River. At that point, the creek was 500 feet wide and several feet deep. The rest of the lot's waterfront was marsh and too soggy to walk on. The lot was on a quiet street within a mile of the office. The only drawback was the marshland—too swampy to access the river. It was more than a hundred feet from the good land to the river on the swamp side. I convinced the owner, Mr. Kellow, that he could use half my purchase price to dig a canal giving his eight other swamp front lots access to the river. He would profit by raising the price of the other lots by thousands of dollars. I even found a contractor who would dig it for the right price. He agreed.

The problem with our proposal was that to dig the canal, we would have to pay the full lot price up front—no installment sale. We still owned the house in Texas and the parcel of land on the future South Loop in Houston. The chance of financing another house was slim until the Conroe house sold. We agreed to rent that house until it sold to offset the payments we were still making. The Houston South Loop was announced shortly before we found the lot, and we were offered considerably more than we paid for our tract of land along the new highway. I was hoping to hold on to that land until the price rose even higher, but the prospect of living on the waterfront won out, and we sold. We now owned our own waterfront lot, and it was 400 feet deep, so I could even have a garden. It also had about a ten-foot slope down to the water, so it was safe from flooding during a hurricane.

Mr. Kellow, true to his word, hired a contractor to dig the canal. In those days, there were no permits required, so construction began in a week. Every lunch hour I visited the lot to observe the progress. The dragline worked on large timber platforms to keep from sinking into the soft marsh muck. The operator always left for lunch before I arrived, so I was able to walk out to the dragline platform on a rickety twelve-inch wide plank to imagine how the finished canal would look after the water cleared. One day, I visited the site in a new light blue suit. I didn't know that the operator had dug through an alligator den that morning, and "Mama Gator" was very unhappy. She lunged onto the platform just as I stepped off the walkway. We saw each other at the same time, and I took off running to shore. She gave chase, but slid off the side. Halfway to shore, I did too, right into chest deep black ooze. I waded to shore faster than I had ever moved before and escaped. But now, I was a mess and had a 1:00 appointment with Mr. Heim and a prospective client. I rushed home, showered and changed, to arrive ten minutes late to face a glare that would have melted an iceberg. When I explained, the new client laughed and we got the job.

Linda and I chose a house photo from *Better Homes and Gardens*, a two-story house we would sink partway into the hill. I drew up the revised plans, pulled the building permit, and became my own contractor for the first time. I had modified the conventional home construction to add some energy saving features (the engineer coming out in me) to the ridicule of the architectural section at RS&H. "Energy is so cheap, you'll never get your money back," I was told. Oil was about $4.00 a barrel, and electricity generated by the city was one sixth of today's cost. When prices skyrocketed during the 1973 oil embargo, I was glad I was too hard-headed to listen to them.

It was now time to clear the lot of the large pine trees and brush. I found a timber company willing to pay for the trees, which were long-leaf yellow pine—a nearly extinct variety. Before they would cut them, Linda and I had to remove the underbrush. We worked three weekends and the brush was piled and ready to burn. Our progress was watched by the neighborhood kids, who were not happy we were taking over their play and fishing place. Shortly after I lit the large pile of brush, I discovered that several aerosol paint cans had been hidden in the pile. One by one they exploded, spreading burning material into the woods. In a few minutes, the fire had jumped to the top of the pines and a major fire ensued. The fire department finally put it out before any houses went up in flames, but none of the neighbors were happy. In a few days, my pines were gone, leaving a number of hardwood trees for shade.

Next came the bulldozer to clear the house site, remove the pine stumps and a few of the trees that were in poor condition. We tied red tape on the trees to save, and grading began. True to form, I visited the lot during lunch. I was in for a shock—only one small group of trees remained, and the operator was starting to take those down, too. The neighborhood kids had removed the tags, and we lost most of the tall trees we planned to save. Linda was heartbroken, but it was too late.

The house construction went surprisingly well after that, until it was time to install the roof trusses. It was a Sunday morning, and the crew arrived at 9:00 AM. The first truss was lifted and fell between the walls! The lumber yard had fabricated them four feet short! The next week they were replaced. Along with the trusses, the plywood for the roof was delivered. The next day, the plywood was gone. Thieves had stolen the entire load. I reported the theft and the police investigated, but to no avail. They told me thieves were even stealing reinforcing rod that had been placed in foundations before the concrete was poured. They suggested deliveries be made as far away from the street as possible, and to keep the police report to file as a casualty loss when we filed our income tax return.

Linda and I installed the plumbing, floors and wiring, and she did the painting. I reminded Dad of his promise to help whenever we built a house, and he showed up one morning ready to work. At noon, he quit and informed me he wouldn't be back. I would have to settle for my part of the sale price when his house was sold. That would be more than enough to pay me for the three years work on his house and my savings bonds that were sold to help pay for it. When his house was sold, I never got my share. I was disappointed but not surprised. We had drifted apart long before.

I was still traveling five days most weeks, and with only one car, the family was pretty much restricted to the neighborhood. Linda was able to catch up on shopping on Saturdays because I had offered an inducement to both children: "The one who behaves best while I'm gone gets to spend the day with Dad." Both loved playing with the piles of scrap lumber as the construction proceeded. Steve especially enjoyed tagging along as I worked on the remaining construction. One day, while I painted the two-story-high eaves of the house, he played and watched. I was busy at the very top of the extension ladder when I felt a tap on my leg. "Hi, Daddy, can I help?" I almost fell off. He was only three at the time.

The construction loan due date was fast approaching, and we were behind schedule. After the "rough in" wiring was complete, I called for inspection and one of the rare corrupt inspectors arrived, exclaiming, "You know, you're taking the bread out of the mouths of an electrician's children by doing the work yourselves." I had taken the wiring examination given by the city and passed, but he would have none of that. He wanted a case of Jack Daniels to approve the work. I refused, and he gave me his alternate, "Rewire every switch and receptacle in this house. If you wired it yourself, I want you to be extra safe. Add a second ground wire to the one required by code. I'll be back tomorrow, and if you're not done, I won't be back again." He was sure we would give in and he would get his liquor.

Linda and I worked all night long, pulling the extra wire to each box, but by 6:00 AM, we were out of wire. She waited at the supply house until they opened, and we installed the last wire just in time for the inspection. But he never showed up. When I called to follow up, he denied everything and told us he had approved the work the previous day. "You did a good job," he sneered.

The day before the construction loan expired was time for the bank's inspection. I was finished with all the work except two sheets of shower paneling beside the bathtub. The inspector checked the rest of the house while I finished. In my rush, I became careless and bumped into a hanging light fixture. It broke, the glass falling onto my wrist and puncturing an artery. Blood was gushing out. I clamped my thumb on the artery to stop the bleeding and completed the work one-handed. The last screw was in place just in time, but when it went through the panel, I heard a hissing sound. I had pierced the gas heater line behind the wall. I turned the gas off, passed inspection, then removed the paneling to fix the pipe. We had our first home designed and built by ourselves. We would move in as soon as the yard was done enough for the kids to play in it. The completion of the rest of the house construction was now in our hands. We were to finish the basement, add a patio and barbecue pit, a swimming pool and a boathouse.

Shortly after moving in, Steve decided he was big enough to start to test who was in charge. He was now four and strong willed. As I was relaxing in my recliner on our second floor balcony, he calmly announced that he was going to do something that I had told him was off-limits. I don't remember what it was, but I recall the results. "Daddy, if you don't let me do that, I'm going to jump off this porch!" Without a word, I got up and went downstairs to the patio, moved all the furniture, returned to my chair without a word.

He looked at me and said, "What did you move that for?"

"Buddy, I won't let you do that, and if you're going to jump, I don't want you to fall on the chairs and hurt yourself."

"Do I have to jump?" he whimpered.

"Of course not, but you can't do what you want, either."

He crawled up onto my lap, hugged me and said, "You're a good daddy."

At four, he also decided he could fly. He pretended to be Batman and climbed up onto the counter, jumped several feet to land on his hobby horse, just like they did in the movies. He had Batman and Roy Rogers mixed up, but that was just the boy in him. He missed and landed beneath the spring-mounted horse, but his right arm got caught in the spring. "Mom," he whined, "I think I hurt my arm. Please don't spank me. It was an accident." It was broken and bent at an odd angle. It was on to the emergency room to get it set. We were lucky that it was less than ten minutes away because this was only the first of many visits. During the recovery, he learned to write left-handed.

The evening I was writing the check for the last doctor bill, he was jumping on the living room couch. That was another "No-No!" As we came into the room, he stopped. His last jump bounced him off onto the side of a marble topped table, and he peeled the back of his scalp down to the skull. We were off to Baptist Hospital again—this time for stitches.

As the scalp wound healed and the stitches were removed, he complained of the itching, but he was forbidden to scratch the wound. One night, he came to us covered in blood from his head to his feet. "I didn't scratch them, honest. I rubbed them on the brick wall. I was just minding you." We shook our heads and smiled. He was right, we didn't tell him not to bang his head on the wall. It reminded me of Ma Perkins' advice in Landon, "If you are faced with a brick wall, don't butt your head against it, go around or go over, but get past all hurdles in life." Steve should have met her. It might have saved some medical expenses. By that trip, he was recognized at the hospital. "Hi, Steve, what happened this time?" the nurse asked as he received new stitches.

It was now time to address the yard. Almost an acre of bare sand was left after the trees were scalped off by mistake. Every time it rained, washed out sand had to be raked back in place. The sand hardly grew anything without addition of some organic matter. We planned on peat moss, but my new RS&H project might provide a better solution.

It was a new process for converting municipal garbage to compost, and it began with the operation of a pilot plant in Largo, Florida. The pilot plant included small-scale equipment to test the process and to obtain the engineering data for a full size plant to be constructed in Houston, Texas, within a stone's throw of my first job at Eastern States Refinery. Normally, the composting process takes several weeks and generates an unpleasant smell. In the proposed plant, garbage was to be converted to a saleable soil conditioner in a week, with little or no odor.

My first trip to the pilot plant was an eye opener. The garbage was dumped on a conveyor belt. As it proceeded to the grinder, a line of "pickers" was stationed on each side. Their job was to remove glass, plastics, wood, aluminum cans, clothing, shoes, toys, and any other material that would not decompose. A magnet removed steel. The "picked" material was sorted and recycled. One would think it would be hard to recruit workers for that job, but there were always some willing to fight the odor because they got to keep some of the "good stuff." At lunch and at quitting time, all the shoes collected would be lined up, matched and taken home. Lots of toys were salvaged, too. Without fail, if a whistle came through on the belt, one picker would grab it and blow to see if it still worked (*ugh!*).

The success in the process was that the garbage went through a 500 horsepower shredder that pulverized it into small pieces, and municipal sewage was mixed in to provide extra bacteria to break down the mix. Next, it was spread into bins that had air blown through the mix to aid in composting and to prevent foul odors. Twenty-four hours a day, the mix was lifted from the bottom of the bins to the top by bucket elevators, speeding up the process. In a week, odor-free compost was ready for sale. It was selling well locally.

I decided to give it a test as an alternative to buying tons of peat moss. I took ten free bags home in the back seat of our car, and they worked fine. Even better than the peat moss we had tried.

I asked "Swede" the operator, "Just how much can I get?"

"As much as you want, but the bags are expensive. If you want a lot, you can have it free if you take it in bulk," he replied.

"If I get a trailer, can you load it?"

"Sure" was the reply.

Each week I traveled to our Tampa office (just a few miles from the pilot plant) for the project and returned to Jacksonville on weekends, a four-hour drive. The next week, I shopped for a rental trailer I could pull behind my Pontiac sedan. Each one I looked at seemed too small. If it was going to be a free load, I needed something *big*. The miser in me overcame engineering judgment, and I found the perfect unit, a wooden trailer seven feet wide and sixteen feet long, with four-foot sides. Compost is light, so I needed lots of volume. I was told it was not for rent. It was to be rebuilt by the rental agency because no one rented that large a trailer, and it had no tail lights or brakes. Both were required by the state. I convinced them to rent it one last time for the trip to Jacksonville. The load would be light and not need brakes, and I was only traveling in daylight. The rental only worked out because the trailer was to be sent to Jacksonville for overhaul, and I could deliver it after unloading. He warned me, "Remember, without brakes—3500 pounds, maximum."

Friday noon, I arrived in Largo for the free load. Swede began filling the trailer while I called Linda to tell her I would be a home by five, six at the latest after taking the trailer to the new lot. As I approached the trailer, I saw Swede using the loader blade to pack the compost down, and the tires looked low. We tied a tarp over the load, pumped up the tires to 100 pounds, and I was off!

I gunned the car and didn't move at all. Maybe it was a little overloaded. Swede pushed with the loader, and I just barely crept forward. Swede waved and shouted something. It sounded like "Go." The engine was roaring so loud I couldn't hear that it was "Whoa!" Then I heard two explosions. I had run over a concrete block, pulverizing it and both tires on that side of the trailer. I had driven a total of twenty feet.

The service truck driver who arrived with new tires tried to jack up the trailer, but his jack couldn't lift it. "Lawsy, whut you got in dere? It sho' be heavy." Swede lifted with the loader as the driver used two jacks. The frame bent slightly, but it was high enough for the new tires to be installed. I had been nervously watching the time of day. It was almost four, and nearing the rush hour. I would have to drive over the high rise bridge crossing Tampa Bay, then through town in heavy traffic! It never occurred to me to call home in the panic of the afternoon's activities.

I left the plant after a push by Swede, and headed for the high interstate bridge. I knew I would have to get a running start on the level approach roadway or I might not make it to the top, so on the highway I tried my acceleration. It was miserable, but another problem cropped up to take my attention away from acceleration. The radiator boiled over! This was not a shock, though. It had been leaking for weeks, and I always brought a three gallon insecticide sprayer full of water in the trunk for such emergencies. In a few minutes, I was back on the road, headed for the bridge. I just barely reached fifty mph when I started up. By midway, it was twenty-five, and by the top, I was just barely moving. The rush hour commuters honked and gave me that special one finger wave as they sped past. At least I made it to the top.

Now it was easy. With the trailer pushing the car, I started down. Fifteen, thirty, forty-five, and I was not even half way down. I tapped the brakes to slow down, but when I did, the trailer swayed into the next lane and pushed the car toward the guardrail. This was serious! I gave up trying to brake and just held on. By the bottom of the bridge, I was completely out of control, moving at sixty miles per hour. The car and trailer were swaying across both lanes and the shoulders of the roadway.

Then it happened. I went off the interstate, down the embankment, through the grass median, onto the shoulder of oncoming traffic, then back across the median, stopping crossways, blocking all traffic. I looked back up the road and saw a great brown cloud where a third of the compost had been thrown up into the air as I zigzagged back and forth. Not a car was moving in either direction. They were all watching the wild ride. That was it. I gave up. I pulled off the traffic lanes onto the shoulder and began to disconnect the trailer, but the wild ride had bent the hitch and it wouldn't let go. I was expecting a patrolman any minute, but in the massive traffic jam in both directions, I guess they couldn't get through.

I finally started home at a speed of thirty-five mph, the maximum speed without swaying. I was too nervous even to stop to eat. Each time the steering wheel moved even a slight amount, I was out of control, even when I slowed to twenty-five mph. It was dark when I got to Orlando, and the overpasses there caused the swaying to resume. It was then I remembered I had no trailer lights, and thirty-five mph was below the minimum interstate speed. Surely I would be stopped if I kept to highways. North of the city, I detoured onto a back road through the Ocala National Forest. It was deserted, just right for a slow speed and probably no patrolmen to notice me. At least I thought so. The heavy load had played havoc with my gas mileage, so I stopped to fill up.

The gas station attendant came running out. "You're trailer's smoking. It's on fire! Get it away from the gas pumps!" Sure enough, the wild ride even got the compost bacteria in a such panic they were working overtime, and the load was too hot to touch. I took off the tarp and sprayed the load with water to cool it down, but that made it even heavier. As I was about pull out onto the road, a highway patrolman stopped me.

"No lights," he exclaimed, "you can't go on the road like that." I agreed to leave the trailer there overnight and come back in the morning, but the gas station operator refused.

"That thing will catch fire and burn me out!" The patrolman looked under the tarp and was met with a blast of steam.

"What is that you're hauling?"

"Compost for my lawn"

"Why's it so hot?"

"It's garbage compost, and it's still decomposing."

"You're hauling garbage from Tampa to Jacksonville? Don't they have garbage you can use there? There's a weighing station down the road, let's see if you're over the 3500 pound limit."

The scales registered 7950! I was over by 4450 pounds! There's no telling how much I had before so much flew out in Tampa. Finally, he asked how far I had to go. It was less than seventy-five miles. He told me to go on—carefully. "I'd never be able to go to court with you and hear this story again without laughing, and no judge would believe it anyway," he laughed. I promised to stay on back roads. I got home about 1:00 AM, after taking a sledge hammer and knocking the hitch loose at the lot. Linda was frantic and I was dead tired, but the adventure was over. I emptied the compost and returned the trailer the next day. The wooden sides were charred from the smoldering compost, but the rental agent did not charge for the damage since the trailer was to be rebuilt anyway.

A similar compost plant was built in Houston, and it worked as designed, producing about 400 tons per day of compost. The developers had left out one factor in building the plant—selling that much compost every day. Soon the market was saturated and the plant closed. Too bad it wasn't built in a sandy area with endless need for organics. Jacksonville had hundreds of acres of barren, mined out land that could have used the compost.

A few weeks before moving into the new house, a tropical depression dropped ten inches of rain on the house, and washed out a five foot bank of sand, which poured into both ends of the lower level, met in the center and then flowed out the sliding glass door opening, filling the downstairs with over fifty tons of sand. Fortunately it occurred before the wiring and sheet rock walls were installed. The family worked the next two weekends shoveling sand. Spreading the compost and seeding the yard to prevent more erosion jumped to the top of our "to do" list.

Months later, I received my notice of my annual IRS tax audit. I was audited for each of the past nine years, but never knew why. There were never errors, but the audits just kept coming. This year, I found out why. The auditor asked why I had a black mark by my name. A black mark was not for good conduct. The black mark came after my 1960 audit in Texas.

It seemed that my former partner in the Wash Tub coin laundry was being investigated on his 1958 tax return. I was audited that year partly to help them locate Chuck, and partly to make sure the partnership was dissolved.

At the time, I was working in Conroe, about thirty miles south of the IRS auditor's office in Huntsville, Texas. My appointment was for 9:00 AM, and I was to bring all my records for that year. Now, I was an engineer-inventor not a bookkeeper, so my records left something to be desired. All bills, receipts, pay stubs, and other records were piled into a dresser drawer, neither sorted nor labeled. I sat in his office with the drawer on my lap until noon. Without any excuse for the three-hour delay in our appointment, he told me we would be getting together after lunch. I was irritated by then, but I carried the drawer to the car and got a hamburger. Promptly at one I was back. He showed up at two.

At five, he came out to the lobby and said, "You'll just have to come back tomorrow, maybe I can get to you then."

I hit the ceiling, "The h—- you say!" (I got that saying from Dad; it was one of his favorites.) I marched into his office and dumped the entire drawer contents on his desk and told him, "Good luck, mail them back when you're finished!" Then I stomped out of his office.

"You'll be sorry!" was the comment from the employees back at Sparkler. They were right. Each year for nine years, I had the opportunity to remember their prediction. Even being polite and accurate in my taxes each year didn't erase the black mark.

This year's auditor was an elderly man who offered to have that black mark removed. All I had to do is withdraw my deduction claim for the stolen plywood. Even with a police report, he claimed I needed an inventory the day before the robbery and one the next day to prove the loss. "If I knew the night of the robbery, I'd have been there to shoot them," I exclaimed.

"True," he smiled, "but this is my last case before retiring, and I need to show my last case was a success. IRS owes you over three thousand in refund even if you drop your claim of the theft loss. I can hold that refund up indefinitely, and you'll spend more fighting us than the few hundred dollars you lose in dropping the deduction. I'll even get paid extra to follow the case after I retire. Remember the black spot comes off, too." I gave in and the spot disappeared.

The compost worked better than I expected. The lawn was planted, and we moved in. It was time for my reward. I wanted a swimming pool, bulkhead, boathouse, and when they were finished, a boat. I knew if we used sand under the boathouse and bulkhead, it would wash out, so rock would be needed. Unfortunately, it would take almost 100 tons, more money than I had to spend. I had to find a cheaper alternative.

The solution came courtesy of the State Highway Department. They were widening University Boulevard and demolishing a concrete block church in the way of construction. I bought the Spring Glen Methodist Church concrete blocks for one dollar a ton, delivered to my lot. The delivery began one afternoon, and the trucks dropped the blocks right where I wanted them. I congratulated myself for my shrewdness. Too soon, it turned out, because the next day when I came home there was the floor slab in ten by twenty foot pieces and the reinforced concrete foundations in huge pieces, right on top of my blocks. The whole delivery cost $90, but I spent each evening and every weekend for the next six months breaking up concrete into small pieces with a sledge hammer and placing them behind the bulkhead. Bad days at work increased my production of broken concrete and relieved stress. I did receive an unexpected fringe benefit from all the concrete I broke up. I recovered over 300 feet of steel reinforcing rod for use in the concrete in the bulkhead and boathouse.

We were in the final stages of completing the boathouse when a friend of Mother's offered to sell us her husband's boat. He was seriously ill and would not be able to use it and wanted it to go to a family that would take care of his "baby," a twenty-eight-foot Richardson Cabin Cruiser with a beautiful teak and mahogany hull. One look was all I needed to buy the "Bet-II," named after John's wife. It was love at first sight.

I made another of those memorable decisions that led to another adventure. Linda and I were hosting an oyster roast for about forty people that Saturday evening. The oysters, shrimp, and beer keg had been delivered and iced down, and we hired a local woman to help serve and clean up (shucking oysters and beer in paper cups tend to generate a lot of trash). We had a few hours until the first guest arrived, so I couldn't wait to get the new boat home. The marina where the *Bet-II* was moored was only twenty-five miles away by river, and we would have plenty of time to drive there, load up the family, and enjoy a two-hour cruise back home. I could then show off my new treasure to my engineering buddies and their wives.

We arrived, loaded up the life preservers and boating gear, and headed home. That year, 1967, the St. Johns River had been partially choked with large masses of water hyacinths, and it was important not to get props caught in the tangle of roots they all carried below the surface. The Corps of Engineers was conducting a herbicide spraying program to keep the shipping channel open. After spraying, the hyacinths gradually died and sank to the bottom.

The trip was exciting for the first hour, dodging patches of hyacinths as we cruised north under the new three mile long Interstate 295 bridge under construction. The weather was beautiful, and our young children were having a great time on their first boat ride. As we approached the Naval Air Station, we slowed to watch the take off of military jets and waved to the pilots. Then it happened! I cruised through a large patch of hyacinths submerged just below the surface. The engine slowed down and the temperature alarm sounded. The cooling system was plugged with rotting and slimy "goop." We were dead in the water. Several unsuccessful attempts to restart failed. There were no other boats near to give assistance, so I took two orange life preservers, climbed to the top of the cabin and began to wave for help. No luck. The pilots we had been waving to assumed we were just being friendly. Several even tipped their wings and waved back. It was now getting late, and I remembered the oyster roast. Why hadn't I listened to Linda and waited to show off the boat? There were no cell phones then, so we were on our own.

By the time I was about to give up, a commercial tug boat appeared on the horizon, heading south. We were headed north, but maybe they could pull us to shore where we could use someone's phone. They slowed and stopped, asking if we needed help. After explaining that they were on the way to the bridge construction a couple miles south, and that they were late, the captain offered to tow us to the bridge, where I could climb up the thirty-foot tall pilings and walk the half mile to shore—balancing on the beams that were in place. We had no other choice, I would have to "tight rope walk" to shore or stay in the middle of the river. He threw me a line and I tied it off to the bow. Off he went, at a fast clip—way too fast for comfort, but he was late for work. We were fishtailing back and forth, spray flying up over the cabin when I tried the engines again. The speed of the tow had washed out the slimy hyacinths and was turning the props. Both engines fired off, and we signaled to be cut loose. I thanked the captain as he sped off to work.

It was now the time for our help to arrive for the party and only an hour until guests would arrive. The house was locked, so she couldn't even start without us. I cruised at top speed all the way home, carefully avoiding any sign of weeds, but I was too late.

No, the maid was there, and the guests were arriving, but the first to meet us to help tie the boat up were all sail boaters! "If you bought a sailboat instead of a 'stink pot,' you'd have been here on time!" they all kidded. The party was a great success with lots of laughter—most directed at me. By the time the last guests left, the story had been enhanced so much by my friends it was not recognizable. One version even had me screaming in terror as a dive bomber buzzed us. Never believe a sailboat owner.

The *Bet-II* was renamed the *Linda Sue* and we enjoyed it for three years, but by then it was leaking slightly and it was time to have the keel re-caulked and the bottom repainted. That was definitely not a do-it-yourself project, as the boat would have to be pulled out of the water at a boatyard. I finally got around to the task. The engines also were in need of a tune-up, so I selected the repair shop, delivered it to the yard, and picked it up a week later. On the way home, everything was working well, and the new paint job made the *Linda Sue* look like new.

Two weeks later, I was bending down to crank my lawnmower, and I noticed that the tide was unusually low. I could hardly see the *Linda Sue*'s cabin. As I continued to pull on the starter cord, I noticed the tide wasn't low next door. Dropping the cord in a panic, I ran to the waterfront. The *Linda Sue* was sitting on the bottom, with her cabin and cockpit filled with oily salt water. I screamed in frustration, and my next door neighbor Walt came over. "Charlie, your boat has been slowly sinking for three days. I'd have said something, but I didn't want to worry you." I couldn't believe my ears! But it was true.

I rented a pump, dove into the slime and plugged the cockpit drains, closed the cabin windows, and added plastic sheeting to minimize the leaks and started the pump. The *Linda Sue* slowly rose off the muddy bottom and finally was afloat. In my rush to examine the damage, I jumped into the cockpit and as soon as I hit the oily deck, slid on my bare back through the cockpit, down the stairs into the galley. The beautiful teak and mahogany hull had been covered with gasoline from the fuel tanks and oil from the engines. The cruiser looked almost as beat up as my bloody back. I quickly found the source of the sinking. The boat yard that had finished working on the boat two weeks before had re-caulked the keel timbers with oakum as was customary, but had run out of material a foot short. They had filled the gap with several coats of paint, which lasted only a few days. The bilge pump kept up with the leak until the battery finally went dead. If Walt had told me of his observing it going down, I could have recharged the battery and saved the boat. When he moved away, we didn't hold a good-bye party.

The damage was extensive. Both engines were filled with salt water, so I drained them, flushed both with fresh water, and filled the engines with oil—crankcase, cylinders, heads, and even submerged the carburetors, starters, and generators in motor oil. I hoped to preserve as much as possible. The oil, gasoline, and salt water had saturated the mattresses, cushions, curtains, life jackets, and more importantly, it had seeped into the teak and mahogany. Several rises and falls of the tide during the week I had been out of town had thoroughly saturated everything.

I immediately called the boat yard, described the faulty work, and made an appointment to meet the owner at 8:00 AM the next day. When I arrived, a notice was posted on the door: *Closed Permanently—Bankruptcy*. A short time later the boatyard reopened, but the new owners refused to consider repairing the *Linda Sue*. Another boat yard salvaged the boat, and we traded it in for a new cruiser.

My next brainchild came two years later. I was out of home projects and unable to relax. What time we spent on the patio and around the swimming pool was frequently interrupted by mosquitoes. I bought a fogger, but the breeze off the water quickly blew it away. "Let's screen in part of the patio," I suggested. Half of the patio was covered by the upstairs balcony, so it seemed to be a simple project. Linda can testify that none of my projects were simple. Once I got started, they always expanded and grew into large ones.

It started with screening in part of the patio, a less than 200 square foot project. Then, "How can we keep the bugs from coming down through the balcony floor? It has half-inch gaps between floor planks."

"Why not screen the balcony, too? It's got a roof."

"As long as we're at it, let's enlarge the structure to include all of the patio and the barbecue pit."

I decided this was a "do it yourself" project and added lighting and wiring. As the plans grew, I realized that extending the existing roof at the existing slope would lower the outside wall to less than five feet. That meant tearing off the roof over the balcony and building a flatter roof. "Oh, well I'll be doing it myself, and that's just a little more materials." Now instead of a simple screening, the plan had expanded to a two-story structure containing almost 1000 square feet!

This new challenge would add some spice to my life, and I tackled it with enthusiasm. On Steve's tenth birthday, the basic structure was up, the roof was complete, and I had progressed to the point of installing framing for the screens. It was almost time for his cake and ice cream, and I had only one more two-by-four to install in the top of the second floor wall. I decided to take just a minute more to install the board and then get cleaned up for the festivities. The board was a little too long, and no matter how much I pounded, it just wouldn't go in place. I climbed the two-story ladder to get a better swing and positioned myself with my belt even with the roof. Balancing just off the side of the ladder, I grabbed the hammer with both hands and swung upward at the board. It moved! Now for the final blow. Swinging up as hard as I could, my hammer missed! I heard a ringing sound and saw the hammer head slowly moving away from my forehead, then I blacked out.

Linda heard that the pounding had stopped and came to see if I was finished. I was! She found me two stories below lying on my back on the concrete beside the swimming pool, surrounded by a large pool of blood. My forehead was a mess and blood was seeping out of my nose, eyes and ears. I had landed on the back of my head, and the cool deck had smashed it open, too. I came to as she came downstairs. I was dazed, but still alive. The hospital was only a few blocks away but as she prepared to rush me to the emergency room, I refused to get into the car until Linda hosed my blood off the cool deck. I remembered jumping off the sea wall onto a broken Coke bottle at Jacksonville Beach when I was twelve and running to the hospital, two blocks away. Those bloodstains remained for over a year, and I didn't want that to happen here.

I only remember waking up in surgery and hearing the doctor as he stitched my head up. "Hit himself in the head with a hammer?" he chuckled. "What next?"

"It's not funny," I responded, and he went on silently. I had a severe concussion and a bunch of stitches, and my skull had a lump the size of a peach on the forehead and another on the back, where I had landed. Dizziness and severe headaches remained for months, but the joke, "Hit yourself with a hammer lately?" lasted for years.

I returned to work looking like a prizefighter that had lost the fight, but was able to function. A couple weeks later, complications began. I could hear and remember conversations, but I could not remember what I heard over the telephone, even seconds later. My right ear was somehow not passing messages to my brain. A speakerphone solved that dilemma. My neurologist prescribed powerful painkillers for the headaches, but I was not getting better. Flying on a commercial flight on my weekly trips to Tampa and South Florida resulted in immediately blacking out as soon as the altitude changed. This was solved by flying on a private plane at altitudes of 1500 feet. Even riding more than two floors in an elevator without stopping blacked me out. I could no longer drive for fear of passing out, so my secretary drove me everywhere for business meetings.

Six weeks into the recovery period, Linda and I attended a meeting where we sat next to a physician we had met at our beachfront condominium. He noticed my unusual behavior, and after describing the symptoms, he arranged for an emergency two day battery of tests at Shands Hospital in Gainesville. During a stressful memory test, it happened. My brain stopped functioning.

I couldn't repeat anything. My brain had begun to swell and knocked me out. It turned out that the pain medication was masking the brain swelling, and as I continued to work, the swelling increased, threatening permanent damage.

I was given blood thinners and taught to recognize the feeling that preceded the swelling. From then on, when that feeling occurred, I went home to bed immediately and ceased taking painkillers that kept me from feeling the impending swelling. Within another month, I began to improve, and nine months after the accident I had recovered. The casual condominium meeting had saved me. At another critical point in my life, someone had been sent to prevent catastrophe.

MICKEY DAYS

Just after the final manual for the Saturn V was completed, Mr. Shivler, RS&H president, introduced me to Stan Graves, an old friend from his WWII Navy days. Stan worked for the Disney organization and was responsible for selecting a Florida firm to assist in design of Disney World. Stan explained the project would involve three separate tasks, the new "town" of Lake Buena Vista, The Disney Preview Center, and developing several hotel sites. The projects would vary greatly from conventional design services and require more comprehensive management. I was to have all of RS&H resources at my disposal and to report directly to the RS&H president. A new position of project director was created. The project would be under the supervision of Roy Disney, Walt's brother. Walt had passed away from lung cancer, and Roy was carrying on for him.

Our work was done in cooperation with Disney World's master planning consultant, Adam Krivatsy—one of the most proficient planners I met in my fifty-year career. He was a down to earth, practical man, with the ability to visualize both the appearance and the effect of his proposals. He even considered the engineering and construction constraints sufficiently to include them in his planning. He and I would work together for several years on the Disney project and Orlando's Orangewood, a community planned for a population of 30,000. Sea World was its anchor commercial activity.

Adam and I met on the Disney property south of Orlando to plan the site layout. Orlando was a small cow town surrounded by pastures and orange groves, not really a city yet. The focal point of the hotel area was to be Lake Buena Vista, a small lake inhabited by a few alligators. It was located a few hundred yards from Interstate 4, adjacent to an existing interchange. The lake was visible from the air, but completely obscured from the ground by dense pine trees, vines, and brush. It's hard to imagine the area in those days, but some of the blackberry vines were as big around as a thumb and reached up as much as thirty feet into the pines. We had to find the lake through the "jungle," so Adam and I, armed with machetes, began the search. We were a strange sight, two highly placed professionals in business suits, hacking wildly at the underbrush and vines. By lunch, we broke through, and it was indeed a prime spot for the first Disney building to be opened to the public.

The lake was surrounded by muck ten to fifteen feet deep. We could not walk within 150 feet of the lake without sinking into the swampy soil, so we piled the vines and underbrush we had cut down on top of the muck and made a path to the lake shore. It was a beautiful location, but terrible construction conditions.

After our success in opening the path to the lake, Stan retraced our steps and agreed this was the spot. We had work to do before it was finally approved, though. Walt's brother Roy would have to be convinced, and a narrow path wouldn't do. He was not one to hike through underbrush and prickly vines. Roy was a man who had to see more progress first hand, and to show it prematurely would be a mistake. The architectural sketches were needed, along with a master plan for the entire area, and the swampy area near the lake had to be prepared sufficiently to allow him to walk up to the very edge of the water—with dry feet.

It was time to get to work, but a problem had to be overcome. The project was in the middle of union organization attempts, and we had to be careful not to interfere with either side. Clearing was needed, and the only labor available was from a flood of auto workers who came to Orlando during an auto workers strike in Detroit. They had come to work, along with other union members. RS&H was not a licensed contractor, so we could not hire laborers. We had to work through another Disney contractor. The problem was he had no spare equipment for this project. Our company would have to rent the dozers. Even with the liability concerns, our partner in charge approved the rental for such good potential.

A brand new dozer was delivered at 8:00 AM, right off the show room floor. As it backed off the trailer, it disappeared! All we could see was the tip of the blade sticking out of the muck! The driver jumped off just before he was buried, too. It was not a good start for me at all. I never even called the office. All they could do was yell at me, anyway. Eventually, another dozer pulled it out, and there was little damage. The operator had shut it off and yanked the key out when he jumped off. A day's hosing, cleaning and re-lubricating, and we were back in business, but it stayed on high ground from then on. My Detroit labor crew had never handled axes and brush hooks and that was all we could use to clear palmettos near the water. To keep from sinking, I had them lay the palmetto fronds, brush, and trees on top of the muck, and walk on them like a mat.

The walkway was in, the muck partially covered with tree trunks and palmettos as we were told the "Mickey Mouse" (the Disney plane) was on the way from California, and we had only a few hours before Roy would arrive to inspect. In those hours, the laborers carried buckets of sand to cover the path to the lake. I cautiously walked on the mat of branches and sand floating on some ten feet of muck. It held, even though it was "squishy." As long as we walked Roy carefully to the edge of the water, all would be fine.

Sandy, the Disney PR man, was driving, and he had another plan. As I held up my hand to stop him, he ignored me and drove onto the walk path and right to the edge of the water. We looked on in horror! Is the chairman going under? He didn't, and we were relieved. As he looked approvingly at the lake, he remarked, "This is a perfect site!" Then "Charlie, this looks pretty mushy, do you think we can build on it?"

"No, Mr. Disney" I replied, "the muck will have to go just like at the park, but there's far less here." We all walked to the high ground and let Sandy back the car out. With three less passengers, it was light enough to make it. Roy and I spread the plans out on the hood of my car, and he invited me to present them in California the following week.

Author and Roy Disney Reviewing Plans for
Disney World's Lake Buena Vista Preview Center—
Copyright 1968, Walt Disney World Co.

Our presentation was held in the Glendale, California, headquarters of WED
Enterprises, Disney's design team. WED was formed by Walt in 1952 to oversee the design and construction of Disneyland in California. He used his initials
(Walter Elias Disney) for the company name. The company was assigned responsibility for Walt Disney World prior to his death in 1966, and continued
under the leadership of his brother Roy. WED Enterprises was located in a
two-story building with strict separation between the artistic employees and the
financial arm of the company led by Roy. After Walt's death, rivalries between
the two groups continued. The engineering staff that coordinated design and

construction for the Florida Disney World joined the two WED groups, and an uneasy truce resulted.

I went to my first meeting along with Adam. We were to present the master plan for the Preview Center and the Lake Buena Vista hotel complex adjacent to the center. Costs for work at the park were skyrocketing, and budgets were strained. Many of the artistic side of the family were opposed to spending any money outside their area—the amusement park, but building the Preview Center with its exhibits and scale model of the park would keep public attention on their "baby." It was a compromise to be battled out in the "War Room." I quickly learned that its nickname was accurate.

Adam started by presenting the master plan outline. He was from California and not as suspect as our Florida group. I followed his presentation with the engineering and architectural details, along with a preliminary cost estimate. The overall Disney World project was running thirty percent above estimates for most contracts to date, and there was great concern that our project would follow that trend. I explained that out-of-state designers often experienced cost overruns, partly because their drawings and specifications were different enough from local designers to cause contractors to add larger contingency amounts. In addition, contractors spent more money and experienced delays dealing with clients located so far away. A difference of three time zones aggravated the problem. I presented our record of bids coming in within five percent of budget with as many below as above estimates, but few believed the data. After much discussion, we were given the go-ahead for the Preview Center, the entrance road, and the hotel sites. The fact that the hotel sites would bring in much needed income greatly helped in reaching the compromise. We were the new kids on the block—except for Florida drainage engineers and surveyors, all the other designers were from California.

The design process was theoretically to be a simple task. The WED staff had designed the building interior and exterior even down to the landscaping. The RS&H responsibility was to produce construction drawings, specifications and the construction contract. We would also receive and evaluate bids for WED and oversee construction. When I returned to Florida with the details, our architects immediately wanted to make changes to the design, something I had been cautioned not to allow. I began to realize the difficulty of my task. I had to convince our people that changes were not permitted. Only after appealing to the company president was I able to hold the line.

The bidding for the building was completed shortly thereafter, and we were on budget to the amazement of Disney personnel. After that success, many more assignments were received.

It was during design of Lake Buena Vista Boulevard serving the Preview Center and the hotel complex that I met five people who would have a huge impact on my future. Stan Graves and Bob Foster who represented the Lake Buena Vista project were the earliest. Later would come Bill Evans, Disney's landscape designer, Charlie Sepulveda, their superintendent for landscaping, and Lindsey Robertson, Adam Krivatsy's landscape planner. Bill and Charlie introduced me to the nursery and landscaping talents that had produced the amazing topiaries and planting techniques that amazed most visitors to Disneyland. Charlie also demonstrated plant propagation methods that I was to use years later when I started my own nursery. Both Bill and Charlie emphasized that the landscaping of the entrance road to the Preview Center and hotel complex would be the most important task of the assignment. It was to be the first public view of their project and had to exceed the California park's beauty. I had no idea of how to accomplish that. RS&H was just starting to enter into the planning business and was not yet prepared to take on this responsibility. Adam had worked closely with me on the planning of the project, and he offered Lindsey's talent to complete the landscape plans.

We had only three days to meet the deadline, so Lindsey flew to Orlando to assist in preparing the drawings. All day Saturday, he sketched out his concept, and on Sunday morning, he put me to work—preparing my first landscaping drawings. I'm sure he was frustrated with my lack of skills, but he patiently corrected each mistake. The drawing was twelve feet long and was stretched out on the office conference table. We each worked on separate ends, and by Sunday night, he was actually asking advice on some options he was considering. By midnight we were flying through the plan, each of us drawing furiously. It was new and exciting, and I knew then I would eventually move into landscaping.

The next morning, we were finished. The long drawing was cut into shorter sheets, title blocks added and the landscaping design was complete. Plans were approved at WED, and the project was bid. Again, the bids came in on budget. RS&H now had the confidence of all three WED groups—artists, engineers and financial. More assignments were on tap for RS&H.

The new project was a large hotel complex to be located at the main entrance to the property, several miles south of the park. Adam and I spent a short time planning this major complex when it became apparent that it was a mistake. It was too far from activities, had no infrastructure, and would drain resources from the park itself. In addition, we believed a new entrance from Interstate 4 would eventually be built, cutting several miles off the trip from Orlando to the park. Walt's dream of Epcot Center would demand this new entrance when it was constructed. This proposed hotel complex would then no longer have the traffic volume. It was difficult to turn down such a large project, but it was the right thing to do. Adam and I presented our conclusions in the War Room, to the astonishment of many. A consultant was actually turning down a huge assignment! Roy accepted our recommendations and the project died. Since many of the artistic camp were also opposed to spending on that project, we gained credibility that lasted through my assignments with Disney.

I found myself traveling to California regularly to meet to coordinate our work with WED staff members, who now accepted RS&H as part of their "family." Trips were hectic, as time for travel was limited. I began to understand why their costs were running above estimates. I made three to five trips a month, and even made two round trips in the same week. The travel scenario was to complete work at RS&H by seven in the evening, hop the 9:00 PM flight in Jacksonville, arrive at the Mikado Motel in California by 3:00 AM, Florida time (midnight in California) meet at WED at 9:00 AM, review work all day, check out, eat dinner and catch the 10:00 PM "red eye special" to Florida, arrive about 5:00 AM Jacksonville time, shave, shower and report to the office by 8:00 AM. I traveled coach and couldn't sleep sitting up in narrow seats, even when exhausted. The coach section was thick with cigarette smoke, which added to my discomfort. By the third trip in two weeks, I was worn out. Each trip would be over sixty hours without sleep, and I needed more sleep than that.

I solved that sleep problem on the next trip. I arrived at the Delta flight early and was first in the boarding line. I selected an aisle seat, and immediately after sitting down, I opened the "Barf Bag" and held it under my chin. My seatmate slowed down as he saw he was assigned a seat next to someone who would be sick on the four hour flight. After whispering to the flight attendant, he was assigned a seat far away from me. After take off, I lifted the armrests, stretched out and slept fine.

Roy heard of my sleeping arrangements and took me aside during a break in a meeting. "Charlie, is it true you are sleeping in coach?" he asked. With a smile he continued, "I heard the story of how you get three seats for the price of one."

"Yes, that's the only way I can get any sleep, and on a one day turn around, I just have to get some rest to function."

"Well, that has to stop. From now on, you are always to fly first class. We consider you one of the family, and all our people fly first class. From now on, spend at least one night here before returning. All meetings will now be two days." I thanked him for his generosity and from then on, I was able to meet with all three WED groups on the same trip.

My next assignment was design of the Administration Complex. Disney personnel and consultants could coordinate construction and minimize the delays in communications with California from this area. The three-hour time difference no longer delayed projects as much as in the past.

Another project was to create a residential area for the newly formed town of Lake Buena Vista. The community was required to have full-time residents to comply with Florida law, so about a dozen employees volunteered to move into the mobile home park we designed for that purpose. It was located in a pine woods area, hidden from the highway by a dense thicket, and had few amenities.

The day the bulldozers arrived to clear the roadway was hot and humid. As I walked through the thicket, I stepped over what appeared to be a log. It moved, quickly coiled and prepared to strike, rattles vibrating. I made my first ten-foot jump without a running start, and ran out to the dozer. "*Rat-*

tler," I shouted. "*At least ten feet long!*" It actually looked like it was twice that big at first, but after it died, it shrunk to eight feet, just like a caught fish when you measure it.

The operator went after the snake, pinning it under the dozer track. He locked the other track and stepped on the accelerator to grind it to a pulp. Instead, the soft sand let the rattlesnake spin out from under the track and into the cab with the operator. He could jump ten feet too. Out he came, as the dozer continued slowly on until it stopped against a tree. After cooling down, we returned and found the carcass. The rattler was dead, but we didn't wait around to check its pulse. From then on, I watched where I walked.

My next project had the support of both WED groups. Construction of the WDW Service Area was a critical milestone in the park construction. Its buildings would include a food preparation and storage warehouse, communications center, general warehousing, and the huge shop building where the exhibits and ride components would be manufactured by Disney employees for installation in the park. In this facility, provision was made for welding, carpentry, plastics molding, plaster working, wiring, audio, painting, etc.—all the details that had made Disneyland in California such a success.

The Disney concept was to duplicate those California manufacturing facilities for the Florida park. They had planned to use un-insulated metal buildings to keep costs low. I advised their staff that the Florida climate was not as forgiving as that in Anaheim. By the time the buildings were built to cope with the heat, hurricane proofing, and provide the humidity control for the most delicate plastics to be used, we could nearly pay for concrete wall structures. These buildings would be much more durable and flexible for operations during construction and after completion, could be converted to other uses.

I found myself in between two camps—the artists, who insisted "as cheap as possible, so we can tear tin buildings down and build permanent structures later," and the engineering and financial staff, who were looking for the best long term investment. This battle was not won in a single War Room session, but several, with the final decision to be made just before the 1968 Mothers' Day weekend. Roy and his wife invited Linda and me to join them on the Mickey Mouse, Disney's private Gulfstream Jet for the trip. We four were the only passengers, with two pilots and a flight attendant. We were surrounded by numerous tropical plants being brought back to California, each strapped into seats like passengers. It was to be my second exposure to the Disney landscape staff and added to my decision later to start a nursery.

The War Room battle this time was fierce. Neither side wanted to yield, but the deadlock was broken by Roy, after I presented contract prices for pre-cast double tee walls and roof. The cost proved to be within the budget for steel buildings, provided we could avoid the thirty percent overruns they were experiencing on other contracts. By the end of the session, almost all supported my plan. After weeks of wrangling, I had finally won.

While the battle raged on, Linda had been enjoying a private tour of the Disney Studios and models of the Florida park. We had been in California an extra day, and it was now Friday. Roy suggested we both stay in California as his guest, and he would make the Mickey Mouse available to fly us to San Francisco for the weekend, all at his expense. "It's the least I can do for infringing on your Mother's Day weekend," he explained. I graciously accepted, but suggested we fly commercial, to keep costs down and so that his crew could have the weekend off, too. With a smile, he agreed. That weekend, Linda and I enjoyed the best side trip we had taken, and we returned to LA well rested.

The trip back to Jacksonville was a pleasant one until I arrived at our office the next day. Our architects refused to design such buildings. I was told, "Imagine our reputation if we designed a plain concrete building." Nothing would sway them. I had a contract, time schedule, and personal commitment to bring the four buildings in on time and on budget. Now RS&H would not accept the assignment, and my neck was on the line. I remembered Ma Perkins' advice from Landon—*Remember, you are prepared, don't ever give up.*

I informed Don Edgren, WED vice president, of the roadblock and requested that he join me in Florida to negotiate a contract direct with a manufacturer of pre-cast buildings. They would be responsible for the design and construction of all the buildings except for the communications center. I would bypass the RS&H architectural division and have the civil engineering and industrial/power divisions design foundations, floor slabs, mechanical and electrical systems, and the manufacturing support utilities. Ma Perkins had been right. I went around, and the buildings were all finished on time and under budget. This time I was given a Mickey Mouse watch and a personalized Walt Disney World engraved nameplate.

Working for Disney was the only project that Suzanne, then seven, and Steve, five, could relate to. NASA, going to the moon, defense, and industrial projects all were beyond their comprehension, but Mickey Mouse and his friends they understood. They continually wanted to go see the park, but it wasn't open. Their trip to see the Preview Center, with its scale model of the completed park, exhibits, and film only heightened their desire to visit. As soon as the park was open, our family was treated to a an all expenses paid stay in the new private condos we had designed along with tickets to the park. Now they knew what Dad did during all those trips away from home.

During the three years consulting for Disney World, numerous projects were completed and summer vacations were never interrupted by work. Three summer trips took Linda and me to Jamaica, where we enjoyed our get-aways with our close friends, Dan and Dora Sherrick.

Little did I know that wheels were set in motion for a huge change in my career. Our firm was being considered for a project in Jamaica, one that would divert water from the north side of the mountains on the island to Kingston, relieving the drought and providing additional hydroelectric power. Because I was the only employee with experience in Jamaica, I was asked to join the RS&H partner in charge of the environmental and process division for the trip to Jamaica. I jumped at the opportunity. I should have *run for my life* instead.

Chuck's plan was to fly to Ft. Lauderdale in his private plane, drive to Miami, and then take Air Jamaica the rest of the way. We met at Craig Field in Jacksonville, loaded our luggage, and took off. As soon as we left the ground, a warning siren sounded and several lights flashed in the cockpit. From the pilot's seat, he told me the reason we were flying this leg of the trip in his plane was that his instruments and controls had been acting up, and most didn't work at all. They would be repaired while we were in Jamaica. There was no danger though, he had been flying this way for weeks without incident. I was not convinced, as he had a reputation for flying on the ragged edge of safety. Some friends even refused to fly with him. I would soon join that group.

The trip to the aircraft repair shop in Ft. Lauderdale went smoothly until we started to descend. A different alarm sounded, and Chuck exclaimed, "Wonder what that is?" I didn't want to know, I just wanted my feet on the ground—and soon! I got my wish, and we left for Jamaica later that day, this time on a safe, commercial flight.

Chuck and I spent a few days exploring the project's proposed site and meeting with local officials. It became evident that the successful firm would have to make "appropriate donations" to be considered, and later we dropped out of consideration. It was on to Florida and home. I planned to take a commercial flight back from Miami, but Chuck refused.

"I called the shop and my plane is repaired. It's even been flight tested, and we will fly in daylight. I'll get you home quicker than National Air Lines, anyway. Don't waste money on a ticket when you can fly with me free." He was boss, so I agreed—reluctantly.

Dick Jones, one of Chuck's employees from Gainesville met us in Miami, to drive us to the repair shop. He needed to discuss another project. We arrived in ample time to get home by dark, and the weather was clear. I relaxed a little. Then the two continued talking and talking and talking. It was getting late, and I suggested continuing the conference later. Chuck refused and we went to dinner. "No sense flying on an empty stomach," he exclaimed. The uneasy feeling in the pit of my stomach was definitely not hunger! There were no flights from Ft. Lauderdale to Jacksonville by then. I was stuck. It was after eight before we left the runway.

"The weather is fine all the way, so don't worry. In two hours you'll be home." Forty-five minutes later, the sky to the north was filled with lightning. It looked like we were heading into a *big* storm.

"Chuck, did they say a storm was ahead when you checked the weather?"

"Actually I checked the weather five hours ago, but not before we took off."

"We better check now," I replied. He did and found a huge thunderstorm with high winds lay about fifty miles to the north.

"I guess we better fly around it," I exclaimed when we heard the report.

"No way!" he replied, "I just got my instrument rating. I'll file for instruments, and we'll fly on through. It'll be fun."

Onward we went, into the jaws of the storm. Over the deafening sound of thunder, the straining engine and the roar of the wind and rain, Chuck shouted, "Get out the instruction manual and turn on the light." He finally was filing for instruments, but late. We were already "socked in," and the plane was bucking like a bronco.

"Read the first question."

"Chuck, just call for help!" I yelled. It was now so loud I could hardly hear. Lightning was flashing on both sides, and the wind and thunder made repeating necessary. We were losing valuable time, and I didn't want to admit I was scared and about to be airsick.

"No way," he replied. "I don't want them to think I'm a novice. Read the filing instructions and I'll tell you the correct response. Write it down, and then when we've got them all answered, hand me the list. I'll read it off quickly, and they'll think I'm a pro."

This was getting ridiculous. By now, I could hardly write as we were being pushed all over the sky by the wind.

"How many times have you flown on instruments?" I asked when I finished the list.

"This is my first!" he responded. I was sure we were doomed!

He rattled off the items, and by the time we received clearance, we were out of the storm. We had flown socked in for over thirty minutes! I was soaked with sweat. By the dim cockpit light, I could see he was grinning.

We landed safely at Craig Airport. It was almost midnight. "Wasn't that fun?" Chuck asked. I didn't answer. I was giving thanks that those prayers were answered. I would *never* fly with him again, boss or not!

A few weeks later, Chuck and all his family except one son were flying a rental plane near Messina, NY. He was flying in a storm through the Adirondack Mountains—filing for instruments when the mike went dead. They had flown into a mountain with no survivors. I shivered, remembering our ordeal filing for instruments, and realized that he had lost valuable minutes preparing his list of answers. It cost him and his family their lives. It could have been me if we had been flying near mountains the month before. My prayers were for his remaining son. I never again flew on a private plane that did not have a professional pilot.

Chuck's death left RS&H a huge void to fill. After searching outside the firm for a replacement, it was decided to transfer me from the Disney and Orangewood projects to fill his position. Jack Potts, who had been assisting me for many months and had earned the respect of both clients, was placed in charge. I continued with Ludwig and FPL work in progress, and my workload increased dramatically. I would now be required to supervise the environmental and process engineering staff members in Jacksonville, Tampa, and Hollywood, Florida, as well as assuming much of the marketing responsibilities.

One of my first tasks after taking over Chuck's process engineering group was to transfer the commercial development of Chuck's patents and research to our partner company. We were joint-venturing on a process to recover nitrous oxides that were a major air pollutant and convert them to useful products. The trip to Ohio for the negotiations was in winter, and I was flying with Don Whitfill, another RS&H engineer and a close friend at night in a borrowed plane. Ray Smith, our *professional* pilot in the two-engine craft, was flying along the eastern side of the Appalachian Mountains as a fierce storm poured over the mountain peaks from the west. As we proceeded north, he received word that airports were being closed by heavy snow and ice ahead of us. After about an hour, Don and I (one on each side of the cabin) used spotlights to look for ice on the wings as the pilot struggled with the controls. Ice was building up! The wing de-icers successfully knocked off large sheets of ice as we proceeded, but by then all airports in our path as well as those we had passed were closed! The only airports east of the mountains were beyond our fuel range. There was no choice but to try to cross the Appalachians to clear air behind the storm front and find a field that was still open.

Just as we neared the peaks of the mountains, the ice slowly began to overpower the de-icing equipment. Ice was now building up on the leading edge of the wings and spreading. We slowly began to lose altitude just as we passed over the mountains in West Virginia. Our destination airport, Akron, was still open. We still had ice on the wings and both of us continued to watch, even though the de-icers had long since stopped working. Somehow it was better to watch than to look at each other, even though our necks were aching from the tension and constantly turning toward the window.

About a hundred miles from setting down, the Akron airport was closed down. Ice had started building up on those runways, too. We were low on fuel from the additional weight and drag and had no choice but to land. With pillows over our faces and crouched in the "crash position," Don and I prayed. Ray turned on the landing lights. They barely shined at all through the ice covering their lenses. The field lights were still on, but it was difficult to land with landing lights to help see the pavement of the runway and patches of ice. "Hang on, we're going in!"

The landing was surprisingly smooth, but as we taxied toward the terminal, we saw that most of the lights were turned off. We descended the stairway and saw how close it had been. There were over four inches of solid ice on the leading edge of the wings! Again, we knew that prayers worked.

The cleaning crew opened the locked door to let us call a cab to get to our motel, and we slept soundly that night. The meeting was successful, and the trip back was uneventful. Don and I didn't mind at all. We had enough excitement the previous night to last a lifetime.

RS&H converted from a partnership to a corporation, and I was promoted to vice president and now I was a part owner through company stock purchase plan for officers. The next five years were prosperous for me and the company, but the Disney work slowly died out with the completion of the park.

CLASH OF THE TITANS

It was late in the 1960s that I met my first multi-millionaire. Daniel Ludwig was actually a billionaire, and one of the least known of the "mega-rich." I knew who he was because of my experience bringing in one of his supertankers at Eastern States almost fifteen years before. I remember how huge the vessel was, dwarfing the tankers in the Houston Ship Channel. It sat so low in the water that the keel brushed the channel bottom. Part of the cargo had been offloaded downstream so the tugboats could push it to our dock. After unloading, it had been even more impressive, the deck rising more than twenty-five feet above the dock. His fleet numbered about sixty of the largest supertankers and bulk carrying vessels in the world. He also controlled ports, hotels, cruise lines, real estate, cattle ranching, orange groves, banking, and insurance. His other holdings included oil, gas, coal mining, and minerals—located all over the world.

He was a perfect example of the Horatio Alger "rags to riches" novels that inspired me during that first difficult summer after moving to Florida. He was born in Michigan in the 1890s and left school after the eighth grade (a little more than a year older than I was when I decided to drop out and smuggle bubble gum). Just like Alger's heroes, Mr. Ludwig worked his way to success. Much of his fortune had been made after WWII, and his business genius was well known and either feared or respected, depending on whose side you were on.

Mr. Ludwig owned two large tracts of waterfront property containing several thousand acres fronting on Biscayne Bay and Card Sound south of Miami. Florida Power and Light's Turkey Point Power Plant was located between the two Ludwig tracts.

He had announced his plans for the northern 2000 acre tract in 1962. Seadade was to be a huge seaport and industrial complex north of Turkey Point. The port included an oil refinery, a 300- foot-wide shipping channel, and "Port Ludwig," a forty-foot deep dredged ship anchorage containing more than 600 acres. The plan was soundly defeated after a huge protest by environmentalists.

The 1960s were a time of attitude change in South Florida. For the previous ten years, the area had seen phenomenal growth. Environmental concerns were routinely ignored in favor of the booming economy that resulted from the growth. Higher densities, more dredging, new communities, vast profits, all began to lose their luster. Traffic, crime, pollution, long lines, lack of parks, and loss of a "sense of community" all became concerns of the citizens.

I attended many public hearings and began to hear the ground swell of opposition to uncontrolled growth. I thought it amusing to attend zoning hearings and hear a newcomer from places like Brooklyn testify in her unmistakable accent, "There are already too many Yankees here. Close the gate. We're full! Send them back home." Invariably she would be applauded by the other people who had recently migrated to Florida. I remembered that when we moved to Florida in 1947 no one in our school had ever seen anyone born out of state. After just twenty years it was difficult to meet a native Floridian!

Port Ludwig was not the first major project in Biscayne Bay blocked by concerned citizens. Four years earlier a plan to create an 8,000-acre jetport in the bay met with fierce opposition from a local group who dreamed of forming a large park covering most of south Biscayne Bay and the numerous Florida Keys adjacent to the Bay. This national park would include the Bay, the islands, and the reef to the east. Their efforts were rewarded in 1968, when Congress made this "rare combination of terrestrial, marine and amphibious life in a tropical setting of great natural beauty" part of the National Park System. Biscayne National Monument was established October 18, 1968, at a White House signing ceremony.

The Florida Power and Light Turkey Point Generating Station adjacent to Mr. Ludwig's southern property included two operational oil-fired generators, and two nuclear generators that were under construction. Permits for the nuclear units were delayed by strong local opposition. The opponents centered part of their battle on their claim that the heated water from the operating units was causing damage to Biscayne Bay National Monument marine life. The two new nuclear units would increase the damage to an unacceptable level. The door for FPL's Turkey Point permits was closing fast. Faced with insurmountable opposition at the local and federal levels, FPL decided to counter the criticism by constructing a discharge canal several miles south of Biscayne Bay to Card Sound.

Unfortunately, Mr. Ludwig's proposed residential city land blocked access to Card Sound. FPL had powers of eminent domain and planned to condemn a strip of the Ludwig property, cutting it in half. This canal would isolate the waterfront from the rest of the tract and would compromise his ability to develop the acreage. The story is told that the initial clash came as McGregor Smith, president of FPL, went to New York to see Mr. Ludwig to inform him of the plans to condemn his land for the canal. Mr. Smith pulled out his harmonica, played "Dixie," and told Mr. Ludwig, "Stand up, you Yankee SOB, I'm playing Dixie." Well, as you can imagine, Mr. Ludwig didn't stand up. He was not a man to back down, either. Mr. Smith was ushered out, and the battle was on! Eminent domain or not, FPL was in for a battle. They began constructing the canal before condemnation was completed, further enraging Mr. Ludwig.

During my first meeting in New York, I asked Mr. Ludwig if he had been in Florida recently. "No," he replied, "not since 1962, that's why you're meeting me here. I don't plan to ever set foot in the State of Florida again." He had not forgotten the port, but now he found himself in an awkward position. The coalition that had supported the park and opposed his port was now attacking his enemy. My task was to develop plans for the community and to obtain permits for its construction.

FPL's permits for the two nuclear units were stalled at all levels pending out-come of the condemnation and environmentalist opposition. Hundreds of millions in other lawsuits were filed. The environmental groups did not accept FPL's new canal proposal and continued opposition. They didn't want any discharge at all. By this time, dozens of groups joined the opposition. Some even pushed for the existing oil-fired units to be shut down until cooling towers could be built to eliminate using Biscayne Bay for plant cooling water. The latest claim was since Biscayne Bay and Card Sound are federal waters, the existing Turkey Point oil fired generators were killing federal plankton (miniature marine animals). Surely, the government couldn't allow more killing by the nuclear plant. The "dead federal plankton" would turn Card Sound into a sewer. Mr. Ludwig enjoyed hearing the latest FPL roadblock, but neither side was winning. It was a complete standoff.

My first task after meeting with Mr. Ludwig in New York was my introduction to FPL management, to explain my responsibilities. Mr. Ludwig wanted them to know he was serious in his pursuit of the new community. It was not a good day. I felt like a minnow being thrown to a shark. I was given about five minutes before McGregor Smith, FPL president, informed me of the futility of my efforts and let me know I was not smart enough to stand in the way of eminent domain. "Eventually Mr. Ludwig will lose, and that's that. Period. Now, get out of my office and back to Jacksonville!"

He assigned FPL's attorney, Bob Gardner, as liaison and said he never wanted to see me again. Meeting's over! I had been told *"Run for your life. You will destroy your career following such a foolish task."* It was the shortest meeting I ever attended. At least I had missed his playing "Dixie" on his harmonica.

As the plans for the development of the community proceeded, I proposed a compromise that could improve Mr. Ludwig's plans and solve FPL's need for a solution to the cooling water discharge. But the plan required cooperation between the two. That was not going to be an easy sell for me.

Mr. Ludwig was no novice in the development of residential communities. Westlake Village, California, a residential community of approximately 50,000, and a large residential community in the Bahamas were two of his projects. He had also developed the Princess Hotels in Bermuda, Bahamas, and Mexico. There was no way to put something over on him.

None of his people dared comment on my plan for fear that Mr. Ludwig might not agree. It was Mr. Ludwig alone who would decide. At 9:00 one morning, I received a call in my Jacksonville office. "Charlie, this is D.K. Ludwig. I would like to meet with you to discuss your proposal—just you and me—don't bring anyone else. Let's have lunch."

I agreed. "When do you want me there?"

"Today."

"Mr. Ludwig, it's after nine, and I'm in Florida"

"I know perfectly well where you are, I called *you*!"

"I'll head for the airport and try to hop a plane to New York, but I won't be able to make a formal presentation on short notice."

"There is no need for fancy exhibits. I expect you to be here by one. If you have to buy a plane to get here by then, do it, but don't charge it to me!"

My secretary, June rushed me to the airport because there wasn't even enough time to park and run to the terminal. She dropped me at the entrance, and I was the last passenger to board the 9:45 Eastern Air Lines flight.

At one o'clock, I was ushered into his office. He smiled and said, "I knew you could do it. Let's get to work." Over a glass of milk and a peanut butter sandwich, we got down to business. First—the quality of his property. It was virtually all only a few feet above high tide—too low to build housing or roads without massive amounts of fill. In the past, much of the coastal Miami property was built on soil dredged from Biscayne Bay, starting about 1915. Fill from his defeated refinery and port would have been ideal, but that opportunity was gone. With the recent designation of the Biscayne Bay National Monument, dredging from the Bay was not possible. The southern third of the property fronted on Card Sound, but with the public furor over FPL's plan for dumping heated water into the sound, we better not plan on dredging there either. He agreed. He had been beaten by environmentalists on the port in 1962, and the climate had become even more restrictive.

Trucking fill dirt in would raise the cost too much for the lots to be affordable. Therefore, all fill would have to come from on the property. My proposal was to plan his community with several miles of canals, using the canal material for fill. The underlying limestone would make good fill material, and could even be used for road construction. To this point, we were agreed. Then came my proposal, a more difficult suggestion.

The community would have to be built with water and sewer service to each lot. That was a hard pill to swallow. Most competitors built with septic tanks and let the community build utilities after the developer was gone. Our firm was in the process of such a project on the west coast of Florida, and costs were enormous. Roads had to be torn up and rebuilt to install lines. I continued, "If we build without sewers, the porous limestone would allow septic tanks to leach into the canals, creating a health problem." Even though permits were still being issued for canal developments with septic tanks, I believed the State and Corps of Engineers would be hard pressed to continue approval much longer. Many such canal communities were experiencing deteriorating water quality. Even if permits were issued, stagnant, smelly water would hurt sales. His project would take several years to construct, and he shouldn't depend on septic tanks. He didn't look happy.

What about the initial cost? How could he compete with septic tank developments and still make a profit? We're still a long way from Miami. Both were good questions. My answer was, "You can't! *Unless…*" He glared into my eyes, but after years of surviving the "Big Eye scowls" from my dad during disciplinary lectures, I was ready.

My plan:

1. Cooperate with FPL.—He was not impressed with the start, but he didn't throw me out.
2. Get FPL to dig the canals and fill the developable land.—That was a little better!
3. Plan the development and designate where each canal is built to maximize profit.
4. Construct enough canals to dissipate all the heat from the plant without sending heated water into Biscayne Bay or Card Sound, assuring FPL of permits.

5. Get FPL approval of the concept before spending any more money on our firm.

6. If we get the Turkey Point permits released, ask FPL to reimburse you for our planning costs.

He listened attentively. Then, he asked how I came up with such a plan. I explained, "When I put a pencil to the costs for developing your land, it became obvious that the land would be too expensive to develop and still be marketable. It was too far from Miami, had marginal road access, was far from shopping and amenities, and would be a permitting nightmare. I figured if I had to deliver that message to you, I would be walking back to Florida. My plan was simply a matter of self preservation." He laughed and agreed to consider my proposal.

Now, Mr. Ludwig was known for his frugality, so not spending more money until he decided suited him well. He would let me know in a few days, but in the meantime, "Go back to Florida and wait, and I don't pay for travel time, so you're off the clock till you get home." It was almost quitting time anyway, so I nodded agreement. Wow, a billionaire—and now I knew why.

One of his employees in the Bahamas had told me of an experience he had earlier. Mr. Ludwig arrived at the Freeport Airport carrying a tattered leather suitcase. The catch was broken and a piece of clothesline was tied around it to keep it from opening. After he emptied the contents at his personal villa, he handed the empty suitcase to Ben.

"Ben, see if you can get this fixed, but don't spend more than $3.00. It's not worth more." Well, getting anything fixed in Freeport in the '60s was a challenge, but Ben found a way. He purchased a brand new leather case, had the latch and lock removed and installed in the old suitcase by a local shoe repairman. Proudly, he presented it to Mr. Ludwig, who asked, "How much?"

"Three dollars, sir."

"It's a good thing, if it was more, I'd have fired you." But he smiled as he said it.

Ben didn't mention the $75.00 for the case, only the $3.00 to have the lock stitched in. The rest was job insurance.

Now, I have to mention here that Daniel Ludwig was not the cheapskate this story might imply. He just didn't believe in wasting money. Before the end of this project in 1971, Mr. Ludwig established the Ludwig Institute for Cancer Research, which he funded with all of his foreign investments and continued to fund the research until his death some twenty years later.

His approval of my plan came the next day, but with the provision that he send an associate to our offices to monitor progress. My first assignment was to prepare a formal outline of the plan and illustrations for a meeting with Bob Gardner, my contact at FPL. He also authorized computer costs to test my theory and be sure the canals would work.

Soon after the approval, Mr. Ludwig's associate, Harry, arrived to monitor the progress of the project. My office was in the partner's suite, and we arranged an office for Harry's nearby. In marched Harry carrying a canvas bag containing a full set of barbells and weights. Harry liked to keep in shape. Upon being shown his office, he exclaimed, "Oh, no, Mr. Ludwig told me to stay in your office the whole time and be sure you didn't work on any other project until his was complete." He continued with his routine, "I'll be here at nine every day, exercise for a half hour, and then we can get to work. Any work on other projects must be complete by 9:30. But first I must have two cups of hot water with one half of a fresh lemon squeezed in each, and a little sugar." June (my secretary) was listening just outside the door. "June, you can shop for the lemons, but no more than a few at a time—they must be fresh!" he continued.

This was not a satisfactory arrangement, but before I was able to tell him so, Jimmy Shivler, president of RS&H walked in to meet him. He assured Harry that RS&H would be devoting our best people to this project. He would also waive the rule of "officers only" in the suite. "You are welcome to use Charlie's office." I was doomed!

It was time to call Mr. Ludwig and explain that I was responsible for over seventy-five employees located in three separate offices in Florida, and I couldn't stop everything for his project. The call was never made, though. Jimmy told me to just "wing it" for a few days and see what happened. The next weeks were terrible. Every call I received was followed by Harry's question, "Was that a call on this project?" Then he would write a note in his journal. I resorted to scheduling meetings with employees early in the morning and after hours, but our clients were not that flexible. Complaints were mounting even though my staff was doing all they could to manage without me.

Just as I was at the end of my rope, my good friend Don Whitfill offered to host Harry for a day, allowing me to catch up on some much needed work on other projects. Don was responsible for the computer analysis of the cooling canals. Harry lumbered into Don's small office, dropped his barbells onto the floor with a *clank*, and sat down. The day wasn't over before Harry returned to guard me. I had ample encouragement to finish this project with lightning speed. Harry was under orders not to attend any meetings with FPL, though—I would report them directly to Mr. Ludwig.

The computer work had progressed enough to show that my canal concept was feasible, but the research was based on some assumptions that had to be confirmed by Bechtel, FPL's engineers. In desperation, I called Bob Gardner to schedule a preliminary meeting in Miami. That way I could get away from Harry and check on my employees in the local office. It would be two days of freedom, but poor June. Harry even had her doing light shopping for him, and the clanking of his weights was driving her to distraction, even with the door closed.

The meeting in Miami went well, and I was given the information I needed. Bob and I agreed that the project should be kept under wraps until the entire concept was developed. FPL engineers would have to verify our calculations before any meeting with the Board of Directors, and they were having trouble programming heat transfer in such a complicated maze of canals. Bob and I both were sure this project would work, but selling it would have to be done carefully. One misstep might be fatal with such high stakes and the volatile "titans."

On the second day after my return, I received a call from New York. "Charlie, this is D.K. Is Harry there? I need to speak with him immediately!" I gave Harry the phone and stood by trying to hear, but it was a short call.

"Yes, sir. (pause) When? I'll leave now." That was all. He asked for the airline guide, and in a few minutes asked June to make his reservation for a flight to Mexico, then call him a cab. What was going on? I just had to find out if he was going for a short time or for good, so I volunteered to take him to the airport, detouring only to pick up his luggage at the motel. It was already packed! "I always pack in case Mr. Ludwig sends me on another project." Harry was leaving!

On the way to the airport, the story unfolded. There had been a big accident at Mr. Ludwig's port in Mexico. The captain of one of Mr. Ludwig's large cargo vessels had been drinking, and he rammed it into the loading dock. The ship destroyed 300 feet of dock, shutting down the entire operation. Harry was an expert in port construction and was to get the port running again as soon as possible. He gave me a slip of paper with a shipping address for his weights. He said goodbye, and we never saw him again. June threw away the last half lemon.

I called Mr. Ludwig to tell him Harry had made his flight and was on the way to Mexico, then brought him up to date on our progress. He was pleased and assigned Gary Alvey, another of his men to take Harry's place, but this time from his office in Miami. Gary stayed in Miami and didn't have to move in with me.

This project now required me to negotiate another hurdle. It was now time to meet with the next player, George B. Hills, founder of RS&H. Mr. Hills had asked me frequently to update him on my projects because they included many new ideas that fascinated him. This project was especially important to him because it included FPL, a publicly owned power company. After WWII, RS&H entered the electric utility field as consulting engineers and was well-known for success in design and construction management for municipally owned power plants in Florida. In the early years, Mr. Hills made a commitment to provide services exclusively to municipal clients. Even though my work was for FPL's opponent, it might benefit FPL. He insisted on a weekly meeting on my progress, so that he might be able to explain our involvement to any of his old friends who might misunderstand.

Christmas 1970 came in the middle of our project. Linda and I were invited to the two Ludwig Christmas parties, one in Miami and another in Freeport, Bahamas, all expenses paid. We would take a private jet to Miami for the party there and continue on to Eluthera Island to inspect another large RS&H project. That afternoon, we continued on to Grand Bahama Island where we stayed in Mr. Ludwig's private villa at his Xanadu resort.

His Xanadu villa was like something out of the movies. It was a lavishly furnished, two stories high, with an elevator between floors. It included a small private pool, two huge solid marble sunken bathtubs with gold fixtures and chandeliers above each tub. It adjoined the Xanadu Tower, a high-rise Mr. Ludwig built as a rental condo facility. I was given the opportunity to purchase the top floor suite as an investment by Gary, Harry's replacement, but the project was taken off the market before I could buy it. Later, the government ruled the Xanadu Tower to be an investment requiring federal regulation. Mr. Ludwig refused, leaving the whole building empty. Later, Howard Hughes would spend his last days in that very unit we were offered. I missed another "too late" opportunity. Meeting two "titans" in one project was enough.

On the return from Freeport, we landed on San Salvador Island to see Columbus' landing site and visit one of my other projects, another land development. It was a memorable trip. This project included a proposed marina near Cockburn Town, but the Bahamian permits were held up by concern for marine life. It was the first project where we proposed creating a mitigation area to replace the fish feeding area to be destroyed by the construction. It included replanting undersea grasses in a nearby cove, creating a larger feeding and breeding area than that damaged by construction of the marina.

At that time, San Salvador had no tourist resort areas at all. It was site of spectacular coral, excellent fishing, and the Columbus' Landing Monument. It had more amenities than some other Bahamian Islands, and with adequate tourist facilities should be a viable project. The island had been used as a down range tracking station for the Atlantic Missile Range in the 1950s during development of America's military and space missile development programs. It included a small landing strip and a few small buildings. From the air, it seemed ideal for development. The inland was well above sea level, with its highest point over 300 feet in elevation. The interior contained several large lakes, which normally would be filled by rainwater for a good drinking water supply, but the samples we took showed the water to be salty and unfit for drinking. Other water supplies would be needed, and we could design those.

The whirlwind Christmas trip was completed, and we returned to Jacksonville to continue the project. Harry was gone and I could work in peace. But no, another adventure awaited me. I was on the phone with a client when Jimmy Shivler entered my office, took the receiver out of my hand and hung up! Not even a good bye to my client. He closed my door and sat down. "Charlie, we have a problem, and it's up to you to fix it! The husband of one of your employees is in a rage, walking the halls looking for her! Get him to leave! By the way, he has a gun! We don't want the police involved or any publicity. You know him, so just convince him to leave." With this, he walked out.

My wife, Linda, drove to the office and took "his target" to our house to hide. I then approached her husband in the hallway. He had been drinking.

"Let's get out of the hall. I know you're upset, and this isn't the place to talk," I offered.

"Charlie, just tell me where she is!" he demanded. We sat down in the spare conference room, staring at each other.

"She left the building five minutes ago, so you're not going to find her here. Let's just sit here for a few minutes while you cool down." I poured some coffee and sat with him. "You're a professional man, not a thug," I continued, "please unload and put the gun away before you ruin your career. I promise that if you do, we won't press charges. As soon as you're ready, I'll walk with you to the door and to your car." He looked like a tire that had a leak—he just slumped down into his seat.

It seemed like hours that we sat and talked, but it was only a few minutes. "Let's go, I'm okay now," he said, and he thanked me as we walked to the door. It was over. Back to work!

After several weeks of computer work, we completed the analysis, and Bechtel, FPL's engineer, concurred. The concept would work! It was time for the formal presentation to FPL Board of Directors. By now FPL's logjam of permits was larger than before, and Turkey Point Nuclear Units were nearing completion. The original discharge canal was excavated within the condemned strip of land, even though the condemnation was blocked in the courts. Without permits, it was useless. FPL's situation looked bleak. The Board presentation went very well, no posturing, no animosity. It looked like the canal plan was the only way out. McGregor Smith was actually polite to me this time, but never attended my future meetings with his management.

The plan was then presented to permitting agencies after Ludwig agreed to drop further opposition. FPL, concerned about the potential for future residents of the community harassing them, offered to purchase the entire tract of land. Then another hurdle loomed ahead. The State by this time was claiming wetland jurisdiction over the entire parcel, blocking further construction. After weeks of negotiations we convinced the State to accept a quit claim deed for the waterfront third of the tract in exchange for a deed and permits to construct the canals on the balance of the property.

Bob Gardner and I attended the Florida cabinet hearing to approve the agreement. Several other FPL officers flew in to witness the procedure. By this time McGregor Smith, president of FPL, had retired and a new president had just taken office. He heard of the swap of deeds and called during the cabinet meeting instructing Bob Gardner to block the deal! It seemed that years of work were going down the drain!

Bob handed over the phone for me to explain how critical this agreement was to FPL. The new president objected believing that stockholders would revolt if he gave away that much of the land they had paid for so dearly. He had been in office only a short time and was still under close scrutiny by both management and stockholders.

I agreed to give FPL a formal affidavit putting the reputation of RS&H on the line, stating that in our professional opinion, no other option was available for permitting Turkey Point. I also agreed to include in the affidavit that if the agreement was not approved, the state would gain jurisdiction over the entire parcel. The Corps of Engineers would most likely follow suit and make the entire FPL purchase virtually worthless.

He relented, and we returned to the cabinet meeting just as the FPL deed exchange came up on the agenda. As soon as Governor Askew announced the staff had recommended approval, the state official who recommended approval rose and announced *he had changed his mind, and now opposed the transfer of deeds!* Again, Bob and I could see years of work going down the drain!

The Governor responded, "Too late. All in favor?" It was unanimous.

As we gathered outside the capitol, the crowd of FPL observers began congratulating themselves for their victory. The press was approaching! Bob and I quickly silenced all discussion and ushered FPL's folks into taxicabs with the admonition, "No comments to the media. Receiving the federal permits is still ahead and there are many opponents who don't agree with this vote. Don't give them ammunition to block us again!"

A huge barbecue was held at Turkey Point celebrating the receipt of federal approvals based upon "FPL's environmentally sensitive solution." Reports in the media were actually positive. Bob and I attended along with the Board of Directors, EPA officials from Washington, along with local, county, and state officials and of course the press. It was held on the site of the hunting compound where McGregor Smith brought friends and business associates to hunt turkeys.

As the food and beer was being enjoyed by all, one of the EPA officials shouted. "Look, dead fish!" The discharge canal from the power plant was filling with dead fish—2000, according to the next day's headlines. We soon found out that the plant operators had chosen that precise time to dose the condensers with chlorine to remove algae build up.

"At last we can construct the new closed loop canal system and fish won't be able to get near the plant anymore. I'm glad we got the permits so this accident won't happen again," I exclaimed. The EPA official nodded, and the matter faded away a few weeks later.

It had been a long, stressful battle, with many nights of lost sleep, but in the end, it was a huge success for Ludwig, FPL, and our firm. With the State now claiming jurisdiction over all wetlands, Mr. Ludwig would never have been able to develop the land. Without the urgent need for a solution, FPL would have been required to build expensive cooling towers. Turkey Point operation would have been delayed further, and ultimately the consumers would have paid dearly. Turkey Point Nuclear units were on line during the 1973 oil embargo, reducing the amount of oil needed for power

Turkey Point Unit 3 went operational the next year, 1972. Unit 4 followed the following year. The canal system was redesigned to fit on the remaining acreage. The canals continue to function to this day, as cooling system and a viable wetland habitat. The plan worked, millions in lawsuits were settled, and both the titans won.

FPL hired our firm to complete the preliminary design of their new headquarters, provided I was to supervise the work. After approval of our conceptual design, we were asked to meet with the Board to review the details and to assure FPL leaders that the work would be directed through our South Florida office, so that board members and any stockholders that were interested in reviewing the progress could do so conveniently. As I prepared to present our recommendations, the head of RS&H's marketing department insisted on observing the presentation in Miami. At the conclusion of my presentation, he broke in and announced, "We will transfer all the work to Jacksonville, and I'll be making all future reports." With that statement, our contract ended.

I was assigned power plant site selection responsibilities for all of FPL's service area north of Ft. Pierce, Florida. It was the first engineering assignment for a private utility. Mr. Hills would later approve the contract. This time, the marketing department was not involved. I was given a five week vacation in Europe to attend the International Association for Water Pollution Research International conference in Vienna, as a preview for my presentation on "Thermal Pollution Abatement" at their next international meeting in Israel. Unfortunately, I never got to that second meeting. I cancelled after the Tel Aviv Airport massacre. With two grammar school children, the risk of travel to a "war zone" was too great. The "September Massacre" at the Munich Olympics confirmed my decision.

The trip to Europe was a once in a lifetime opportunity. Linda and I ordered a new Mercedes Benz 300 SEL for pick-up at the factory in Germany. The start of our trip had to be postponed a week because of a business commitment requiring my testimony at a Corps of Engineers hearing and a last-minute meeting in Miami.

The Corps hearing lasted so late that by the time I got back home to meet Linda and pick up the luggage it was daylight. Ray White, one of my engineers drove, allowing me to "unwind" from the nerve-wracking meeting. As he drove us to the airport, I realized the passports were left at home along with the travelers' checks. I went on to catch my flight. Linda returned to the house, retrieved them and caught the next flight. She joined me that evening in Miami, and we were finally off on our dream vacation. We arrived in London after a sleepless all-night flight and boarded a connecting flight to Stuttgart, but our luggage missed the plane. My adventures were following us to Europe.

I guess I looked pretty grubby after being up for two nights because the next morning after we checked into our hotel the manager offered me a razor and soap to use until our luggage arrived. Five star hotels expected their guests to look and smell good. I later found out that bath soap did not come with European hotel rooms, so from then on we bought some before checking in.

It was now time to pick up our car. We were met at the factory by the manager who took us to our new Mercedes. I had wished for this car for thirteen years, ever since I had been offered a dealership to sell used Mercedes Benz vehicles shipped to Houston from Germany. U.S. Government new anti-pollution regulations and lack of financing killed that deal because the cars had to be modified before sale in the U.S. The cost of conversion would have eliminated the profit.

There it was, just as I imagined it. The 300 SEL 4.5L was a brand new model, not yet available in Europe. Ours was so new, the serial number was 0000070. But as we approached closer, the chrome lettering was not 300 SEL 4.5L, but 300 SEL 3.5L! I was sure this was someone else's car. Where was mine?

The manager explained that all 300 SEL 4.5L's were delivered with 3.5L chrome markings to prevent theft. The new model was a hot target for car thieves in Europe. The correct chrome markings were stored in the trunk. The U.S. dealer would install them free as soon as the car arrived in the States. I checked, and sure enough, there they were—hidden under the spare tire. We got in, checked out the new leather smell and prepared to return to our hotel to begin our drive through Europe. The battery was dead, and it had a flat tire! By the time a new battery and tire was installed, the luggage had arrived at our hotel. Finally, we left Stuttgart for the trip to Vienna, stopping in Salzburg for two days.

This was our first trip to Europe, and we were enjoying every minute of it. It was September, the summer crowds were gone, and the weather was perfect. The only cloud on the horizon was our hotel reservations. When we modified our itinerary to accommodate the last minute Corps of Engineers hearing in Florida, we shifted the London visit from the first week to the fifth week, leaving the entire month on the continent intact. Unfortunately, American Express computers couldn't do anything that simple. Four weeks of reservations were modified to only one day in each hotel.

The first complication appeared in Switzerland, on our visit to the famous mountain peak—The Jungfrau. The Grand Hotel had no reservation at all, even though we had a written confirmation. The manager apologized and explained he only had two single rooms available, and they were at opposite ends of the hotel. We accepted the rooms, and immediately raised the eyebrows of the other guests as we visited back and forth to retrieve clothes that always seemed to be in the other room. The rooms had no bathrooms, so guests shared the common rooms on each floor. Linda found out quickly that the "Bain" she entered was the men's shower. It was her turn to *run for your life,*" but really the gentlemen just laughed. It was a minor inconvenience until our arrival in Vienna for the week long International Association of Water Pollution Research.

Our reservations in Vienna were at the Parkhotel Schonbrunn across from the Schonbrunn Palace, the summer residence of the Habsburg Emperors. The palace was truly a beautiful site, with ornate décor and beautiful gardens, one of the most picturesque in all of Europe. The Parkhotel itself was formerly the guest quarters of Emperor Franz Josef I, and the fanciest of the accommodations we had reserved the entire trip. On our arrival, we were told of the one night reservation, and that we would have to check out in the morning. We informed them we were here for a week and showed them our confirmation. They would have to honor our reservation, and we went to our room to prepare for the banquet that evening.

The other conference attendees shed some light on the hotel situation. The King and Queen of Belgium along with the Crown Prince of Japan and his entourage were jointly touring Europe, and their itinerary was the same as ours for three of the five weeks. All reservations in the best hotels were preempted by the royal visitors. Almost all the conference attendees were in less costly hotels, so they were not "bumped."

We were in for an interesting journey. We had both noticed the thousands of flags, banners, ribbons, and other decorations during the drive. The cities all looked like they were prepared for a festival. Now we knew why. I still was not going to be pushed around. We had reservations, and we would stay put for the week.

The next morning as we left for the meeting, Linda locked our luggage, "Just in case." It turned out to be a wise choice. When we arrived at the hotel that afternoon, our bags were sitting in the lobby, and the clerk demanded the room key. I kept the key and refused to pay the bill. Two could play at that game.

"We have already moved someone into your room, and you will just have to leave," exclaimed the clerk.

"Not until you get us another room," I responded.

"There are no other rooms in Vienna. The two royal families and the press have all hotel rooms filled. There's not a room available."

"We'll just sleep in the lobby, then."

"That's not possible, the royal party is arriving. Please speak softly," whined the clerk. Timing was in our favor now.

"I'm going to start making a scene, very loud!" I threatened. That did it.

He ushered us in to see the manager, who was a little more resourceful. He apologized and found us a private home to spend our week. It was only a short distance from the hotel. He assured me that Villa Elsa was even superior to Franz Josef's guest house. I was doubtful, but the options were nonexistent. We gave him the room key, paid the bill and headed for Villa Elsa.

If I was to find my way back after the evening entertainment, we better find Villa Elsa in the daylight.

The highlight social event of the conference was scheduled that evening. Wein-Reigen Burgenland, "Heuriger" wine festival, on the shore of Neusiedl See on the Austrian border with Hungary. We would have to check in to Villa Elsa, change for the festival, and drive to the charter buses parked in central Vienna, and afterward return to our room.

Villa Elsa was not what we expected. It was a dark, castle-like brick building surrounded by brick wall, topped by a wrought iron fence. It reminded us of the old castles occupied by vampires in the horror movies. A locked gate, flanked by two brick columns greeted us. I pressed the gate signal and the front door creaked open and there stood Elsa, at least eighty, wiry white hair standing in a dark doorway. "Come in," she beckoned, "Das Spaces, no?"

Linda was shaking her head and whispering, "No way I'm going to stay in this place! It's too spooky."

"Just for one night—we haven't any choice now," I responded. Elsa hadn't heard. Even in mid afternoon, the house was dark, with few windows to brighten the centuries-old walnut paneled walls and ceilings. We walked up the circular stairway behind our hostess. It seemed that she only had one light bulb on that dark stair, and at most fifteen watts. Even I was getting the creeps. Our room was a pleasant surprise. It was spacious and very well furnished, including a huge feather bed. The room had windows and lamps, and wasn't so dark after all. It was getting late. We changed for the festivities, drove to our meeting place, the Imperial Polytechnical Institute that had been founded in 1815, years before most American Engineering schools. There we boarded the charter bus for our adventure.

Vienna is a first class city for those who appreciate architecture and history, with opportunities for endless sightseeing. But if Vienna itself is spectacular, the countryside in the Bergenland to its south is even more fascinating. I loved the wide-open countryside, rolling hills, quaint villages and farms, many roofs thatched with straw. We were headed for Rust, where roofs and chimneys serve as nesting places for thousands of storks. There we disembarked for our boat cruise on Neusiedl See, Europe's largest steppe lake on the Austrian-Hungarian border.

As our boat approached the border, a heavily armed Russian patrol boat chased us away. In such an idyllic setting, it was hard to remember that the Communists were still in power. It was now time for dinner and the evening entertainment, the traditional Heuriger.

Our Heuriger was a small restaurant-tavern belonging to a private vineyard. It was open only for the new wine festival by the same name. The hosts served only what the owner's family raised on their farm. The grape branch hung above the door told us it was open for our evening meal and entertainment. Just inside the door was the Fasslrutschen, the barrel slide down to the basement. The custom dates back to the middle ages when wine farmers were required to pay a tenth of their harvested wine as taxes. The farmers built large barrels to ship their wine tax to the emperor. Sometime later, sliding down these huge empty wine barrels became tradition of Heurigers.

As each person slid down the tunnel of polished wine barrels, he emerged in a traditionally decorated Austrian Wine tasting cellar, the site of the festival to celebrate the opening of the "new wine" casks. Austrian folk dancers met each person and made sure he or she didn't fall. The ceremonial feast included Gypsy music, folk dancing and endless pitchers of new wine. It was a night to remember.

Getting back to Villa Elsa was, too. By the time we got back to our car, it was the wee hours of the morning, and as I left the parking lot, I made a wrong turn and got hopelessly lost. The new wine hadn't helped either. The streets were empty, we couldn't read the signs, and began a typical engineer's trek. First, don't ask for help. Second, follow streetcar tracks—they always lead to the center of town, and I could find my way from there. Off we went following the first tracks we crossed. I hoped I had turned toward town, but there were no signs. Naturally, it was the wrong way. By this time, I was so far from town that the tracks were being repaired. The granite blocks between the tracks were gone! Off the road into the shallow excavation went our new Mercedes—thud! I stopped and got out. We were bottomed out on the remaining tracks. Fortunately, this new model had air operated controls to raise the car several inches with the push of a button. Up went the car and I proudly drove out. Maybe it was time to abandon Rule 1 and ask for help. I drove the opposite way on the tracks toward town this time and stopped to ask directions. I forgot I didn't speak German. All I could think of was saying "Schonbrunn?" Then I drove the way he pointed. Several Schonbrunn's later we were at Villa Elsa. Then I remembered the gate and the bell. It was after 3:00, and Elsa would not be happy. She wasn't. "Ah Das Heuriger," she repeated following us up to our room, wagging her finger at us both and shaking her head the whole time. If I had shaken my head at that time, it would have fallen off!

The next morning she wakened us to a wonderful breakfast and a motherly smile. She even helped us with our laundry. Her house was the best place we stayed the entire five weeks, and her hospitality will long be remembered. We both were saddened to have to say goodbye to that fine lady. The reservation mix-up turned out to be a blessing in disguise.

By the time we were headed back to England and home, our tour had included Switzerland, Italy, France (both Paris and the D-Day landing sites), Germany, Netherlands, and Belgium, where we left the car to be shipped back to Florida the first week of October 1971.

The short flight to London was uneventful. As soon as we left the London Airport, our cabbie remarked, "Do you folks notice this weather? This time of the year, it's usually cool and rainy. It looks like you Yanks have a fine week ahead. Hope you enjoy it." It was just as he predicted. The weather was perfect, as it had been for the whole trip. We only experienced one rainy day in the five weeks we were gone. One of my first observations on the plane was at last the people were speaking English. For the past month, we had struggled with communications. All the tour books led one to believe everyone spoke English, so we did little to prepare for the language barrier. I enjoyed eavesdropping on the couple talking in the seats behind us until their conversation turned to nasal congestion and nose blowing. I decided I hadn't missed much.

That last week of our vacation, we used public transportation in London. I longed for our car in storage at Antwerp. We had sold both of our vehicles in Florida before leaving on our European vacation. My promotion entitled me to my first company Buick when we returned, and the Mercedes was scheduled to arrive shortly after our week-long visit in London. We had paid in full for the car and the shipping before leaving Florida. On arrival, we would only be required to pay the import duty. Those carefully made plans were interrupted. No sooner had we arrived in London than the U.S. Longshoremen strike was announced. The shipping agent refused to ship the Mercedes during President Nixon's Taft-Hartley cooling off period. We would have to make do with the company car I was scheduled to receive on our return until the strike was settled.

We finally arrived in Jacksonville and were happy to see our family again. Five weeks away from the kids seemed an eternity. I rented a Chevy Vega to use until I got to work the following day and received the keys to my new company car.

The next day, I received another setback. President Nixon's wage and price freeze that was imposed during our trip froze fringe benefits as well as salaries, and my company car was vetoed. Now I was faced with no car at all! I was stuck with a sub-compact rental for the duration. For over five months we waited for the Mercedes. When it finally arrived, we were in for a surprise. We didn't have to pay the shipping cost increase due to the strike because we prepaid for shipping, and even better, there was no import duty. The duty had been replaced by a ten percent import surcharge that was not applicable to imports paid for before the surcharge went into effect! Another benefit of the strike was discovered when I went to register the car and buy a Florida license tag. No sales tax was due for vehicles owned out of state for more than six months. We were two weeks beyond that six month rule, and the delay saved us several hundred dollars in taxes. Our total cost for importing and registering the car was less than $275! By March, we were finally driving our own car.

A NEW DIRECTION

Now that I was an officer of the corporation, it was explained to me that with that position came responsibilities above and beyond projects and clients. I now had a responsibility to get involved in outside activities in the community and in professional affairs.

The 1960s were a time of transition for consulting engineers. There was increasing pressure for large firms to go public, pressure resisted by RS&H until 1970. Our partners were convinced that the primary responsibility of architects and engineers was to their clients, not to outside stockholders. Our new corporation stock ownership was restricted to the original partners and selected Licensed Architects and Professional Engineers.

Kickbacks to public officials from contractors had been a problem for years, and the engineering profession was also under increasing pressure from public officials for donations, often disguised as "campaign contributions" in non-election years. Many public contracts were awarded without public notice, often to those who contributed. The National Society of Professional Engineers was leading a fight by many engineering societies to return a selection of Professional Engineers to a process based on qualifications and experience, blunting the favoritism that had crept in along with the expectations for "donations" to the elected official. In 1970, I received a request from the RS&H president, Jim Shivler to join him for a conference call in his office. He was leading the effort for reform and was slated to be the national president of NSPE in 1972.

The call was from a member of my engineering society. At that time, American Society of Mechanical Engineers (ASME) consisted of over 100,000 engineers focusing on technological excellence, public safety, a strong code of ethics, and a desire to increase engineers' responsibility to society. Jim was told of a nearly completed attempt to delete critical portions of the ASME code of ethics, changes that would go against the efforts to reform engineering procurement and reduce the decades-old practice of payoffs. He was asked to send someone to New York to explain why the change would damage the efforts for reform. I was selected for the task. I had been active for years in local and southeast regional ASME activities, but never at the national level.

My presentation to the Professional Practice Committee was successful, and I was invited to become a member of the committee. Even though my workload was too great to justify accepting this position, Jim insisted, and that began my lengthy service to ASME. It turned out to be a time of great changes and progress, due to the dedication of hundreds of unpaid volunteers. During that time, ASME and other engineering societies were successful in establishing many programs to improve engineering practices, including establishing employment guidelines for professional conduct of engineers and their employers.

None of the successes of work at the national level was more rewarding than joining the NSPE battle to remove patronage and reform the selection of architects and engineers for public work at the national and state levels. The effort culminated in the U. S. Congress adopting the Brooks Bill in 1972. Under this legislation, all architectural and engineering projects had to be advertised for competition. No longer could contracts be awarded without competition or "under the table." All federal contracts would now be based on qualifications of the applicants to perform the work and at a reasonable fee. Respondents submitted their experience and other qualifications to perform the design services. The three most qualified firms were then ranked in order of proficiency, and a detailed description of the project was provided to the top firm, which then determined hours and fees to accomplish the work. Fees and responsibilities were then negotiated and a contract signed. Recognizing that the two parties may not come to an agreement, the law provided that the agency could break off negotiations with the architect or engineer and negotiate with the next most qualified firm. Payment for obtaining contracts and automatically awarding work to "favorites of elected officials" was virtually eliminated at the federal level. Within a short time, the procedure was adopted by state governments.

This reforming process came with many casualties, all the way to the executive branch, where Vice President Spiro Agnew admitted to his lawyer in 1973 that he had accepted kickbacks from Maryland contractors because the practice had been "going on for 1,000 years." Agnew resigned, was disbarred, and the spotlight on his actions helped the reform effort gain swift acceptance.

The law got its first real test in Florida, and as was the case in many of my adventures, I got to be the "guinea pig" to take it to court. RS&H had gone through the selection process in the city of Cape Coral. I had made the presentation along with Lee Doughty, my Tampa engineering manager. We emerged in first place, even though another firm had significant support locally. Our firm headquarters was in Jacksonville, over 250 miles away, and the work was to be accomplished in our Tampa office, but we had no previous experience for that city.

Lee and I were asked to sit in the hallway, waiting to begin negotiations on our contract when the city manager emerged and announced that the city had terminated negotiations and was moving to the next candidate.

"We never negotiated, and the law requires negotiations be made in good faith," I exclaimed.

"That's too bad," was the reply. "Go back to Jacksonville; you're through here."

A quick call to Jacksonville resulted in a most difficult task for me. "Charlie," said our president, "you are to file a lawsuit naming the mayor and the entire city council as defendants. If this precedent stands, the entire effort for reform is dead—not only in Florida, but probably nationwide. The stakes are too high to '*run for your life*' this time. You will be the primary witness, and I'll arrange for the Florida Engineering Society (FES) to testify in support."

"Jim, how can I be the star witness against a new client and then ever hope to negotiate a contract under those conditions? Even if I do, what kind of relationship will we have during design? They'll all hate us."

"You'll just have to work that out," was the reply.

It was only a few days later that I received word that the trial was scheduled for 7:30 in the evening. "We want this settled quickly," said the manager.

I had no experience in court and entered the courtroom with great misgivings. There at his bench sat the local judge in his blue jeans and cowboy hat, with his boots resting on top of the bench. "Mayor, what are these guys from up north in Jacksonville trying to pull?" he began. Oh no! I was doomed! This was not like the court sessions I had seen on TV.

I was called as the first witness. Since this project's construction of underground utilities required tearing up many city streets, diverting traffic and making sure no other utilities were damaged, only the most experienced engineers should be hired. I also testified that hiring less qualified firms often resulted in higher construction costs and delays in construction. The representative from Florida Engineering Society testified the purpose for the law was to protect the public safety by being sure the most qualified professionals were hired, and a key element was that both parties must negotiate in good faith. He concluded, "In the entire time this law has been in effect, no firm has been unsuccessful in negotiating a satisfactory contract with a public body."

It was time for the city's witnesses. The entire city council was present along with their staff. We were greatly outnumbered. The summary of the city's testimony was that the City had a right to hire whomever they wanted, and no state or federal law should interfere.

The judge stated, "It's late, so let's not continue tonight." The facts were clear to him, and he would issue a ruling in a few days. The whole "trial" took less than a half hour. None of the city council members even looked our way as they left. I was sure we had lost and returned to report to Jimmy that we didn't have enough time even to rebut the City's claims. I wasn't optimistic about the outcome, but at least if we lost, I wouldn't be faced with trying to negotiate a contract with a hostile client.

A few days later, we were called to Cape Coral for the judge's ruling. It seemed every meeting was scheduled for after working hours and that meant getting home to Jacksonville in the wee hours of the morning. By this time, I was sure we had lost our suit and this visit would be a waste of time and money. I was determined to make something positive come out of the trip, so on the way to Cape Coral, Lee and I stopped in Ruskin, tomato capital of Florida. We joined the laborers picking in the field. Lee had obtained permission from the owner in advance, but the sight of two gringos dressed in suit and tie, stooped over picking ripe tomatoes was a sight none of the Mexicans had seen before.

We unloaded our sacks into a National Air Lines cargo box and sealed it for my flight back home after the meeting and continued on to our courtroom face-off. I had a large garden at home and was now deeply into my "growing our own food" phase. These tomatoes would give me a chance to learn the art of canning food. Fortunately the air conditioning in Lee's Cadillac dried our sweat off in time for the fateful meeting.

We entered the courtroom to face the glares and scowls of the city council members and their staff. A few actually grinned at us, anticipating their victory. This did not look like it would be one of my better experiences. At least the tomatoes were in the car—they couldn't toss them at us. The judge, still in his cowboy boots, passed out his ruling. I was shocked. It was over a dozen pages long, confirmed our position and ordered the City to negotiate in good faith. We had won, but what now? How could I ever repair the relationship to a point where we could work together? The City was smarting from the court opinion and was determined to embarrass our firm.

The Mayor informed me of his rules for our negotiations:

1. Only one person could negotiate for our firm, and it was to be the key witness against the City—me!
2. The negotiations would be with the entire council, supported by their staff with any member allowed to ask questions.
3. The session would be attended by the public, and the local press would be invited.
4. I was to stand in front of the council at all times, and allowed no

props, no calculator, no assistants.

5. The negotiations would be broken off if we could not agree within thirty minutes.

On our drive back to the Tampa airport, Lee and I were unusually quiet. Before us lay a very uncomfortable session that I knew we would have to face. I checked the tomato box as luggage and left on the flight to Jacksonville where I decided to recommend we withdraw from the project. The return was an ominous one. My tomatoes had disappeared, and National had no record of the shipment. I should never have answered the baggage clerk in Tampa when he exclaimed, "This smells like tomatoes."

Jim Shivler was waiting to congratulate me the next morning. "Jimmy, how can I possibly negotiate under those conditions?" I asked. "It's impossible!"

"I'm depending on you to succeed. No matter what, I want a contract. You just find a way," he replied. "But, be sure we make a profit."

The fateful night came. The city council room was packed as I began my presentation with, "For projects like yours, the FES has established fee guidelines based on a percentage of construction costs, and your project size falls between six and seven percent of the cost." I was immediately interrupted.

"You are so *skillful and experienced*, we believe you can use that *great talent* to save a significant amount." They all laughed at his emphasis on the words I used during the trial. He then mentioned a fee below five percent, far less than our projected costs.

A silence filled the room as I was obviously caught off base. They all smiled at my discomfort. Lee Doughty, my project manager watching from the audience looked ill because he was responsible for completing the work with a profit.

We only had fifteen minutes left to agree. "I think we could do a professional job for you for that fee," I responded, "provided we do the job as a team, with your staff providing information and support. If you furnish surveys for the project and furnish base maps with scale aerial photographs and profile grids printed on drafting film, we'll agree to that fee."

The mayor looked over to the city manager who nodded approval. Even the local firm that was feeding him information to unseat us couldn't finish the project for that fee. "Agreed," came the reply. It was done! Lee was speechless.

Afterward, the council members, staff, and the mayor approached me. "The battle is over," he exclaimed. "We're all on the same team, and Mr. Space, I want only one more assurance from your firm. When we go for permits, if they stonewall us the way we did you, I want you to kick them in the teeth the way you did us!" He laughed, and we all shook hands and agreed.

The project went smoothly from then on. It was completed with few problems. Thanks to the city staff's cooperation throughout that project, Lee even earned us a modest profit.

Another of our ASME goals was to reform engineering pensions. The transient nature of engineering employment was eliminating pension benefits for many engineers. When an engineer left an employer for another job, he almost always lost any pension benefits. Many engineering companies had no plan at all, and a program was needed to allow individuals to build a nest egg for retirement.

The Engineering Society's efforts to make pensions portable from one employer to another resulted in President Ford signing into law the Employee Retirement Income Security Act (ERISA) in 1974. The purpose of the Act was to protect Americans' retirement benefits by establishing uniform standards for employee benefit plans. The Act created the Individual Retirement Account, or IRA. Engineers could now save for retirement on their own in tax deferred accounts. The Act also gave retiring workers or individuals changing jobs a means to preserve retirement plan assets by allowing them to transfer, or roll over, plan balances into IRAs. By 1978, the 401-K legislation passed, providing a vehicle for employers to establish retirement programs that were easier to form and administer.

Before the 1970s, many engineers were hesitant to get involved with the legislative process, many for fear of being perceived as non-professional. With the great expansion of legislation affecting engineers, it became obvious that more involvement was needed. Engineers from industry had testified for years, but because of Congress' perception of their advice not being independent of the influence of their employers, it became necessary for the engineering societies to find a new way to provide advice.

In 1973, ASME began a pioneering endeavor for our engineering society. The Congressional Fellow Program began. Under this program, ASME selected engineers from a number of qualified applicants to serve as consultants on the staff of key congressional committees. The engineers are given a leave of absence by employers to serve on the committee, a procedure that preserves the independence of the fellow. The fellows who occupy these positions have a unique opportunity to offer their engineering knowledge for the public good, while learning valuable public policy skills for the benefit of their employers when they return to private employment.

Barry Hyman became the first Congressional Fellow. Serving on the Senate Commerce Committee, Hyman was instrumental in drafting comprehensive energy legislation that established the Corporate Average Fuel Economy (CAFE) standard and required energy efficiency labeling on household appliances.

The success of his ASME fellowship greatly increased the demand for fellows. I was privileged to serve on the Congressional Fellow Selection Committee for two of those early years, and as chairman of the Professional Practice Committee. This program now includes fellows in all three branches of government and at state levels. The ASME program inspired other engineering societies to undertake fellowships of their own, greatly increasing the engineering impact on Capitol Hill, in the White House, and in federal agencies.

During those years serving at the national level, I continued service at the local and southeastern regional levels. It was during one of these regional meeting I was faced with another close call.

Meetings had been getting longer than necessary, and one of the policy board members started a tradition in hopes of curtailing members from talking on and on as engineers like to do. He brought a skeleton of a jawbone of a donkey to the meeting. As soon as a member got long winded, it was passed slowly his way, with the comment, "You win the jawbone of an ass award." Partly due to the jawbone, this April 4, 1977, meeting in Huntsville, Alabama, adjourned ahead of schedule, and I was able to rush to the airport and catch an earlier flight to Atlanta. I got to my seat three minutes before the flight left the gate. After the short flight to Atlanta, I was able to catch an earlier Delta flight and arrived in Jacksonville three hours ahead of schedule.

After arriving home, I found out the true value of the Jawbone Award. My original flight was on Southern Airways flight 242 from Huntsville to Atlanta. Following is the news description of the flight:

"The 81 passengers and crew flew through scattered thunderstorms, some severe with icing, turbulence, and large hail. Two tornado watches were in effect with wind gusts predicted in excess of 70 MPH. At 14,000 feet, hail broke the windshield of the DC-9, and shortly after, one engine failed. Less than a minute later, so did the other engine. They were too far from the nearest airport in Cartersville to land, so the pilots headed for Georgia's State Highway 92, a narrow two-lane road through heavy pine trees. The DC-9 clipped a pine tree, hit the ground, broke up and burst into flames when it hit a gas station. Of the 81 passengers on board, 60 were killed along with the crew and eight on the ground."

I shuddered and gave a prayer of thanksgiving that I had been spared.

Another airline adventure occurred during a trip to a formal ASME dinner in Washington. Soichiro Honda, founder of Honda Motor Company, and his wife came to the United States to be honored for his generous donation to ASME. I was selected to escort Mrs. Honda to the formal banquet. My flight was on Eastern Air Lines, and as we approached Washington, the air traffic controller routed our flight into a long holding pattern. We continued in the pattern and the banquet time was nearing. I knew that I would have to skip the trip to my hotel and proceed directly to the dinner, but how could I get changed into my tuxedo? After more than an hour circling, the passengers were beginning to complain, and after another thirty minutes many were getting angry. I had to change on the plane if I had any hope of arriving on time.

Many readers know that an airline rest room is not very large, but I had no other option. I wiggled and strained for several minutes dressing and was finally finished, cummerbund, bow tie and all. Just as the seat belt light for landing came on, I emerged from the lavatory to the stares of my fellow passengers. "Look," someone shouted, "it's just like Clark Kent changing into Superman in a phone booth!" As I strolled back to my seat in my tuxedo, applause broke out. The tension had been broken.

We taxied to the gate, and one of the smiling passengers shouted, "Let Superman off first!" They did, laughing all the time. I got there just in time to escort Mrs. Honda to the head table. In 1982, the Society established the Soichiro Honda Medal in recognition of Mr. Honda's achievements in the field of personal transportation.

I was fortunate to be able to serve ASME for many years, as National Vice President for Professional and Public Affairs for four years, Member of the Board of Governors for two years, the ASME Executive Committee, and on many policy boards, councils, and committees. These assignments took me to meetings all over the country, to Canada, and to Puerto Rico. During the peak years of service, I was able to bring my family along in the summer, giving our two teenagers exposure to many different parts of the country.

Monthly meetings in New York also were an opportunity to shop, especially during holiday seasons. Linda enjoyed those trips. On one occasion when I was there alone in early December, I decided to buy an old-fashioned model train to add to our Christmas village under the tree. An advertisement contained the perfect model at half price, and it was located in a shop "just a few feet from a subway station." I decide to delay my return until the next afternoon and pick up the train. That began a day I will never forget.

The next morning, before entering the subway, I called to make sure the train was in stock. It was, and I cheerfully asked for the name of the subway line and the station near the store. I forgot to ask just how far it was from my room in The Engineers Club in Manhattan.

I boarded the train for my first trip on the New York subway. I noticed that no one else was wearing a suit and tie. The further we got from the city, the more uncomfortable I felt. The train rose out of the ground and up onto an elevated track and entered the slums. Now I was sure this was a bad idea. My station soon came into view, and I looked down hoping the streets were deserted. They weren't. Doorways were occupied by rough looking men, some huddled under cardboard, sleeping. Others gathered around steel drums filled with burning wood to keep warm. Groups of men wandered the streets. I decided to stay up on the platform, abandon my bargain-hunting, and take the next train back to town. But then I saw the store. It was right across the street from the bottom of the platform stairs! Surely, I could make that distance safely.

It was cold, and they were watching me from the street corner, so I decided to walk fast and wait in the store. I made it, trying to avoid the glaring eyes. I bought the train and some accessories and left to wait on the platform. The stairs were blocked by several men who were watching me. The store manager opened the door and yelled at them, and they left. The next train was almost an hour later, and I didn't want to sit outside alone on the platform that long.

I saw a hardware store a half block away and headed to its door to wander around inside and waste some time browsing. As I reached for the handle, a clerk locked me out, waving a "Wholesale Only" sign. I headed quickly toward a grocery store a block away. Strangers were not welcome, and I found out later that the hardware store locked me out fearing vandalism from the men following me.

As I turned the corner, it was as if I had entered a different world. The streets were clean, the sidewalks were swept, and well dressed people walked the streets. The men all had beards and wore white shirts and long black coats. Each touched his black hat in greeting as I passed. Women shopped at the open stalls as others pushed strollers along the sidewalks. Children played in the streets. It reminded me of movies of the 1890s. I had stumbled into a Hasidic Jewish community. It was like an oasis in a desert. I spent the rest of my time wandering among the shops and friendly people, in complete comfort and safety. After time was up, I turned the corner, rushed back to the platform and returned to Manhattan to pack and return home. As I passed the hardware store, I noticed the "Wholesale Only" sign was gone.

My next shopping experience was my last in New York. I was entering the East Side Terminal to catch a bus to LaGuardia Airport. I was loaded down with my suitcase in one hand and a large shopping bag in another when a man opened the terminal door for me. Another pushed me in growling, "Hurry up!" I went to the Eastern Air Lines counter to check in prior to boarding the bus to the airport, put my bags on the scale and reached for my wallet. It was gone! I remembered then the "Hurry up" guy that bumped me. I had less than a dollar in change to buy the bus ticket, and eat dinner. Linda was meeting me at the Jacksonville airport, so I would be okay there, but I had to get to the airport here first. The lady at the counter watched as I retrieved my ticket and knew I was in trouble. She gave me three dollars for the bus ticket which I mailed back with a thank you note as soon as I got home.

Upon arrival at LaGuardia, we found the flight had been cancelled, and my new flight left from Newark. After explaining my situation, I was given a free bus ride to Newark this time. As I boarded, I paused to let an elderly couple on the bus ahead of me, never expecting them to be on my flight. I boarded my flight and there they were, in the seats next to mine. They were Texans who lived near our former residence in Conroe. When the flight attendant served drinks, my two new friends bought me one in thanks for my courtesy. Once again someone was there in my hour of need. From then on I always kept one hand free to hold on to my wallet.

For the first years of my career, I had restricted professional activities to ASME, but my work now expanded beyond mechanical engineering. I was in charge of several disciplines—civil, mechanical, structural, sanitary, electrical, and environmental engineers. The new responsibilities dictated broadening out to new fields. I sponsored a field trip for the local high school class in urban ecology, was invited to join the Rotary Club, became active in the Florida Engineering Society, National Society of Professional Engineers, American Waterworks Association, the International Association for Water Pollution Research, and others. I also served as a member of the Engineers Council for Professional Development (ECPD), the national college-accreditation review committee and several committees. Later, I was asked to join the Board of Directors of the Better Business Bureau.

I enjoyed serving in the many extra curricular activities, but they did have an impact on my career. While the RS&H management was led by a Professional Engineer, the activities were a positive influence, but as he prepared to retire, internal struggles overcame the benefits. Soon I would retire from public service to build a new career.

FAMILY TIMES

I was traveling out of town with our only car almost every week in the mid '60s, and Linda was left at home raising two young children—a difficult task with no father present for five days in a row. Weekends were hectic with catch up shopping and time together with the kids. My sixty-plus hour weeks during those days often meant finding time out together whenever we could. We spent many Saturday evenings with friends and developed close friendships with two couples that had children near the ages of Suzanne and Steve. They understood the strain of careers and family raising, and we were able to spend many enjoyable hours together, sometimes with the families and sometimes adults only. One of these friends, Dan Sherrick, met a man on one of his business trips and had been invited to spend his vacation at San-San, a private home on the north coast of Jamaica. The home was complete with pool, beach, cook, maid, and houseboy to serve us. Dan and Dora invited us to join them, and we accepted. The cost was $70 per week per couple including the servants! Even in the 1960s that was a bargain.

Our two children were not yet in public school in 1967, and too young to accompany us. It was a whole week off without any of the demands of parenthood, and we all thoroughly enjoyed the week in Jamaica where we swam at the private beach and in the Blue Lagoon, a spring-fed tropical cove a few yards from our villa. The Lagoon Club had been closed to the public the previous year, so we had it all to ourselves. We also went sightseeing and shopping, ate the most delicious meals featuring native foods, buying the food at the local market with Kathleen our cook and "boss of the household." Occasionally, we bought our evening fish from a native fisherman as he paddled past the villa. We all went bamboo rafting down the Rio Grande River on two bamboo rafts passing many picturesque native huts along the shore, finally disembarking in a muddy banana plantation near the seaside, while we waited for our car to be brought to us.

The houseboy ran errands and mixed drinks, and the maid did all the cleaning and washed clothes and bed sheets daily. Her washing was by hand in a steel tub during the hours the water was turned on. She had no clothes dryer or even a clothesline. The laundry was wrung out by hand and spread out on galvanized roofing to dry, and then ironed to press out the ridges from the corrugated steel. In the evenings, public water systems were turned off because the reservoir was too small.

One evening our hosts invited us to their home for rum punch and visiting. We were surprised that they did not see their island paradise as we did. We especially enjoyed the casual lifestyle, the hills and mountains, and they couldn't wait to retire to Florida on some nice flat land with lots of people, shopping, and a place where they had water all the time. It was during that visit we found out that rafting rules required landing at Rafter's Rest, a picturesque landing with parking and a gazebo complete with restrooms, a bar, and veranda overlooking the Caribbean. Our host informed us that "unscrupulous ruffians" often dumped their passengers off early and pocketed the fifty-cent fee that was included in the rafting fee charged for each raft. Sometimes, tourists were robbed and left in the banana plantation. We were lucky that all we lost was a dollar.

That first summer I let Dan try the driver's seat on the "wrong" side of the car and driving on the left side of the road. He seemed to do fine. We also learned about traffic signs that first year. As Dan was cruising down the road, a sign *"sleeping policeman ahead"* appeared. We laughed and remarked, "Ha! They all seem to be sleeping." Then another sign appeared *"You have been warned."* Suddenly the English Ford was airborne. When we landed, we understood a sleeping policeman was a speed bump, and this one had been a fat sleeping policeman. We didn't laugh at signs after that.

Both couples returned the next summer to repeat the activities and enjoyed that vacation even more that the first. We even stopped our raft captains from dumping us in the banana plantation, insisting on going on to Rafter's Rest. It was as beautiful as we were told the previous summer.

That second summer, I did some of the driving. I did fine until I found myself in a "roundabout," a traffic circle. I was okay on the straight roads, but going the "wrong" way, on the left side of the street, and on the right side of the car in a traffic circle meant going around three times before I found out how to get out onto the highway.

By the end of that second visit, we decided that the four kids would enjoy joining us. They were all now in school, and this trip would be fun for all.

The third summer, we each took our children along for their first adventure out of the country. That third year, the capitol, Kingston, was experiencing a terrible drought. Water was rationed and turned off every night at dark, power was also cut, and conditions were not as ideal as the two previous summers. We landed in Kingston that last summer with kids and a pile of luggage. It was a three-hour drive along the winding coast highway from Kingston to Port Antonio on the other side of the island.

In the heat and humidity of the coast highway, the three-hour trip seemed like six. Kathleen, our cook, welcomed us and informed us the water would be off at six, three hours earlier than the previous year. We better shower quick. She saw we needed it.

We found out quickly that the casual vacations of the past two summers now were replaced with planning some activity each day that the kids would enjoy. Dressing was not one of them. Steve was the only boy and, at five, was not welcomed by the girls. He spent the week dressing in a closet to preserve his modesty. We tried taking them to the local open air market, but the raw meat hanging in the open (covered with flies) was not attractive to the kids or the wives.

The beach was fun and so was rafting, especially when they took turns riding through the rapids on plastic air mattresses. We were shocked to see the effects of the previous week's tropical storm on the river. The fifty-inch rainfall in three days had flooded the river and wiped out villages along the banks. Hundreds of trees were knocked down. No one knew how many people washed out to sea, but we could see brush and debris lodged forty to fifty feet up in the remaining trees. When we arrived at Rafter's Rest, even parts of the landing were damaged. That rafting trip was the highlight of the kids' fun.

The previous two summers, we had been told of the beautiful Blue Mountains with their spectacular views, giant ferns, and native plants. A rail line crossed the mountains from Port Antonio to Kingston, and we planned a day trip to explore the mountains on the single car train. Linda, Suzanne, Steve, and I volunteered to take the morning train. The Sherrick family would drive the car to Kingston and return by train while we drove back.

Early on Friday morning we were some of the first to board the train. I brought cameras and wanted to get window seats on the side facing the Caribbean for the best views. As the car filled with native Jamaicans, something was wrong. This wasn't a sight seeing train. It was market day, and the locals were bringing their wares for market in Kingston, on the other side of the mountains. On and on they crowded, even the chickens and a couple pigs. Most had not showered since the water was turned off. This was looking like a mistake, but at least we were on the viewing side of the train.

Up and up we went, past an impenetrable forest. Even at the top, there was no view. The trees and brush had grown taller than the train. Now we knew why there were no other tourists on the train. When we arrived in Kingston, I "blabbed" how disappointing the trip was, and the Sherricks cancelled the trip back. One of the two Ford sedans we rented to get from Kingston to our villa had been turned in as soon as we arrived in Port Antonio, the nearest town. The remaining car was an English Ford with barely room for four. We were eight, and had to make do. The first cloud we experienced was not a rainstorm. We found out the girls were "touch me nots." With four adults and four kids in that small car that was a problem. We were crammed in like sardines, and the whining started immediately. It was three in the front and five in the back of the English Ford—a four-hour long "touch me not" drive. When we arrived, it didn't take long to get out of the car.

The Blue Lagoon Club, the small resort/pub was a short walk from our villa, and it was still closed that year, but now had a caretaker to prevent vandalism. We were able to swim there when "Dudley" wasn't drunk or swimming naked in the water. We all watched as civil unrest resulted in local employees burning down the historic hotel in Port Antonio. It was the favorite spot of Errol Flynn, the movie star from the 1930s and '40s. I remembered seeing him many times in movies—he always played the hero of the film. That year, rumors of drug smuggling added to the civil unrest. It looked like we would have to find another vacation spot the next year.

We still had an enjoyable vacation, and all four kids even spent one day in a Jamaican school to compare it with those at home. They had a better appreciation for American schools after that.

Up until that year, both Suzanne and Steve were too small to enjoy long trips, so we spent vacations near home—at the beach, around the swimming pool, and sightseeing, but by the summer they were ten and eight, we began taking them on some of my business trips where they could see new places and meet new people. Sometimes the trips were a complete surprise to both, many times because my work schedule was so hectic that they were planned at the last minute. The air of mystery and doing new things was a key to keeping them interested in doing things as a family.

Vacations easily kept us together throughout their teen years. For a short time, we were able to compete with their "cool" friends for their attention. Between this age and leaving home for college, summer ASME trips with the kids included Washington DC, New Orleans, Minneapolis, San Francisco, Salt Lake City, and Quebec. Most of the trips were extended beyond the length of the meetings, and a couple even included camping along the way.

Our camping phase came next. It resulted from fond memories of camping at Cedar Point State Park on the St. Lawrence River between New York and Canada during my youth. We purchased a Coleman "pop-up" tent camper and began some adventures "roughing it."

For our first trip, we visited the Smokey Mountains and stayed in a campground near Cherokee, NC. There we were able to get used to "roughing it" and living in those close quarters. We planned a week of sightseeing, hiking, and fishing in a pond in the campground. We even donned swimsuits for a swim in a mountain stream—that proved to be a short dip. The water was cold, and the kids decided to play on their inflatable plastic floats, like those used in Jamaica. All of a sudden I heard a shout, "*Dad!*" Steve's raft was out of control, swiftly going down the rapids. I retrieved him, and we cut short the "swim." The only drawback to the campground was the odor of the sheep pen that was nearby. It didn't take long to decide to try another site. We relocated our campsite to Bryson City, making sure to avoid pastures.

The next year at vacation time, we followed the recommendation of a friend of Linda's brother, and arrived at Fall Creek Falls State Park in central Tennessee, to find that it was the favorite destination of thousands of campers. It was Fourth of July week, and since it offered dozens of activities, it was crowded. We got one of the last campsites. This park offered organized craft classes, fishing, rock climbing, cave exploration, biking, golf, tennis, basketball, miniature golf, wildlife viewing, horseback riding, sightseeing, swimming, canoeing, hiking, and one of my favorites—blackberry picking. That was not in the brochure, but I improvised. The park included three waterfalls: Piney, Cane Creek and Fall Creek Falls, one of the highest waterfalls east of the Rocky Mountains, dropping over 250 feet into a pool at its base. Cane Creek Cascades added to the scenery. For Linda, the availability of showers, plumbing, and a nice lodge were important.

The trip was filled with family fun, fireworks, and I even convinced everyone to pick blackberries and prepare a huge cobbler in our tent-camper. Going overboard with enthusiasm was one of my common experiences. After the cobbler success, I decided we needed to go on to the next level. We all picked as many berries as possible while they were available and canned blackberry jam in the tent. Our neighbor campers raised their eyebrows at that activity, but after a trip to town, buying supplies and copying a recipe from a library book we actually succeeded. Libraries and canning were not on the kids' list of favorite summer activities, but they compromised.

Florida Caverns State Park was selected next for another weekend camping trip. It was near a long canoe trail along the Chipola River, and I bought an inflatable plastic two-man raft for the trip. Our campsite was near a spring-fed creek flowing into the river, so I had to try it out. The engineer in me made plans. I paced off one hundred feet along the stream, tossed a leaf into the water, clocked the time it took to go the hundred feet and calculated the one mile trip's time. It would be fifty minutes. Linda and Steve drove to meet Suzanne and me at the bridge an hour after we pushed off down the stream. Suzanne planned four trips, the first was Dad and Suzanne, then Dad and Steve, followed by Linda and me, and finally Suzanne and Steve by themselves.

With the two plastic paddles along just in case we had to use them to get to the river landing, we were off! Quickly we floated out of view toward the river. We entered a dense forest, but the stream continued on at the same speed. Then, we abruptly slowed down. We had entered a huge swamp. Within a few minutes the raft came to rest against a log, and we stopped completely. Surrounded by tangles of spider webs, fallen limbs, and water moccasins, we slapped at swarming mosquitoes. I was lost, but guys never say that out loud. "This is exciting, Dad, which way is the river?" I didn't have a clue. The swamp continued as far as I could see in every direction.

Once the initial panic wore off, I looked into the water and saw the weeds were slightly leaning in one direction and started paddling. Several times, I got out into the murky water to pull the raft over sunken logs. At least when we slapped the paddles loudly into the water, the snakes avoided us, but the spider webs were everywhere. Pushing aside the tangled webs, we finally ran up against a long, low dam. I climbed over pulling the raft and the shallow stream bed reappeared. Suzanne followed, and we paddled for what seemed hours before reaching the river. There at the landing were Linda and Steve. They had been waiting over two hours, and Linda was afraid we were lost. Me, lost? Imagine that!

As we dragged the raft up the landing to the car, Steve remarked, "My turn now, we've been waiting a long time!" I hated to disappoint him, but that was the last raft trip. When he heard the details, he realized why.

The next summer brought another camping vacation, but this time nearer to home than Tennessee. This year we decided to try the north Georgia mountains.

Waters Creek was a big change from the previous summer camping trip. On this year's trip to north Georgia, we chose a more rural setting, and I even promised, "No canning jam this year—all fun." Waters Creek was near

Dahlonega, GA, and the eight sites in the campground were deserted. We could have our peace and quiet and still explore the area.

Three of four of us loved the rustic setting, but Linda noticed the camp had no plumbing, no showers, and only pit toilets. After several "Aw, Mom's" she graciously agreed to stay for a day or two. We pulled into our campsite, right next to the creek. We had the entire campground to ourselves, so it would be peaceful and best of all, there would be no line at the outhouse.

As with all our adventures, fate would intervene in the form of a local farmer named Shelnut. On our second day, he asked Suzanne and Steve if they would like to go on a horseback ride. Both kids jumped at the chance after making sure we approved. He was a typical, gracious farmer who was genuinely interested in campers having a good time, and he refused any pay "because it wouldn't be right to be paid for being neighborly." Earlier, in Jacksonville, Suzanne had spent a week with one of her friends at a horse camp, caring for horses, riding, and staying in the bunkhouse, and she dearly loved horses. Steve was a couple years younger, so this riding adventure would show us he was grown up.

When the three returned after a couple hours, the farmer asked if they would like to ride again the next day. Linda saw how excited both kids were, so she smiled and agreed to another day, then another two. Soaping up in the cold creek water had to do as a substitute for hot showers. In spite of the minor inconveniences, we all really enjoyed the stay.

Friday, Mr. Shelnut dropped a bombshell. "Mom and Dad, Suzanne and Steve are having such a fine time riding, we three would like you to join us on a trail ride up the mountain in the National Forest. It has some spectacular views, and both kids are great riders." I had just recovered from a near fatal brain injury, and Linda had not quite healed from major surgery, so we both had valid reasons to decline, but one look into those excited eyes melted away our excuses.

After we agreed, he told us the trail ride would have to wait another day. Linda and I were to share riding on his other horse, "Big Red." This was news to us, riding double. We barely could ride at all, and never considered that we would ride together, especially on a horse called Big Red. That name sounded ominous.

He continued, "Big Red hasn't been ridden in a while, and I'll have to break him again before you ride.

"Break him, like a bucking bronco?" I replied.

"Well not that bad, but he is strong willed. After I break him, you'll both be fine."

We looked at each other. What had we gotten ourselves into? "My horse, Midnight was that way," said Suzanne. "I just jerked hard on the reins a couple of times when he acted up, and he quit. You'll both be okay."

The next morning, we went to the corral and met Big Red. He was *big* alright. Shelnut said that the horse was now ready, and lifted Linda into the saddle. He held the reins as Big Red pranced a little, then calmed down. Suzanne and Steve were waiting on Midnight, a gentle mare. I climbed up and sat behind Linda on the horse's back. "Mrs. Space, you hold the reins, and Mr. Space, you hold onto your wife's waist until Big Red gets used to you both."

As Shelnut handed Linda the reins, Suzanne advised, "Remember, Mom, if he drops his head, it means he's trying to buck. Just yank his head up to stop him." The look on Linda's face showed she was not convinced. Big Red knew she was no match for him. He must have felt the two bodies trembling because as soon as Linda grabbed the reins, he bolted!

Linda didn't yank on the reins as instructed. She dropped them and jumped off the horse into Shelnut's arms, leaving me to fend for myself! Away we went! Big Red was racing across the field headed for a barbed wire fence! I was riding bareback holding on to the back of the saddle with both hands, bouncing up and down with each stride. The reins were out of reach. About two lengths before the fence, Big Red jammed on his brakes, if that is how you describe tragedy. I was still about two inches above his back when he stopped abruptly. The saddle hit me in a very tender part of my anatomy, and I slid off onto the ground, groaning. All four witnesses to my ride were trying not to laugh. If video cameras had been invented by then, we would have had a prize winning entry to *America's Funniest Home Videos*.

I was ready to go back to the campsite and sit in the icy water of the creek! "Come on, Dad, be a good sport," convinced me to continue the ride. It was time to revise the plan, though. Shelnut took my place behind Linda and lengthened the reins so he could control Big Red. Suzanne and Steve rode double on Midnight, and I inherited Cody. Off we rode across the meadow into the Chattahoochee Forest with Linda and Mr. Shelnut in the lead. Our ride was to follow a narrow trail up Crow Mountain. We had just entered the forest when Cody seemed to realize Shelnut was no longer his rider. *Aha!* an amateur. He pranced sideways, no matter how hard I pulled on the reins to straighten him up. *Bam!* He mashed my leg into a tree trunk. I kicked him, and he backed off. Not a minute later, my leg was between Cody and another tree.

Shelnut broke off a holly branch and whacked Cody on the rump, handed the prickly branch to me and said, "Next time he does that whack him good." I did, just as soon as he moved off course. Three whacks later, I was in control. The trail steepened and narrowed. It now was just wide enough to pass single-file without sliding off down the mountain. We had been on the trail a couple hours when Linda's surgery began to bother her. Another few minutes, and she couldn't go any further, she had to get down and walk a little.

Now, picture three horses with five riders in single file on a trail less than three feet wide, a wall of clay and rock on the right and a steep drop-off to the left. Not much room to maneuver. Shelnut told us of a wider spot a few minutes ahead, and we continued. "Wider" meant just enough room to pull the horse against the bank and dismount on the two-foot wide shoulder. Everyone dismounted, with me last. As they all watched, I whacked Coby to force him against the bank. As I swung my leg over the saddle to dismount, Coby got even for the holly branch. He sidestepped to the edge of the drop-off. I dropped to the ground that was no longer there. Fortunately (I think), I was still holding tight to the reins, and I swung under the horse onto the trail. As I lay on my back under Coby, he stepped back, one hoof right on my groin. This time, nobody laughed.

We made it to the summit and the view was fantastic. Our trail ride continued back down without incident, but after four hours in the saddle, everyone was ready to get back to camp and rest. About a mile from the stable, Midnight showed how much she wanted Suzanne and Steve off their backs. It was hot, and she bolted and galloped full speed back to the pasture and creek with Steve and Suzanne holding on for dear life. Suzanne was in the saddle and Steve was bouncing about a foot above Midnight with each stride. After dismounting and thanking Shelnut for such a fine ride, we limped back. Linda and I sat in the cold stream until we were cool and numb. As a last insult, one horse stepped on our hamburger grille basket, flattened it, and rode off into the sunset.

We were now prepared for our next year's three week, 4,000 mile camping trip through the western states—another adventure covered in "Dad's Worst Shortcut."

After we returned to Jacksonville to recuperate, we called back to invite farmer Shelnut to come to Florida for a week and visit in our oceanfront condo unit, but he politely refused, explaining, "I've never been as far as even Atlanta, and I don't aim to start now. Besides, the horses would miss me."

DAD'S WORST SHORTCUT

The old urge to seek excitement had overcome me again. It was time for a *real* adventure. As you know, men are notorious in never asking directions and taking all possible shortcuts, and lastly never admitting that any situation is out of control. That's me!

It was 1974. Suzanne was thirteen, and Steve was eleven. They were approaching the time when it would be boring and "uncool" to go on a vacation trip with their parents. It would be our first driving vacation throughout the West. I was determined to make this an adventure that we would remember, *and we all did!*

This was the plan: Visit close friends that had moved away from Florida earlier. All our kids had grown up together and our friends' new homes were close to our planned route. We would also visit the small town in Texas where both Suzanne and Steve were born. On the way, we would visit the most spectacular places in the West:

The Badlands of South Dakota
Mount Rushmore
The Black Hills of Dakota and Wyoming
Devil's Tower
Bighorn (Custer's Last Stand)

Lake Powell

The Grand Teton Mountains

Carlsbad Caverns

Flaming Gorge

Salt Lake City

Grand Canyon

Zion National Park

Bryce Canyon

Yellowstone Park

Arches National Park

Jackson Hole, Wyoming

We would take our Buick, with four bicycles strapped to the bumpers, and tow our four person pop-up camper and camp all the way—all in three weeks. Is that a great plan? Our route was carefully planned to be on split second timing. (It's an engineer thing—schedule, schedule, schedule.) Unfortunately, we lost a wheel on the camper the first day before reaching Atlanta. The last we saw of the wheel was as it bounced down the shoulder of I-75 and into the woods. It took a day to find a new wheel and get the bent mounting bolts repaired.

On to our second stop at the home of our friends Dan and Dora Sherrick. They moved to Illinois after our Jamaican vacations together. We visited and even took time out for the kids to ride Renata and Sherrie's horse. Suzanne was a good rider, but Steve hadn't learned yet. Both Sherrie and Renata were also riders, so Steve couldn't let three girls outdo him! After the three rode around the ring several times, it was time for Steve. He was too short to reach the stirrups, so we boosted him up into the saddle, and off he went. Halfway around the ring, he started to slip in the saddle and lean outward. As the horse sped up, the tilt increased. Steve wouldn't give up while we all were watching, though. Around again, and he was now leaning parallel to the ground, his leg hooked around the saddle horn to keep from falling. In that position, he couldn't rein in the horse. Finally, the horse slowed down and the panic look on Steve's face disappeared. He smiled and calmly said, "Next?" We all hooted as we helped him down.

It was now on to the Badlands of South Dakota, where in the 106 degree heat, we had our second blowout. The tire was replaced, and we continued to Mount Rushmore to see the monument to the five presidents. Shortly after leaving, we had our third blowout! Our trip took us next to the Black Hills of Dakota and Wyoming, Devil's Tower, Little Bighorn (Custer's Last Stand), another blowout, then to our camp site at Yellowstone Park. That night, we got caught by a hail storm, and if you have never sat out a hail storm in a camper with an aluminum roof, you have never really tested your hearing. Finally it was over, except for the ringing in our ears.

We were warned about recent attacks by overly aggressive bears in Yellowstone, so when Steve woke Linda in the middle of the night whispering, "Mom, there's a bear trying to get into the tent!" She was up in an instant.

After the initial panic, she answered, "Go back to sleep. It's just Dad snoring."

After exploring the wonders of Yellowstone, we continued on to the Grand Teton mountains of Wyoming, where the family enjoyed a white water river ride down the Snake River. It was then on to Flaming Gorge and into eastern Utah—finally arriving at Jim and Ruby's house in Salt Lake City by the end of the first week.

Finding new tires after each blowout slowed us up some, but we stayed pretty much on schedule. We all were ready for a rest prior to going to the Grand Canyon, Zion, and Bryce Canyon, then meeting them for a week cruising on Lake Powell in their forty-foot long houseboat.

The day we were to meet them, we were exploring Bryce Canyon, a beautiful but rugged Utah Park. Early in the afternoon I actually broke the unwritten male code and asked a ranger for directions to the marina! I was looking for a shortcut.

The normal route was on a paved road, about a 200 mile trip, but the shortcut I chose was much shorter—sixty-seven miles, but was it a passable road? The ranger confirmed the shortcut saved over 100 miles on our way to meet friends at Bullfrog Basin Marina. It was passable but *only in daylight*, so we better get going. He didn't know we were in a car with a trailer. I estimated the trip to take a couple hours, so we should be there by dark.

The road to the town of Boulder, the beginning of the shortcut, was paved on the top of a narrow mesa, in places only two lanes wide, with no shoulders. At one point the road narrowed to one lane with a sheer drop-off on both sides of the pavement. *Pow!* Another blowout, and we had the road blocked. Fortunately there was no traffic. We were in the middle of nowhere. After fixing the flat, it was *really* getting late! Now, there would be no spare tire for this leg of the trip.

It was dusk when we stopped in Boulder, Utah, at the beginning of what was called the Burr Trail. It was only a sixty-seven mile "road," not quite dark, so I'd try it even with no spare tire. I figured we could take it slow and average thirty miles per hour. I broke my rule, "Never ask for directions" for the second time in one day. At the trading post where I stopped for last minute advice while the family waited in the car, the owner looked out the window at our rig—Buick, four bicycles and pulling a camper. He laughed and said, "It's not a road, buddy, it's an unmarked jeep trail—four-wheel drive only, *never at night*. For you, not day or night in a car pulling a trailer! You better turn back to the main road." He showed me a map with ominous names like The Gulch and Rattlesnake Canyon. Me, admit defeat? I don't think so.

"You're still going? Okay, if it starts to rain, stop immediately and wait for rescue. The streams have no bridges, and you have to drive through the stream beds, gullies, and wash outs. If you get stuck in one and it rains, you'll be swept away. Be sure to stop at each gully and check it out before driving through. If there's any water, stop. *And* always keep to the main trail or you'll get lost and may not be found alive. [There were no cell phones then.] Finally, if you give up, don't turn back, because your car can't possibly make it back up the cliffs." *Cliffs? The ranger didn't mention any cliffs.* Oh well, it was too late to turn back, and he was just trying to scare me (I don't scare). I persisted, and he insisted we call ahead to arrange for a rescue if we didn't make it. *Rescue?*—Not me. Naturally, I didn't share that tidbit with the family, but I did call Bullfrog Marina and leave a message to be put on the bulletin board for Jim and Ruby. *"If we don't arrive by* 10:00 PM, *send a rescue team. We're coming on the Burr Trail."* He shook his head as I left. Another brainless tourist!

The American Southwest.com—used by permission

What I didn't know was that we would have to drive down almost 3000 feet to the Colorado River and the lake, and most of the drop was down the Waterpocket Fold Cliffs. We were unable to take photos of the trail as darkness was fast approaching. By the time we reached this point, it was dark, and we couldn't see just how steep the decline was. If I had seen the drop, I would have turned back. The photos used were taken by travelers with more sense. They took the trail years later, after it had been paved.

Starting Down the Cliff—(Copyright)
Photo courtesy of Kate Burgess—used by permission

Off we went. What? No road or signs? Onward. We reached the top of the Waterpocket Fold Cliffs at dusk and slowly started down the switchback trail. In the shadows, visibility was poor, and we soon were in trouble. The brake fluid was now boiling. The brakes failed, and I had to run off the trail and up embankments to slow down, then back down to the trail and start again. Much of the time the headlights didn't light the road—they shined out into the night sky.

It's Getting Worse—(Copyright)
Photo courtesy of Kate Burgess—used by permission

Where was the edge? Where is a Jeep when you need it? Nervous wrecks after only ten minutes, we continued and finally made it to the bottom without going off a ledge. It had taken over an hour to negotiate three miles!

Now it was pitch black, and we were still thirty miles from the trail's end. Three more hours to go, given our fantastic top speed of 10 MPH. At least in the dark my panic and sweat didn't show. All the bicycle wheels had hit bottom while driving through a dry stream bed and were bent, but the car brakes had cooled off and were now operating, so we went on. Linda and I were terrified, but both kids thought it was a great adventure. As we proceeded over a rise, the headlight beams rose above the trail out into endless darkness. I would then stop the car to use flashlights to be sure we weren't driving off a cliff or into a washout. Twice we stopped just short of going over a precipice. Each noise in-cluding opening electric windows to use flashlights was imagined to be another blowout. With the spare tire shredded a few hours earlier, another blowout would strand us in the desert.

"Dad" was losing his cool now, and the panic was showing through. As we bounced through several stream beds, we were sure each one would get us. After a short while, everyone realized we really might not make it, and

303

the car got real quiet. I was sure we would have to stop and wait for rescue. I was glad that I took the advice about calling ahead. It would be embarrassing to admit defeat, but it was better than a serious accident. We continued on at a snail's pace.

The only living things we saw were jackrabbits, and I think they were laughing at us as they ran across our path. What's so funny? After three *more* hours in the dark, we still weren't there. Had we turned off the unmarked trail? Then, we drove over a rise and saw a single electric light bulb on a cabin several miles ahead. We all cheered. That was the brightest 100-watt bulb I ever saw. We finally arrived at Bullfrog Basin Marina—more than five hours after entering the trail. We pulled into the marina parking lot after midnight, terrified, with a ruptured shock absorber on the car and about fifty rivets broken on the camper. Our Coleman lantern fuel cans were leaking—worn through by the sandstone grit that filled the trailer. Tin cans of food were crushed, four bike tires bent, and a bumper broken. It was over two hours past the time to send a rescue team. I went to the office to retrieve the rescue notice. I was in for a shock. The marina operators had gone to bed and not posted our rescue message. We found out the next day that it had been lost. It's a good thing we weren't.

Only the kids could say *"Great Shortcut, Dad!"* Linda just rolled her eyes and shook her head. Jim and Ruby did too.

The Burr Trail turned out to be a cattle trail used in the 1870s and more recently as a uranium prospector's Jeep trail that was used during the uranium boom of the 1950s. It had been all but abandoned by the time we decided to try it. In those terrifying hours on the trail, we never saw a sign of another human being. It has since been improved with part of the trail now paved and the balance improved to a gravel road. Even the washed out stream beds now have culverts. But don't try it at night in a car with a trailer and bicycles! You'll miss the views.

We spent the next weekend cruising Lake Powell, including exploring cliff dwellings that were accessible for the first time that year, as the lake was now full. On our way back to Florida, we visited Arches National Park, Carlsbad Caverns, and Conroe, Texas, where both Suzanne and Steve were born. It was a marvelous trip, one we will never forget, especially with the blowouts and shortcuts.

You would think that adventure would have cured me from taking short-cuts, but it didn't. I guess it's a *"guy"* thing.

SKIP YOUR
FORTIETH
BIRTHDAY

It was 1975, time to put the "Run for Your Life" nightmare behind me and stop dreaming of the past. I was nearing forty, with a wife and two children and a successful career. What was I going to do with the few years left for me? I had become reconciled that I would die by my fifties as Mother had so often reminded me, so time was wasting away. For most of my grown life, death had hung like a cloud over me. It was time to chase the cloud away, and I was sure that a new direction would do just that. I had gotten the idea for a change from our friend Dan Sherrick, who had just finished reading *Shifting Gears*, a book glamorizing a mid-life career change.

As I lay there in the cool October breeze, I had to plan something new. I was letting my inability to idle well urge me on to something different. I had always been told to watch out for "the big 4-0." Men do strange things about that age. I was no exception. It was just a few weeks away—the most dangerous time.

I had no idea which direction to take until Richard Moe, a friend from work, told me of his change. He and his wife had bought property on the St. Johns River, in Fruit Cove, an area south of Jacksonville that had been settled many years ago. It was a perfect area for rural living—raising citrus, fishing, shrimping, gardening, and relaxation. For the kids, the schools were superior. Fruit Cove was in St. Johns County where schools retained accreditation when Jacksonville's schools lost theirs. There was even plenty of room for horses on your lot. That sounded like a perfect plan—away from traffic, air pollution, paper mill odors, and the rising crime rate. I might even be able to find a church home in the country. I had given up long ago looking for a "Follow the Bible Only" congregation.

As the big birthday approached, I began my search and quickly found an old house for sale, just a few lots south of Richard's. The kids were excited, and Linda was kind enough to hide her reservations. It wouldn't hurt to just look, so on a weekend afternoon we headed south, past strip malls and traffic lights, finally crossing the bridge into Fruit Cove. As we turned into the dirt driveway, we saw a pasture that would be perfect for a couple horses and the rest of the four acre lot contained dozens of camellia and azalea bushes and a large citrus grove planted with at least a dozen different varieties. This was really looking good! It was October, and the trees were loaded with fruit. The house was a plain two story structure, covered by asbestos shingle siding. That siding would have to go first. I had enough exposure to asbestos in the refinery to kill several people. No need to risk dying even earlier than I expected.

We met Francina, the owner, and she took us on a tour of the house. The entire house, including bathrooms was paneled using long leaf yellow pine. Even the ceilings were pine! The house was shaded by old live oak trees, had few lights, and the aged dark paneling made it look even darker.

But the view of the three mile wide river at sunset was spectacular. A walk out the 400 foot long dock allowed us to look back at the house and imagine the improvements it would need. The seven foot high ceilings on the second floor would certainly need raising, but the downstairs would be fine. The roof shingles needed replacement, but that would come with the raised roof. The two-story, six foot wide front sunroom would need widening, but since we were going to raise the roof anyway, it would be easy—if we widened it before the new roof went on. My mind was spinning with ideas. Linda's was just spinning. We had built our existing house from scratch, and she remembered the struggle. It would not be easy, but both kids would be teenagers by the following spring and this time they could help. After seeing my enthusiasm, Linda graciously agreed. Suzanne and Steve were hesitant to leave all their friends, but the promise of a horse convinced Suzanne. Steve just had to have one, too, so he wouldn't feel left out. I had beat the deadline. It was my fortieth birthday!

We made an offer, contingent on an inspection for termite damage and a clearance letter from the inspector. The offer was accepted, and we began to make plans for the renovations. There was not much time to plan for all the necessary work. While the inspection was conducted, the title work, survey and deeds were prepared. We still had to complete a few projects at our old home to prepare it for sale. The time went by quickly, and we visited the new house several times to take measurements for the plans I was drawing for the remodeling. I discovered one board in the kitchen that had a small spot of dry rot, but since we were planning to replace the pine with sheet rock, it was not a concern.

It was an exciting time for all and the anticipated project crowded out thoughts of the office and its deadlines. At the time I was responsible for four groups of engineers, two in Jacksonville, one in Tampa, and one in Hollywood, Fla. I traveled extensively, and many of the house plans were completed on weekly National Air Lines flights. It was a busy period, with no time for idling.

The fortieth birthday party was followed by planning something else that was new and exciting. We were all going to learn to snow ski that winter. With all the paperwork on the house in the hands of realtors, inspectors, and attorneys, I just couldn't sit still and wait. I was either at full speed or sleep. Idling was not in my vocabulary. So, it was off to Utah and the famous deep powder of the Wasatch Mountains.

Our dear friends, Jim and Ruby Madole and their family, had moved from Jacksonville to Salt Lake City and invited us to visit. That winter, I was scheduled to attend an engineering society meeting that allowed the family to visit Salt Lake during spring vacation and learn to snow ski. This was the first time when the teenagers had a big advantage over their parents. They both laughed at us as we tried to practice walking in ski boots. They adapted quickly, and we didn't. It was worse when we put on the skis.

As they glided down the slopes, it was, "Get up, Mom. See, it's easy!" It wasn't easy for us. Fortunately we were finally able to negotiate the "bunny slope" for beginners, and they went on to more difficult runs. At least now we wouldn't be seen sitting in the snow as they passed by. After a week, though, Linda and I had learned to ski well enough to succeed on the moderately difficult slopes and looked forward to many more trips.

If you decide to learn to snow ski at an "advanced age" (over thirty), I recommend the first trip be at least a week long. That way you can get past the worst part of learning and people laughing at your clumsiness. If we had gone home after only four days, we would never have tried again.

On our return home, we received the title binder and survey. Next, the mortgage company informed me that they received the termite clearance letter, it complied with the contract, and all the papers were in order. We could close on the house. It had been three months, but the dream was finally coming true—our own house in the country.

After closing, I could hardly wait to begin work. Our house in town was on the market, and we would have to be ready to move with little advance notice. There was little time to spare. Francina moved, we cleaned out the house, and immediately began removing the paneling in the six foot wide sunroom to begin the expansion. During this task, I discovered a small area that had been damaged by termites, but it was confined to the corner that was being demolished so I gave it no concern. The pine was beautiful—straight grain long leaf yellow pine. That variety of pine was almost extinct from over harvesting in the post WWII building boom. We were eager to save it for use in the renovations. It did have its drawbacks though. It was so hard that it could not be nailed without drilling holes first, and removing the old nails required a long crowbar. Even then a large number simply broke off and the nailed end would be sawn off.

Next came the task of more demolition—tearing off the asbestos siding. This task required more safety precautions than others. Wearing a government-approved mask for asbestos removal, I wet the entire side of the house and began carefully removing each shingle and placing them in plastic bags, being careful to dampen the dry side of each one to prevent dust flying. The plastic bags would keep asbestos dust from escaping during handling after the shingles dried. I finally had them all removed and hauled off.

After that, construction went swiftly, even though we decided to move another outside wall at the same time as the sun porch walls. This made room for a new fireplace and hearth. Owen (my brother-in-law) and his crew joined us to help with the framing. It was now time to remove the old roof and replace it with a new one. The work had to be planned carefully because the house had relatively new wool carpeting we planned to keep, and we didn't want any of the pine paneled ceilings, walls, and floors to get wet and warp. The upstairs wall and ceiling paneling had been left in place to stabilize the house while wall height was increased and the new roof trusses were installed. The rockwool ceiling insulation and paneling would be removed two days later, after the new roof was on and dried in.

The materials for the new roof were delivered and placed next to the house for easy access. The weather bureau forecast sunny skies for the next three days, and we started ripping off the entire roof in one afternoon. We were scheduled to start installing the new structure the next morning, and within twenty-four hours would be dried in, leaving an extra twenty-four hours for unforeseen delays or rain. The plan was perfect (we thought).

Weathermen should be paid only for correct forecasts, but in Florida, that would mean they would starve. Just after the roof was removed, an ominous cloud appeared across the river. It darkened as it got closer, then lightning, and torrential rain hit. As we stood in the living room, water began dripping upstairs, then pouring through the ceiling light fixtures, down the stairs and out the front of the house. By the time it was over, four inches had fallen and the entire structure was soaked! The water had even short circuited and blown most of the fuses. This project was not looking like fun anymore!

We squeegeed out as much water from the wool carpets as possible and dragged them into the yard after the sun came out. It took everyone to move them. We hoped they would be salvageable, but even after the sun had dried them, they still smelled bad. Mrs. Nichols, our next door neighbor defined the smell best: "like wet sheep." A measurement showed us they had shrunk too much to use.

It was now time to survey the damage to the rest of the house. The rock-wool insulation was the first casualty to be removed. The wet insulation lay between the old ceiling and the new trusses which were only a foot higher. Suzanne and Steve crawled through the small opening, loaded dozens of bags of the soggy mess and handed them down to us for transporting to the dump. As the insulation was removed, the wiring was exposed. It was a knob-and-tube wiring system from decades before. Bare copper wires had been stretched between porcelain insulators screwed into the framing. None of the wires in the attic were insulated, and those in the walls were insulated with paper and cloth! At least we had found the reason the power was off. Only the dry insulation prevented short circuits. The wiring was so old that the switch and receptacle boxes were made of porcelain. The kids found several dead rats that had electrocuted themselves by burrowing into the insulation and touching both bare wires. All this hazardous wiring needed to be removed and replaced with new wires. Our budget was being damaged as much as the house.

Now it was time to tear down the old pine ceiling and framing. Much of it was still salvageable because the dense pitch-filled pine didn't absorb much water. Steve especially enjoyed tearing down the ceiling paneling. He could hold on to the new roof trusses and just stomp the ceiling boards until they came loose, a perfect job for a boy who had just entered his teen years.

Tearing out the pine was much faster than removing the nails. The boards were piled in the yard for Linda to remove the nails and stack the boards for reuse later in the project. For days the pile of nail-studded boards grew, but eventually, she got to the bottom of the pile, still sitting on top of the boards to hold them for nail pulling.

I heard a scream and came running. There under the boards she had been sitting on was a coral snake that had made a new home under the boards! She had been calmly sitting on the snake's new roof, pulling nails. Linda was terrified of snakes. It was "run for your life" time again, and she did. Northeast

Florida was home to three poisonous varieties: coral snakes, rattlesnakes, and water moccasins. Our new lot had all three!

Linda had been deathly afraid of snakes ever since she found a snake in our playroom when Steve was about four. We heard him scream, then *bam, bam, bam, slam!* The first three were Steve coming up the stairs, four steps at a time. The next sound was his door slamming. He didn't like snakes either.

Linda's next encounter was a snake in our garden. Fearing that it would get the kids, she took up the garden hoe as a weapon and by the time I saw the results, the snake looked like it had been through a bologna slicer. She had protected them all right.

While all this work was proceeding on the house, I was still traveling throughout the southeast for our firm. As soon as I returned each Friday, all four of us would spend weekends at the site, sleeping on the floor on sleeping bags. The old windows and doors were gone, and the house was open to the outdoors, leaving the generous mosquito population with tempting meals. Soon, each sleeping bag had a No Pest Strip placed at the head and foot. The smell was not too bad, and the mosquitoes kept their distance. Much of the novelty had worn off by now, but at least we were making progress.

In the middle of our replacing termite damaged wood, our eighty-year-old neighbor, Mrs. Nichols, shouted, "Mr. Space, help, come quick!" Oh, no! I thought it was another snake. If Linda sees another one this soon, she'll never want to live here until I get doors installed!

As I ran toward her, she handed me a shovel. Slowly crossing her yard and heading for a tunnel they dug under her foundation was a family of armadillos, Mama leading four babies. "Whack them!" she shouted, "they're damaging my foundation."

"I'll get them," I replied, but I declined to use the shovel and went back for my rifle. I had shot Linda's coral snake, so a few armadillos were no match for me. I fired at the last one in line and missed. They all ducked into the tunnel before I could reload.

"City folk, *ha!*" Mrs. Nichols snorted.

The next day she was waiting for the armadillo parade. As soon as they appeared, I heard, "Mr. Space, come quickly." I was ready this time. I had a loaded shotgun ready. As I charged to her rescue, she said, "Stop! Watch!" In four seconds it was *whack, whack, whack, whack*! At her feet were five dead armadillos. She actually killed two with the first whack. She looked at me, smiled and said, "That's the way we do it in the country. If you have any bothering you, just call me!" The family didn't laugh out loud, but their huge grins told the story. They had seen the whole episode!

One week during the kids' summer vacation, while I was out of town, Linda, Suzanne, and Steve went to the house alone. Even though it still had no doors or windows, the house was several hundred feet from the road, and we had neighbors within a hundred feet on both sides. Safety was not a concern. Sometime in the middle of the night, voices woke Linda.

"Let's stop at this empty house."

"No, let's get out of here," was the reply.

Another voice, "We're sinking; we've got to stop."

"I'm getting out at this dock to hide this stuff."

"Maybe we can come back to get it tomorrow."

By now she was fully awake, fearing they would come to the house and find the three. Linda had brought Steve and Suzanne to her room, urging them to keep quiet. There weren't even any lights she could turn on and scare them away and no telephone either. That would have been a perfect time for a cell phone, but they weren't invented yet. The chattering and noise continued for what seemed an eternity. Banging, cursing, scraping sounds. Finally the noise stopped. What now, would they come to the house and find the witnesses? No, an outboard motor coughed and sputtered to life. They left the three alone, shivering in the dark bedroom, even though it was summertime. It had been a close call!

The next morning no one slept late. As soon as it was light all three headed out the dock to the boathouse. It was filled with stolen goods—liquor, boat supplies, fishing tackle, guns, ammunition, electronics, and everything the gang of thieves collected from the line of homes and boathouses along the river. *And*, they would be back! Linda called the sheriff and an officer known as "the singing deputy" came to their aid. Disguised as a fisherman in ragged clothes and a straw hat, chewing on an unlit pipe, he pretended to be fishing with his cane pole when the gang returned.

"Get off that dock, old man," they ordered. "We've got some stuff in there."

"Eh, that stuff yours?"

"Yep, so just git—you're trespassing on private property." Then they got out of the boat. This one must have been bigger than the previous night so that it wouldn't sink from the weight of all that loot.

As they approached the "singing deputy," he pulled out his badge and gun and arrested all four. He took them away without mentioning the family staying in the old house. They were local teens, and the judge released them to their parents. The parents must have been effective because we never heard of waterfront burglaries in the neighborhood again. Later, we heard that the "singing deputy" went on to a career in entertainment.

Guess what we made top priority after that night's adventure? Doors and windows, which meant the new siding had to go on first. It seemed like nothing could be done unless there was something else finished first. Our house in town was under contract to a new owner, so we would have to speed up to be able to move. As the closing date approached, it was obvious we wouldn't make it in time. Bruce and Mary Smith, our new next door neighbors, offered us the use of the "Roach House," an appropriately named abandoned fishing cabin his parents had moved to the back of their lot to make way for their current house. It had functioning kitchen and plumbing, but we used our own kitchen and bathroom during the daylight to avoid the several hundred foot walk. "Kitchen" was a loose term, because it had only a stove. Our sink was sitting on the ground in the yard. One had to fill a bucket using the garden hose, heat the water on the stove in the kitchen, and carry it outdoors to the sink. It was easy to empty the sink by pulling the stopper and lifting it off the ground to drain. Our furniture was stored in the Roach House, ceiling high in all the rooms except the bedrooms we slept in. "It's like a camping vacation," I explained. No one bought that story. In fact, the Roach House turned out to be our last camp-out. One evening I came home from work and the tent camper was gone—sold. I was tired of roughing it too, so I didn't miss it.

It was at the time we were replacing the stairway to the second floor that the stairs collapsed, and Suzanne fell through and got a nail stuck in her knee. After the first aid, the damaged board was removed exposing the stair supports. I found termite damage that had not been reported to us. The center wall supporting the entire second floor was almost destroyed. This was a huge setback.

I began to investigate further. I found that the termite report had not been sent to us even though the contract required we be furnished a report showing no infestation or damage. The mortgage company requested our copy be sent directly to them prior to closing and they approved the report without our review. A copy was not given to us until our attorney demanded one. The termite letter specifically stated that it did not include the damage report required in our contract. I also discovered that the termite inspector who had not reported the damage was a close friend of the former owner. He was aware of severe termite and powder post beetle infestation and damage. Later, a contractor informed us that the realtor had hired him to cover-up termite damage in the house and wood borer damage to the 400-foot dock.

I contacted the termite inspector, who informed me that he knew the house was damaged! "I have no responsibility, even though the contract requires damage to be reported." The realtor ordered the inspection, and the inspector claimed his only responsibility was to the previous owner, the person who contacted him. I was not pleased at all and contacted an attorney friend to investigate. Months later, we received a copy of a letter the inspector had written to the Florida Real Estate Commission after our incident, explaining how real estate salesmen and pest control operators cooperated to avoid reporting damage to a seller "to keep his business relationship." We also discovered some realtors had ownership interests in inspection companies, and reports on those houses were always clear.

I began my own inspection of the structure and discovered that the storage building had been damaged beyond repair. The garage and shop were salvageable, but needed extensive work. The dock and boat house were next. Several of the pilings were eaten by wood borers, and much of the super-structure had recently been patched to hold it together. The house was far more serious. The complete center supporting wall of the house had to be replaced, and even worse, the wooden beams under the entire first floor were beyond repair. We would essentially have to either tear it down or rebuild the house by replacing the old structure from inside the new house. We received an estimate of almost $40,000 just for the house repairs. The dock, garage, and storage building would probably double the estimate, but no contractor was willing to do the job—they all wanted to tear down the house and start over. That would have been financially impossible. We had no choice other than to do it ourselves.

The foundation beams were replaced by removing a section of flooring and tunneling under the floor to remove and replace the beams. Suzanne and Steve spent countless hours removing dirt by filling gallon buckets and pass-ing them up to be dumped in the yard. Once the tunnels were complete, the damaged foundation beams were sawn in short sections and pulled out. Tem-porary shoring was installed to support the floor as the family wrestled the damaged beams out to the burn pile. Then new, pressure treated beams were jacked into place and the floor lowered back down. This was definitely more than we bargained for.

After consultation with our attorney, we decided to go to court for re-imbursement. I have never believed that contingent fees were proper, so I refused to pursue the case on that basis. I paid for the services as the suit proceeded. After several months of investigation, Buck, our attorney, had found a trail of numerous termite inspection reports that had omitted infor-mation on serious damage. Dozens of home buyers had purchased severely damaged structures, and one a short distance from our house sat for months stripped of its exterior waiting for resolution of the conflict with its inspec-tor. It was time for the next task—try to reform the inspection practices that had harmed us and so many other home buyers.

Our suit included the mortgage company for its instructing the termite company to bypass us and send the report to them, the realtor for failure to disclose known damage and for hiring a contractor to cover it up, and finally the termite company for its negligence in preparing a report that violated the contract and informing us that it complied. Florida law didn't address this issue, so the procedure was a civil suit, not a criminal trial. We had to bear the financial burden of proceeding. The suit dragged on for months.

Meantime the repairs continued, and we were able to move out of the Roach House by the beginning of school. The defendants offered to settle the case for about half of the cost of our damages provided that we agreed they had no responsibility for the deception.

Several other homeowners who had purchased termite damaged houses had been following our battle. They urged us to proceed, so that the practice would be stamped out. This was not a decision for just the parents. All four of us met at a local restaurant with Buck, who explained that we had an excellent case, but if we settled, others would be hurt as we were. But, there was always the chance that we would lose. Juries sometimes return strange verdicts. We decided to continue to trial. But then a blow was struck. The judge died, and after more delay our case was reassigned to another judge. All the pre-trial activities had to be reviewed and some repeated. The new judge was irritated that he had been assigned the case and that we had refused to settle. The defendants knew we were paying the expenses as the process continued, and threw up every roadblock possible, hoping we would run out of money.

They were not far off course. The two years had been a struggle. Our house in town and our ocean front vacation condo had been sold, and I had cashed in all of my profit sharing/retirement account. We were passing our financial limit. A second offer to settle was refused, and the trial was scheduled for July 1978, more than two years after we filed the complaint. By that time all the renovations were complete, and we were enjoying the fruits of our labors. At Buck's direction and at the direction of the first judge, we had documented the damage with photos and had saved samples of severely damaged wood. It was time for the face-off in court.

With the move came Suzanne and Steve's reward. We bought horses for each, Skipper for Suzanne and Duchess for Steve. Our Mercedes was not capable of hauling hay, so we sold it and bought a used Chevy Suburban. It was large enough to haul a week's hay in one trip. They learned to feed and care for their horses and spent many spare moments for the next two years riding frequently.

Those years of struggling on the house repair, our finances, and the trial delays were not all grief. We were able to continue our vacations and to add even more new activities that kept the family enjoying each other even during the "declarations of independence" that frequently arise from growing teenagers.

This phase of our lives that started at forty led us into a complete change in direction, resulting in many bumps in the road, but leading to new friends and broader experiences. If you are not prepared for a wild ride, maybe you should *skip your fortieth birthday.* I'm glad I didn't.

THE BIG DETOUR

I had completed another NASA project, the conceptual design for the National Aircraft Noise Reduction Laboratory. This was my second acoustic laboratory, but this time for airborne noise research instead of Navy undersea surveillance. Again I was responsible for preparing the conceptual design to prove feasibility and the funding request to be presented to Congress. The facility was subsequently funded, designed by RS&H and constructed at Langley, VA, renamed NASA Acoustics Research Laboratory.

By this time, Suzanne and Steve were teenagers, with adjoining rooms. I had anticipated stereo noise when I built our house and had used some of the information learned to provide acoustic noise control. Even the military had no concept of a way to combat "stereo wars" between two teenagers, each trying to out-volume the other. The government noise projects were more successful than mine at home! The only effective way to silence the battles was turning off the circuit breaker and shutting off the power.

In quick succession, we completed the following Environmental Division projects:

1. Design of the first full-scale municipal reverse osmosis water treatment plant to remove contaminants from mining runoff in the Peace River in west central Florida
2. Conversion of Jacksonville's River Water Fire Protection

network to a combined fire and potable water system

3. Upgraded the entire Jacksonville water supply and distribution system
4. Designed Florida's first advanced waste treatment plant for Hillsboro County
5. Expanded utilities in several Florida cities and completed several military projects
6. Completed a survey of the hydraulic and thermal resources of the St. Johns River for FPL
7. Initiated a water conservation program for Northeast Florida where water levels and quality had significantly deteriorated.

By 1971, I had been assigned responsibility for environmental permitting of the new power plant expansion at Northside Unit #3, for our company's longest and most faithful customer, the Jacksonville Electric Authority.

RS&H had designed and performed construction management for virtually every JEA project since WWII. By the early 1970s some friction between staff members had developed. Newer JEA employees were not satisfied with maintaining the status quo and expected more from RS&H. Relations with my Environmental Division remained strong as several critical permits were obtained by joint JEA-RS&H staff efforts, and this helped retain work for JEA.

One especially interesting trip was a tour I arranged for the JEA staff to accompany us on a tour of TVA coal fired power plants, so they could become familiar with construction and operation of these large units. JEA had only oil fired power plants and the oil embargo of 1973 convinced them that other options should be considered in the future.

The trip was uneventful until our flight home. None of the JEA Board of Directors was familiar with coal, so numerous photos were taken for their review. I suggested that I also bring home a baseball sized lump of coal for the next Board meeting. It was winter and I placed the coal in the pocket of my coat, a bulky North Sea style great coat with wooden pegs instead of buttons. The bulge hardly showed.

Before the flight we sat in the restaurant of the Atlanta airport waiting for our prime rib dinners. The service was exceptionally slow and flight time was approaching. I asked for the manager, and lo-and-behold, he was a former RS&H employee. He chatted a few minutes as the meal arrived. By then we had only twenty minutes to catch our flight. He quickly had the rare roast beef wrapped in aluminum foil and cancelled our bill with his apologies. I crammed my dinner in the other great coat pocket, and we rushed to the gate, where I dropped my coat on the counter. *thud* went the coal lump.

"What was that?" asked the attendant.

"A lump of coal," I responded, but he didn't believe me and shoved his hand into the pocket to check. He withdrew a blackened hand.

"It's a souvenir," I responded. The flight was in five minutes!

"I suppose the other pocket has another lump of coal?" he asked.

"No, it's roast beef."

I thought we would have to close his jaw for him. It hung wide open! The restaurant manager had followed us to the gate in case we were stopped. He explained, and our group was quickly allowed to board. The rest of the trip went smoothly.

The new officer in charge of the RS&H Power Plant Division had not been as successful in his relationship with the Electric Authority staff. A dock site study completed by that division was released without environmental review and contained a fatal flaw.

Just prior to the release of the report, my staff at RS&H had assisted in negotiation of permits for Offshore Power Systems to dredge and fill a large part of Blount Island, an island created over fifty years ago by dredging of the St. Johns River to eliminate a sharp curve in the original channel. This island contained a large wetland that would have to be dredged and filled. Permits for this type activity were no longer automatic, but required a strict justification analysis.

Offshore Power Systems planned to construct floating nuclear power plants on Blount Island to operate off the East Coast in huge breakwaters to protect them from storms and vessel collisions. These plants would be less costly when built in the planned shipyard and would not need huge cooling towers—an additional saving. Better quality control would be possible in a shipyard, and the plants would be safer to operate. Licensing, training, and regulatory controls could all be standardized. Finally, the remote possibility of an accident would be less threatening as the plants would be anchored far from population centers.

Added to these benefits was a huge boost to the economy. Blount Island was owned by the Jacksonville Port Authority (JPA), a public agency, so land acquisition would be uncomplicated. Even with all these positive aspects of the project, the Corps of Engineers was under enormous pressure to block permits for dredging in wetlands. The permits were issued with one large condition—JPA would have to agree to leave almost 200 acres of undisturbed waterfront untouched to receive the permit.

The officer in charge of the dock study refused to allow environmental review before releasing his report to JEA. Unaware of the prohibition, he recommended building the dock in the undisturbed area. His report concluded, "permitting should be simple, since the COE had just approved the OPS permit." JEA staff provided me a copy of the recommendations, with the comment that RS&H would have to correct the error.

After much internal discussion, I was assigned responsibility for correcting and reissuing the recommendations. A new site would have to be recommended. In addition to the permitting roadblock, the original site required piping the oil across a shipping channel in the river, a potential for mishap. The site recommended in the original report was withdrawn, and an alternate site was selected. The new location was on the same side of the shipping channel as the power plant. It was a fairly straightforward task to revise the recommendations. I assigned preparation of the report's exhibit revisions to Jerry, one of my draftsmen.

Jerry had been hired some months earlier from an out-of-town competitor and had been unable to relocate to Jacksonville without a loan for moving expenses. New employee moving expenses were not reimbursed for non-professional employees at that time. He approached the credit union for a loan, and offered the cash value of his life insurance policy as collateral. I was asked to cosign and agreed, but only if fully secured by the policy value. Little did I know at that time that this decision would forever change my future.

The officer responsible for the original dock report resigned, and I was temporarily assigned to lead the Power Division until a new officer could be recruited. The report was completed and accepted by JEA, and all Power Plant Division projects were temporarily transferred under my supervision.

The new officer was selected the next year, and Ben arrived just before our family left on our three week vacation camping trip through the western U.S., the trip we named "Dad's Worst Shortcut" and described in a previous chapter. Ben was recruited from one of the large engineering firms in the northeast. His family had not moved from New York and he was staying in a motel until their arrival, so we invited him to stay in our home for those three weeks. He could watch the place, make sure the lawn was watered and make himself at home. He accepted and moved in just as we left for the West.

While we were away and he was out, burglars broke in and stole several thousand dollars worth of goods, using our wheelbarrow to transport the items to their boat, which was tied up at our boathouse. Ben arrived while they were loading their loot and chased them away. As a final insult, they pushed my wheelbarrow into the river. Upon our return a few days later, we found our insurance did not cover the coin collections, the jewelry (including Linda's engagement ring and wedding ring), or the cash.

Ben turned out to be my nemesis for the rest of my career at RS&H. While attending a meeting in New York, I was warned by his previous boss that he had difficulty developing a working relationship with clients and employees, but my warning to our president was ignored. I was ordered to take him to Miami to meet Bob Gardner, my FPL contact ever since the successful permitting of Turkey Point Power Plant. Bob supervised our power plant site selection projects.

Bob was a non–smoker, and his *Please Do Not Smoke* sign was prominently displayed on his desk. Ben's first act after meeting Bob was to move the sign completely off Bob's desk, light up a cigarette, and blow smoke in Bob's direction. His displeasure was apparent, and he looked at me with a questioning look on his face. Ben's next statement concluded the short meeting. "From now on, I'm in charge of all of your work. Don't call Charlie, call me." He then put his cigarette out in Bob's pencil holder. Bob thanked us for coming and ushered us out, shaking his head at me, and whispering, "I'm sorry." His call the next day confirmed our contract was over. Two years' effort went down the drain.

THE
GATHERING
STORM

Several months after cancellation of my FPL Contract, Jerry (the draftsman who worked on revising the dock study) was dismissed. Within a few days, I was notified he had defaulted on his credit union loan. The insurance company informed the credit union that Jerry had withdrawn the cash value after pledging it as security for his loan. As cosigner, I was required to pay off his balance.

While in the process of preparing a criminal fraud complaint against him in 1975, the roof caved in!

A local reporter appeared on TV with Jerry, who was rattling off his description of something "not kosher" in the revised report. He claimed the report had been altered to favor another client, instead of to correct a company error. It was interesting that Jerry was not stuttering during that statement, and he always stuttered unless he was reading. Later, I was told he was furnished with a teleprompter to make his statement stutter-free. Jerry had gone to the press to block me from filing charges against him for fraud. It worked. I was ordered by superiors to drop plans to charge him and to say nothing in response to the TV claims. It would all die down if we remained silent. If there was ever a time to take the advice *"Run for your life,"* it was then.

I should have followed that advice and remained silent to all TV questions, but up to that time, I had developed a close relationship with Lloyd Brown, Mike Clark, and Fred Seely, reporters for the Jacksonville newspapers. I expected the same treatment from TV. Four years of open communications with the press had resulted in accurate, fair reporting of the many projects that were in the public eye. I had even received calls at home from the writers and editor before articles were printed to be sure the information was accurate.

I was so sure that the whole story should be available to the public, including admitting the error of the first report, that I responded by opening all our information to the media.

That was my big mistake. The newspapers fairly reported the case, but the TV station turned it into a crusade. Earlier that year, I had made a neighbor (who happened to be the news director of the TV station) angry when I threatened to file charges on his son for vandalism. Frequent "decorating" of our trees with toilet paper had been replaced by the kids throwing hundreds of feet of newsreels in the trees, along with boxes of shredded film scattered on our lawn. The film was from that TV station.

My on-camera interviews were edited to eliminate many key facts. Suddenly I found TV cameramen wherever I went. One crew even waited outside my house to catch me off-guard. A fellow Rotarian advised me to keep my mouth shut, or if I just couldn't, at least keep moving my head so the irregular movements would make the edits obvious when the interview was broadcast. The moving-head suggestion worked. No longer did the cameras follow me wherever I went. But the damage to my career was done. I lost support of our management and found myself abandoned.

I decided it was now time to take the *"run for your life"* advice I had been given earlier. The daily TV attacks were not only affecting me and the company, but my friends, neighbors, and family were all being drawn into the storm. To avoid more harassment for me and all my family, I planned to resign and move to another city. Without discussing it with anyone, I contacted my favorite realtor, aunt of my college roommate. I ask Violet's advice about selling our house. She had been following the media attacks closely and advised me that moving would be unfair to me, my family, and my company. "I know you, Charlie, and everyone else who does knows you did nothing wrong. Don't run, stick it out. The truth will prevail. If you run now, you'll be presumed guilty, and you will be running for the rest of your life." I reluctantly agreed and dropped plans to move.

The fury died down after a grand jury investigation found the illegal activity charges brought by a city councilman to be unfounded, but my career took a decided turn downward and I paid the credit union the full amount of Jerry's loan default. Bringing charges of fraud now would only re-energize the TV reporter, who went on to a career with a national TV network.

The next two years were relatively uneventful at work, with most projects being completed satisfactorily. We continued with the work repairing termite damage to the house and finally were ready to tackle rebuilding of our 400 foot long dock. The materials were delivered, and I was ready to demolish the old structure to save money on the project. I systematically cut two supporting pilings at the water line, climbed onto the dock and cut the deck supported by those pilings, standing on the solid deck, pushed the cut section into the river, then towed it to shore. The plan worked fine until I reached water five feet deep. As I cut the deck timbers, the uncut section I was standing on caved into the river, with me aboard. The pilings supporting that section had been eaten off by borers below the water. As I clutched the chain saw, it revved up to full speed before "going for a swim." It only took one short second for the cool water to be sucked into the hot cylinder—and *crack*, it stopped for good. I let the contractor finish the demolition.

The crew of several laborers dragged the new heavy pilings along the bottom to their designated spot. They were so saturated with creosote pressure treatment that they didn't float. Each piling was raised vertical and installed using a jet pump. As the crew approached shore for another piling, a manatee (a huge sea cow) about eleven feet long and weighing several hundred pounds bumped into one of the crew, surfaced, and blew a snort of water into the air. He had never seen a manatee before, and he screamed, "Sea Monster!" His face turned pale, he grabbed a standing piling, and with one hand pulled himself up six feet, to balance on top. His eyes were as big as saucers. The manatee went one way, the rest of the crew went the other. As soon as it was over, he saw he was sitting on the piling, lost his balance and his three hundred pound body splashed into the river. It wasn't a tsunami, but it was close. He plowed his way to shore, jumped in his car, and to the laughter of his crew, sped off. The next day he was nowhere to be seen, but the crew kept watch for manatees after that. I explained that the manatee was just a gentle, harmless creature that was grazing on seaweed on the river bottom, but they still kept watch for its return.

A ten-foot manatee trying to be friendly—(Copyright)
Photo courtesy of Michael Bragg—used by permission

During the turmoil of the termites and the repairs to the property, I read a small advertisement in the Commerce Business Daily for a Navy project. It was for an environmental study but lacked sufficient information to determine whether to apply. On inquiring, I was told details would only be disclosed to applicants. The deadline for applying was only days away instead of the normal two to four weeks. That convinced me this must be a major project, but why the rush to award and the secrecy? Immediately after submitting our letter of interest I was invited to assemble our hastily selected team members and travel to Washington for an interview. The interview was unusual only in that the selection board was chaired by a full Navy captain, and in dozens of previous interviews, never had a high ranking officer participated in interviews. This had to be a big project!

The interview went very well, and within days we landed one of the largest contracts for RS&H. I was officer in charge of the task force to select the location for the new U.S. East Coast Ballistic Missile Submarine Base, and prepare the environmental impact statement to obtain permits. Our selection was based on our ability to complete the first phase in twelve weeks. I had been issued a security clearance in 1964, and updating it for the Navy would not delay the project.

I accepted the project even though many of the team members thought it to be impossible. Our responsibility was to visit and survey forty-nine potential sites on the East and Gulf Coasts and narrow the list down to a few final sites in those twelve weeks. Criteria we were required to consider were strategic location, mission adaptability, weather, ability to rapidly prepare an acceptable environmental impact statement for the final site and ability to obtain construction permits.

Time was critical because the United States only had one U.S. refit base to support Trident Class Ballistic Missile Submarines and that was located in the state of Washington. Our Atlantic fleet depended on our base in Scotland and the major base in Rota, Spain. Treaty negotiations between Spain and the United States in 1975 resulted in a planned withdrawal of our squadron from Spain in four years, less than half the time normally required for selection and environmental permitting of such a large base. The Chief of Naval Operations ordered studies to select a new Trident Sub Base on the East Coast, and we were responsible to find one quickly.

The treaty with Spain was ratified by the Congress in June 1976 and called for the withdrawal of the squadron from Spain by July 1979. Without an East Coast base, submarines would have to go under the North Pole or through the Panama Canal to reach the west coast base. While in the Canal, the subs were open to attack and subject to local politics delaying the crossing.

The critical need for the report delivery in twelve weeks was emphasized when I was given the briefing on the classified elements of the project. "If your firm cannot deliver on time, you will never see another military contract, so it's up to you to see that it's done on time. And none of this briefing information can be shared with your team. You just *make it happen!*" They continued, "Your firm's work would be reviewed by a team of several admirals, so that should convince you we mean business. Good luck!"

One of the top Navy facilities planners, Don Pledger, was assigned as NAV-FAC liaison with our firm. I explained to Don that I had a team that was in revolt against my leadership since they disagreed on the time limit and the budget, claiming they needed twice the time and three times the budget. I accepted the project, and they were left out of the decision. After a formal complaint was lodged with the RS&H president demanding I be fired, they were informed to "do your best to meet the schedule." Even he didn't know the consequences of missing the deadline, so I was on my own.

I informed Don I had set the deadline for our staff a week ahead of the admirals' schedule as "insurance" against a last minute problem. Each field visitation team included a captain from the submarine fleet, and the visits were completed on schedule. I heard many Cold War stories during the visits and was especially intrigued by our submarines' ability to travel undetected. Some even were able to silently pull up to Soviet subs, bump them, play loudspeakers, and back away undetected. Our high technology was one reason the Russians were hesitant to escalate the Cold War.

As the twelve-week deadline approached, our subcontractor's team of biologists and environmental specialists informed me that I was wrong in accepting the short schedule because even though their work was done, they couldn't get their chapter typed and copied in time.

It was time to cash in my "insurance." The report was shipped to Washington with the environmental chapter blank except for a note explaining the subcontractor's inability to get it typed. A copy was hand delivered to their Gainesville office with the blank chapter and the note. You would have thought a bomb had exploded. Our president was contacted with a second demand I be fired, and he delivered the consolation message back to Gainesville. There was a second chance. Don was holding the reports in Washington for a week, and if the missing chapter was completed, delivered, and inserted in all his copies, the note would simply disappear. My plan worked.

The report was delivered on time and led to one of the largest contracts in the firm's history—to prepare the environmental impact statement for Kings Bay Submarine Base. That report was delivered on time.

The TV channel attack and my pressuring our team to meet the Navy deadline had made enemies and done me in. Shortly after delivery, acceptance, and approval of the first report, I was transferred off the Kings Bay project. For a short time, I continued with directing the Environmental and Process Division, my professional activities, and marketing.

Even though I no longer directed the Kings Bay project, I retained the Navy friendships that had been developed in those first critical months. Linda and I were invited to join a new ski group comprised of many of those friends from NAVFAC and other Washington friends. In the following years we joined the group skiing—first several times at the lodge at Smuggler's Notch (Stowe, Vermont), then Sugarbush, followed by Zermat, Switzerland, and the Dolomite Mountains of northern Italy. For the overseas trips, we adopted the official sounding title of the Downhill Ski Club. Suzanne and Steve were able to join us for three of the trips to Vermont. It was fortunate that we learned to ski in Utah before joining the club.

Changes at the federal level led to my next project, and my last at RS&H. The previous year (1975), the Atomic Energy Commission (AEC) was replaced by the Energy Research and Development Administration (ERDA), which was created to focus the federal government's energy research development activities into one unified agency.

The following June, I presented our firm's qualifications to design a research and development facility at West Virginia University. The Fluidized Boiler Project was to design and construct a test facility to develop power plant boiler designs for burning high sulfur coal without needing expensive scrubbers to eliminate acid rain. The fluidized bed boiler was also envisioned to be capable of burning low grade coal that could not be burned in conventional boilers, allowing recovery of energy from millions of tons of coal that was rejected and stored in scrap piles at the mines. It was to be a state-of-the-art facility, and to cap off my presentation, I announced I was leaving that afternoon to attend the 1976 American Society of Mechanical Engineers summer meeting in Quebec where I was to be installed as National Vice President for Professional and Public Affairs. Upon my return, I would be ready to kick off the project with the full re-sources of RS&H. Little did I know the total impact of that closing statement.

We were awarded the project, and on my return from Quebec, I was in-formed of a reorganization that had taken place in my absence. A marketing department staff member was assigned to replace me as Environmental and Process Division Vice President, and I was demoted to project manager in the Power Division I had previously managed. I even had to report to Ben, the new officer who had destroyed my FPL contract. My career as a division officer was over, and I was asked to vacate my office in the Partners' Suite and relocate to a project manager's office. I was back where I started. Twelve years of successes was wiped out. I was off limits for promotions from then on.

The president and executive VP who had directed me through ten years of success both professionally and at the national level of Professional Engineering ethics and public service were soon to retire. Their corporate successors no lon-ger considered these activities valuable in their new direction for the company. The principles that had served me well for so many years were incompatible with the philosophy of the new leaders so I knew my time was limited.

With my career in shambles, the termite damage trial was the only way I saw to recover. If we prevailed, I could start over.

THE TERMITE
TRIAL

Our day in court had finally come. Gone were the countless delays. Long before, my fellow officers at RS&H warned me of the risk of crusading. They recommended settling out of court, but I was determined to press on and stamp out the deception in reporting of termite damage.

Jury selection took most of the first day and went smoothly until time to interview two jurors. Our attorney, Buck, had identified one as acting strangely. He seemed to be constantly distracted and unable to focus on the interview questions. During the interview he admitted that he couldn't read or write and didn't understand the questions. Over our vigorous objections, the judge accepted him. Another juror was a convicted felon who had appealed to have his civil rights restored. He was accepted, too. Later, a third juror accepted by the judge fell asleep several times during the trial in spite of several warnings by the judge. "Jury of your peers" took on a new meaning that day. We were sent home to return for the formal trial the next morning. We were ready, and it was expected to be an open and shut case.

That evening I was so confident of winning that for the first time I faced a major challenge without praying for help. It was not just an omission. I decided I didn't need God's help this time. I would win this one by myself! The previous several years had seen our church attendance become sporadic. As the months of hectic reconstruction continued, my travels increased and all available time at home was spent working on the house. Church attendance had all but stopped as we worked every weekend. We had all retained our belief and faith in God, in prayer, in Christian living, and in truth winning out in the end. Those beliefs sustained us as we struggled with the financial and physical burdens of the house reconstruction, but we had given up searching for a church home where only the Bible directed policy and practice.

As the court testimony continued, Buck submitted a four page letter signed by our termite inspector. He mailed it to the State, outlining how termite inspectors and realtors deliberately misled home buyers by not reporting damage, even when they found some. After the defendants objection that it might sway the jury (I thought that was the purpose of a confession), and because it was a written document instead of direct testimony, the judge threw it out. I was speechless! The previous judge had seen the letter and allowed it, but we had not gone to the trial yet. His death and the reassignment of a new judge wiped out over a year of legal work.

There was still plenty more evidence, so we continued on with our case. Other termite company representatives testified on our behalf along with numerous witnesses. The photos and damaged wood were entered and accepted along with the summary of costs. The judge continued to urge settlement as the trial continued.

Even though the defendant's written letter was thrown out, a letter from the previous owner was allowed by the judge, a letter claiming I had inspected the house before closing. It was read with emphasis on my "inspections," which were only trips to obtain measurements for the remodeling drawings. The defendants continued to claim they had no responsibility to inform me of damage. It was a "let the buyer beware" situation, and I was an engineer who knew what he was buying.

Then, the bombshell! The defense insisted the entire jury be allowed to visit the house to inspect the damage. Buck objected vigorously because in the two years of "court procedures" the damage had all been repaired. The previous judge had approved the work and insisted that photos be taken for the trial. Now, there was no damage to see. Even the dock and boat house had been rebuilt.

But this was a new judge, and he allowed the visit. We were not allowed to join the group, but a friend of ours was allowed as an observer. The visit was a disaster. Our friend Tom heard the following conversations, none having to do with the trial:

"They have a new car," exclaimed one juror, ignoring the photographs of the damage.

"This bedroom is bigger than my whole apartment," remarked another, ignoring the pile of termite destroyed boards we kept at the first judge's instructions.

"Look at the boat they have, why do they need money?"

"I don't see any termite damage."

"I'll never get to live in a place this nice."

"Land sakes, look at this bathroom."

"Look at those orange trees and the flowers."

"This lot is bigger than my whole apartment complex."

On and on it went, ignoring the pile of damaged wood, the pictures, and the repair invoices of well over $100,000. Storm clouds were forming on our horizon.

The defense attorneys took note of the comments, and their defense strategy was changed. "He is wealthy. He knew of the damage and intended all along to sue. That's why he kept complete photos and samples, not because the previous judge instructed them to do so. The judge that directed them to keep the information is deceased, so how do we know what he said? Ask him to come back from the grave and testify. Our clients had no legal obligation to inform the Spaces, even though it was required by the contract. If the State intended him to be notified, the law would say so." Four days' testimony was destroyed in the jury's bus ride back to court.

The jury came back with the verdict. *Not guilty on all charges, and all court expenses of the defendants, the insurance companies, and all their attorneys shall be paid by the Spaces.* We had not only lost, but the verdict would mean that we would be financially ruined and the termite inspection practice would continue. Many future home buyers would lose, just as we had. It was a devastating walk from the court to the car.

Linda, Suzanne, and Steve sat through the trial, and we were all shocked by the sudden turn of events, but none more than Suzanne and Steve. "That's not fair," they chorused. "They lied! I thought courts were for justice."

As we drove from the city parking lot, the defendants preceded us to the cashier station—and drove out without paying. That was the last straw! Linda broke her silence, "See, they're crooks!" It didn't help. Where were we going to get the money to pay all the attorneys? It was a year before college for Suzanne and two before Steve would follow.

From that day onward, it was difficult to look anywhere on the property without being reminded of the years of hard work, the futility of trying to get the practice eliminated, and second guessing every decision we had made for the past three years. The enthusiasm of our family members was replaced by a "gloom and doom" attitude. Each check we wrote to send the monthly installments for court costs seemed futile. I had let the whole family down in my quest for justice and reform, but worse, I had turned away from God.

The stress of the past five years had taken its toll on my health, and I had been turned down for additional life insurance needed to protect my family. Based on Mother's projections for the past forty years, I had less than ten years to live. My slide had been long and the landing difficult, and a new direction was needed for our lives.

Margaret J. Harris (1865-1919) wrote a hymn in the 1890s, "I Will Praise Him." One phrase best described my situation at that time:

Though the way seemed straight and narrow,
All I claimed was swept away,
My ambitions, plans and wishes
At my feet in ashes lay.

EPILOGUE
TO THE TRIAL

One of the legislators who owned a reputable termite inspection service had been promoting stricter standards in his industry, without much attention from lawmakers. Our three year long case had been followed by many in the industry and in government. It put a spotlight on those current cover-up practices and the damage to homebuyers. Even though the judge had refused to accept the termite company owner's letter detailing the way purchasers were misled, it was widely circulated to lawmakers. The Florida Legislature passed strict laws to prevent undisclosed financial interest in termite companies. They also revised reporting standards by requiring reporting all evidence of previous treatment or damage, and requiring financial responsibility including either a bond or errors and omissions insurance. The primary goal of our three year long battle had finally been met. Not only had the practice been eliminated, it was now a criminal offense, and individual homeowners would not have to spend their own nest egg to seek justice. It was a noble but expensive battle for us, but well worth the effort in the long run, even though we couldn't see that at the time.

An old saying that "the first to plow the field gets to remove the rocks" proved to be true. We got to remove the rocks. If I had foreseen the result of my fortieth birthday decisions, I'd have followed this book's title—"Run for your life."

SHIFTING
GEARS AGAIN

The loss in court meant we would have to liquidate all of our investments and use most of our savings. I realized then that I could no longer win every battle without help. My self-confidence had led me to believe all I needed to succeed was hard work, being right and following a straight path. I was so sure I would win the termite suit, I made a conscious decision not to pray for help before the trial! I was wrong. From the minute I made that decision, my world seemed to fall apart. It was time to return to the Lord.

It was now 1978, time to assess our position and our future course. The termite trial had financially crippled us at a time when both kids were approaching college age. Suzanne was to enter Flagler College in two years. We paid our legal expenses and reimbursed all five opponents attorneys for their court costs, even though it took months to do so. All our savings and my profit sharing and retirement account were gone. Suzanne's year at Flagler would require selling some of my RS&H stock. Our ocean front condo was gone and the proceeds spent on the repairs and the trial. I never believed in contingency fees, so we had been paying our attorney regularly for the past three years. I began selling citrus from our grove to supplement my income.

At work, things were little better. I had been stripped of my position at RS&H and had been demoted two years earlier from division officer to project manager and now managed only one project, the ERDA Research and Development Facility at West Virginia University. When I made the original presentation to ERDA for the Fluidized Bed Boiler Project, I was asked if RS&H was committed to keeping the same project manager for the entire project. Many engineering firms had switched team members on their projects after signing the contract, and they wanted to prevent the *bait and switch* practice on this project. Ben assured them I would remain.

Two years earlier I knew I would eventually have to leave. By the time I had reported to Ben for several months it was apparent that our business practices were too far apart for me to continue beyond the current project. I would stay until its completion, which was scheduled to be another five to six years. This should give me ample time for both Suzanne and Steve to complete college, to rebuild the savings we had lost and to experiment on the types of plants that I could raise and market within six years. I planned to raise all my stock by rooting cuttings.

My long association with the Disney project had resulted in learning landscaping, plant care, and propagation techniques, and after my 1976 transfer to the Power Division, I began to experiment with raising plants in my small nursery, located on an acre on the back half of our four acre lot. The first cuttings were from the dozens of azalea and camellia plants on the property, and they were very successful, so the next year I ordered twenty varieties from a nursery in California to use as an additional source of cuttings. Both Suzanne and Steve worked for me until leaving for college, although it was difficult for me to compete with teenage activities. Half of their pay was for spending money and the rest went into their college fund.

The nursery plot was next to their horse corral. Skipper and Duchess watched as we worked seeming to invite both to stop and go for a ride. Regularly they were able to ride in that rural area where there was little traffic.

Linda and I decided to drive to Atlanta for a business meeting with my engineering society in the fall of 1977. Both the kids were still in high school and old enough to stay by themselves, so this would be their first try. Neither was allowed to drive so we stocked up on groceries, left a list of emergency numbers, and left for Atlanta.

RUN FOR YOUR LIFE

On our arrival at her mother's home, we were met by Nana, who told Linda to call home right away. Suzanne had a crisis and needed help. She was right. Suzanne sobbed into the phone, "Skipper's dead! Steve and I were riding along the road and suddenly the horse started shaking and fell down. I just jumped off in time to keep him from pinning me to the ground. He stopped breathing and was gone, just like that.

"I went to the neighbor's house for help and when we returned to Skipper, some bum put an empty beer can on his body! I need you! I don't know what to do! Please come home!"

I had a critical part in the meeting so I couldn't go home, but we turned around and drove to the Atlanta airport. On the way, Linda asked what she should do with the body. I didn't have a clue, but thought she might be able to have someone with a backhoe dig the grave and bury Skipper in the pasture. Neither of us thought Suzanne could face that ordeal alone. With the disposal issue still up in the air, Linda caught the next flight home. She rented a car and was home to console Suzanne in a couple hours. Steve tried to help, but this crisis required more than he could provide. While waiting for Linda, Suzanne returned to see Skipper again and guard the body so no more beer cans would be left there.

Our neighbor came to the rescue. He contacted the county offices and discovered that they would take care of the removal and disposal because the horse had died alongside the county road and on the right of way. The horse was removed and taken away and the trauma of a burial was avoided. Steve lost all interest in riding and sold Duchess shortly afterward.

In the two years between the starting of the nursery and the termite trial, Suzanne and I attended classes on nursery operations at the local agricultural extension and I looked forward to the change. I anticipated the termite trial to replace our lost savings and provide the necessary funds to start a new career, but with that reversal, it would take longer to recover and be ready for "shifting gears" again.

I had been knocked down, flat on my back, and that forced me to look upward. I knew then that it was time to make a major direction change in my life. The years of success had blinded me to a deeper need. We attended church sporadically, knowing that God and His Son, Jesus are real, and that Jesus came and died for our sins. I believed that telling the truth, paying your taxes, leading an honest life, voting in every election, saying grace before meals, prayers before bedtime, and praying only for major difficulties was enough. I now knew it wasn't. The Lord had not turned His back on me as I thought—I had turned mine on Him. I knew the Bible was the Word of God, but obeying was not a high priority to me. I had been living in a condition of spiritual complacency for many years.

It was time for me to follow the call *"Run for your life,"* but this time instead of running from disaster I would run back *toward* the goal I had abandoned during college days when I became disenchanted with church traditions that were invented by men. It was time to resume the search for spiritual fulfillment and find a new direction for my life and for my family.

I decided that unless I developed a firm scriptural foundation first, repeating my college era search by visiting several churches to find one where I could worship would be a mistake. I had to get back on the right track. Based on my mother's projection, I had only a few years left until the family history of early heart failure would catch up with me.

It had been so long since I had done any serious study, I knew I would have to start with more Bible study—fundamentals first. Study the doctrine of the Scriptures and then brush up on how the Church functioned in the time of the Apostles, before all the additions and modernization occurred. I knew of the Old Testament punishment of the Israelites for falling away, and of Jesus' New Testament criticism of the man-made rules and traditions that had crept into their worship. I wanted to avoid the same path, so I searched for a church that copied the biblical practices of the first century Christians.

Later, I was to discover such a church was called a "Restoration Movement Church"—non-denominational, led by elders, no affiliation except to God, and one that spoke where the Bible spoke, and was silent where the Bible was silent. Why had I missed this discovery during my search twenty-five years earlier?

This new search was short lived. Quinton and Louise Tapley, parents of Suzanne's good friend, Debbie, approached us to visit a small Christian Church in Mandarin, Florida, and we soon became faithful members. Many of the modern practices of my former churches disappeared. Suzanne, Steve, and I were immersed in baptism (Linda had been immersed when she accepted Christ years earlier). We all became enthusiastic members of the congregation and the association with Christians soon dimmed the family's pain and frustration. Their constant support was a Godsend to us at that critical point.

Shortly after the trial, Linda and I took time off for an engineering meeting in Las Vegas and added a side trip to Salt Lake City to see Jim and Ruby and get in some snow skiing. The kids were again to stay by themselves, but this time, Suzanne had her driver's license. The previous week, I had been offered one of the company Buicks for a good price and arranged to bring it home for a test drive. Suzanne was sixteen, and we planned to buy the car as a surprise for her next birthday. We could park our car at the airport and leave the Buick at home *for emergencies only*. This was their first chance to show their maturity by being on their own, cooking, getting off to meet the school bus on time, doing all their homework without supervision (nagging was what they called it). One item on the long list of instructions was regarding the Buick. No driving except for groceries at the fast food market, and *no driving at night*—even for food. Do not cross the bridge into Duval County under any circumstances, and finally, pay attention if you drive.

We completed the meeting and had arrived in Salt Lake when we received a call from my dad. He was at the hospital with both Suzanne and Steve. They had decided our instructions were optional, and drove at night (Strike 1), to the Dairy Queen (Strike 2), across the forbidden bridge (Strike 3). Blinded by oncoming headlights, Suzanne had crossed the center line, struck a truck which broke in two. The car skidded sideways and crashed at a gas station, just short of the gas pumps. The truck driver was still alive, but seriously injured, requiring over 200 stitches to his head. Both Suzanne and Steve were trapped in the wreckage—bruised and cut, but the injuries were not life-threatening. "At least not life-threatening till your parents get home," Dad told them.

"Don't break up your trip, we'll check on them regularly and make sure they are all right. They are scared of the consequences when you get back, so don't let them off the hook. Let them stew for a few days, it'll do them good." We took Dad's advice after talking with them both on the phone as soon as they were out of the hospital, making sure they were okay. As for the wreck, we told them we would discuss it when we got back, not on the phone.

When we arrived back home, both were expecting the worst. They figured the punishment would at least ground them for life and probably much worse. In response to their apologies, we hugged them both and said, "We're glad you both weren't injured seriously. You're both forgiven for disobeying, but you both must accept the consequences of your decision and the resulting actions." When they asked about punishment, we responded that the car was to have been a gift for Suzanne. The car wasn't even in our name yet, so I would have to pay the company full price for the useless car. She had wrecked her own car and would have to buy the next one herself. Then, because Steve was a party to the breaking of rules, he would have to do the same when he wanted a car. They both accepted the decision and life returned to normal, at least as normal as life can be during years of growing up.

The loss of the termite suit had another impact far greater that the financial losses. Living in that house was no longer the joy it had been. Everything reminded us of the loss. Even the kids had to bear some of the burden. Both were in high school, and with our financial reversal, some of their wishes had to be postponed. Suzanne continued work in the nursery and earned enough to finally buy herself a car to replace the one she wrecked. Steve went to work part time at local fast food restaurants and continued helping in the nursery to earn enough for a car. He still put half of his earnings into his college fund, and soon he had enough for his first car, a well used red VW Dasher.

We now had two years until completion of the Fluidized Bed Boiler Project. The design was complete, the contract awarded and the facility was under construction. The money planned for the nursery had disappeared with the court verdict, and it would be difficult to make the change that soon. Suzanne had just started at Flagler College in 1980, and Steve was planning to attend Auburn the following year. Even if we liquidated everything else, what would we live on? I now had to reconsider the plan. My alternative was to request a transfer to another officer, out from under Ben's control.

While pondering whether we could make the transition to the nursery "fly," outside events took control. Like a young bird learns to fly when his mother pushes him out of his nest, the same was about to happen to me.

One of the employees on the project was planning to spend all her savings on a down payment for a house and approached me for my assurance her job was secure because she couldn't afford the purchase if it was not. The same day, I received a call from the client. The project was cancelled! Starting the next day, all engineering was to cease, and the boiler was to be demolished (the demolition order was cancelled later). Federal priorities had changed. I was told later that the cancellation came from the Carter administration after complaints from congressmen representing competitors of the fluidized bed boiler manufacturer.

I immediately informed Ben, the officer in charge, and a high level meeting was called. All department heads in his division met in his office. I explained the cancellation and the orders to stop work. The project was a cost-plus-fee contract, so renegotiating was out of the question. Many employees were now to be idled. "No one is to mention the cancellation under any circumstances," we were all instructed.

I replied that it would be unethical for me to withhold that information from the employee who asked me directly about her job. She was a specialist in a field that RS&H had no contracts and would probably be let go early in the close-down process. It would financially ruin her, and I surely knew what that was like.

"If you tell her, be prepared to resign," Ben replied. There was dead silence in the room. What was so important that an employee should be sacrificed? I found out later that Ben was up for consideration for promotion to executive vice president and the cancellation of his largest contract might delay the vote. In that new position, Ben would continue to control me even if I were transferred to another officer, so another option was closed. In addition, the marketing director who had cancelled my FPL Headquarters contract was slated to become president.

Another part of the organizational changes restricted sale of company stock. All sales were to be limited to fixed number of shares per year. That was the only asset I had to survive on if I decided to leave. I had such a large number of shares that it would take fifteen years for me to sell all my stock if I waited for the new policy to take effect.

I had a major decision to make, but this time I would confer with my church friends and this time *pray* for guidance. No more going it alone. I was not willing to abandon my responsibility to the employee or bet my future on the success of the two new leaders, so guidance was critical.

The next morning as I was shaving, I looked in the mirror and said to myself, "Charlie, you either have to stop going to church or stop going to work." The prayers were answered. I made my decision.

It was "step out in faith and follow your conscience." I chose to notify the employee of the project cancellation and resign as instructed by Ben. It was two years ahead of my planned schedule, and my only available financial asset was my company stock. I did have a good head start on the azaleas and camellias I had started from cuttings. Those would have to do until a larger crop was available. Three years of raising plants on the two acres behind the house convinced me that I could not become a full time nurseryman with that little land. I would need more.

I was allowed to finish details for closing down the project and keep my company car. In early 1980, money was tight and the prime rate was hovering around twenty percent. I sold my stock for enough to purchase more land and expand the nursery. It looked like all my prayers were being answered. I was free to follow my dream, two years ahead of schedule!

As often occurs in life, another roadblock appeared. In lieu of cash for my stock, I received a company note for the full amount. Not even a down payment! I planned to use that money for the land and to expand the nursery. We were on our own, living on a piece of land too small to produce enough plants for a decent living and, with the termite suit loss, no money to buy more land. It was time to pray for help. We did.

The answer came when a stranger knocked at our door. It was a woman who had grown up as a close friend of the family that sold us the house. Her career in Hollywood ended after a serious automobile accident, and she was searching for a fresh start and a new home. The fond memories of her childhood led her to us. She had spent many happy times playing there. She loved horses, so the now empty horse corral attracted her even more. She made an offer for an acceptable amount, and it was all cash, with a small amount withheld for my completing the bulkhead that I had started. Another prayer had been answered.

We accepted the offer, and started looking for a place to live while we made plans for a new home and a new career. No longer were we able to enjoy waterfront living, but times had changed, and we were now able to finish paying the termite trial legal expenses. At least RS&H President Jim Shivler allowed me to keep my company car. Two weeks later, Ben cancelled the car offer. I received a call from the personnel manager to "return the car immediately or we will issue a warrant for your wife's arrest for stealing the car." My protest call to Jim went unanswered. He was out of town.

I had considered selling the property after losing the termite case and I casually looked at real estate suitable for a nursery and a home. I found fifty-five acres for sale few miles south, forty being sold to a cemetery and the remaining fifteen acres for sale. The fifteen-acre tract included a large citrus grove and most of the rest was an abandoned pasture, perfect for converting to a nursery. I made an offer on the fifteen acres, and it was accepted. We insisted on a survey and title insurance, and after some haggling, we accepted full title insurance and a survey to be completed by the seller's son shortly after closing. The survey delay was provided to allow our parcel and the adjoining forty-acre parcel to be surveyed at the same time. The contract provided for an adjustment at the per acre purchase price if the survey included more than fifteen acres.

Quinton and Louise Tapley, our close friends from church, offered to buy a double wide mobile home for us to rent if that would help. We could even store the extra furniture in their barn while we decided on our future. We accepted, and a large group of the congregation moved us in to the mobile home and moved over 40,000 plants in pots to the new property. That help we received in our time of need demonstrated the Christian lifestyle we had been missing during those years where getting ahead and making money were too high on my priority list. It was less than a year after my "retirement," and now the nursery was relocated and we were ready to start a new home. The dream that began with Walt Disney World was now a reality!

EPILOGUE
TO SHIFTING
GEARS AGAIN

I have enjoyed many successes and survived the inevitable failures that come in a lifetime. I have experienced happiness in good times, sorrow in bad. I have seen success, fame, prosperity, self-fulfillment, and self-doubt. I have also experienced the danger of pride, abandonment, love and hate, jealousy, and greed. But until that day when I found myself totally hopeless, I never looked upward. When I did, I found peace, compassion, sharing, freedom from worry, and true joy. I have learned that growing older is mandatory. Growing up is optional. Laughing at yourself is therapeutic.

Unlike the Biblical lament *"The bed is too short on which to stretch out, and the blanket is too small to wrap oneself in"* (Isaiah 28:20, NAS), my bed is now long enough and my covers are plenty wide. God has taken care of us. Some of the best answers to my prayers during the past seventy years have been, "No, my son." Paul tells us: *"And we know that God causes all things to work together for good for those who love God, to those who are called according to His purpose"* (Romans 8:28, NAS). That quote never rang as true as it does today.

My theme for this book has been *"run for your life,"* and that accurately portrays my life's journey up to that time, twenty-five years ago. "Run toward something new and exciting, and run from life's dangers" had been my motto. "*Engineers don't idle well*" had been my creed, but if there is a lasting message for me to leave, it is this: Life is not just a series of short stories, it must have direction and focus—not just focus on the next short term goal, but a better vision for the future, as a servant of Christ.

The twenty-five years since my awakening have been a complete change in outlook and life style. The challenges and adventures continued, but the cloud was gone. I knew then that the best was yet to come.